Iner S. Ritchie, Medical Evangelist

Iner S. Ritchie, Medical Evangelist

Delmer G. Ross

Stahl Center Publications
La Sierra University
Riverside, California

First edition.

Published by
Stahl Center Publications
La Sierra University
4500 Riverwalk Parkway
Riverside, California 92515
U.S.A.

Library of Congress Control Number: 2007920732

ISBN-10: 0-9789294-0-3
ISBN-13: 978-0-9789294-0-4

Printed on acid-free paper in the U.S.A. by
Morris Publishing
3212 East Highway 30
Kearney, NE 68847
1-800-650-7888

To Inelda May Ritchie Christianson,
Dr. Ritchie's younger daughter,
without whose knowledge of her father and dedication
to collecting historical documents and artifacts
this biography
would not have been written.

Contents

Acknowledgments

About ten years ago I was approached by Inelda May Ritchie Christianson who asked me if I would be willing to write a biography of her father, Dr. Iner S. Ritchie, a pioneer Seventh-day Adventist medical missionary to Mexico. While my first reaction was the thought that I was far too busy with existing projects to take on another one, because of my interest in Latin American history, and because I already knew a little about Dr. Ritchie's career, I responded with a guarded affirmative.

After determining that for years Mrs. Christianson had been collecting material to use in such a biography, I warmed to the task. I explained to her that I would be willing to try, provided she was willing to help and could wait for me to complete several projects that I had already begun. Her response was to the effect that she was eager to help and that she had been waiting for years, so a few more would not be much of a burden. Had she been told it would be ten years before I could devote major attention to the project, she probably would have given up on me immediately. My projects have a way of going on and on, far beyond the originally expected termination date.

This particular project got under way very quickly, though. At that time I taught a history course, HIST 294/494, History Colloquium, the main objective of which was to give history majors some experience in tackling research projects as members of a small team rather than as individuals. I assigned selected topics dealing with aspects of Dr. Ritchie's life to student teams in the class. They responded, producing a number of short papers, several of which offered interesting insights or gave me useful ideas. Because all students in the class participated, even though I may not have used their papers, through their comments and questions they all helped. I therefore thank every team and each student who took my History Colloquium classes in 1993, 1994, and 1995.

Maritza Durán took on the project for her senior seminar and honors thesis in the year 2000. Her work helps to provide the chronological outline of major events that is the basis for this biography. At one time she planned to work with me as coauthor on the proposed book, but when she became involved with projects of her own she had to limit her participation. Her help was significant, however, and is greatly appreciated.

I must also thank Rennie Schoepflin and Jeff Dupeé of the Department of History, Politics and Society, and John Jones and Charles Teel of the Division of Religion of La Sierra University. They offered constant and valued support. Additionally, as director of the Stahl Center for World Service, Charles Teel was responsible for the publication of this book.

My wife, Karen, offered constant support as well. She proofread the manuscript and the galleys. So also did retired English teacher, my friend and fellow adventurer on the Colorado

Desert, Bob Carlson. Katie Parsons and Petal Harris, student assistants working for the Department of History, Politics and Society, helped with different aspects of the required research. They too deserve my heartfelt gratitude.

Finally, I must return to Inelda May Christianson. Her knowledge of her father and her willingness to provide access to the files dealing with him in the Stahl Center and elsewhere were invaluable. In appreciation of her friendship and in recognition of her tireless efforts to bring the project to a conclusion, I dedicate this book to her. She richly deserves it.

Delmer G. Ross
La Sierra University, 2007

Introduction

They were Yaquis, a well known and feared tribe of Indians in northwest Mexico that had successfully resisted government efforts to subjugate them for centuries. There were dozens of them, some dressed in outlandish costumes and engaged in a ceremonial dance of some variety, others just standing about. Many carried weapons. Over the years the Yaquis had altogether too often used their weapons against any intruders in their territory. In fact, only weeks earlier they had killed three interlopers. Now among them, like Daniels in a den of lions, were four men who obviously did not belong there. They were foreigners. But these outsiders seemed to have no fear for their safety. In fact, one of the four, a physician named Iner S. Ritchie, was actually taking pictures of the Indian ceremony with his movie camera. The Yaquis, despite being notoriously secretive, seemed not to mind. How could this be?

The answer to this enigma can be found in the life of the physician, a Swedish immigrant to the United States. He was quite unlike most of the interlopers in Yaqui country.

The story of Iner Sheld Ritchie is that of a caring overcomer. An overcomer may face many different kinds of adversity, but

eventually triumphs. There have been many such people throughout history, from the child with a mental or physical handicap to
the owner of a business who loses everything in some unexpected
catastrophe. Instead of allowing problems to defeat them, they
took control of their lives and the situations in which they found
themselves, and building on what they yet had, went on to succeed
in their chosen fields of endeavor.

Ritchie was different from a majority of overcomers in that he
used what he became to help others, no matter what their station
in life. As a medical doctor he had opportunities to help both the
well-to-do and those who were not so fortunate. He treated both.
Throughout the world—including the United States and Mexico,
where he practiced medicine—there are many more poor people
than there are wealthy, so most of his patients had few material
possessions. Many could pay him only with their gratitude. No
matter. His was a life of service, not one of amassing worldly
wealth.

Likewise, many of the other criteria by which people commonly are judged mattered little to Dr. Ritchie. Race, nationality,
religion, gender and other such factors he saw as of little consequence. What he saw as important and worthy of his attention was
a person's health, both physical and spiritual.

Perhaps it is in the nature of any society, but it is a fact that
legal discrimination and social prejudice exist in our modern
world. It is equally true that, despite the standards of society,
throughout the course of American history many open-minded
individuals have made a difference on a one-to-one basis. Many
also fought for systemic or institutional change. Well known and
outstanding Americans such as Susan B. Anthony, Martin Luther

King, Jr., and César Chávez organized social movements to try to alter the way some people felt about their fellow human beings so as to produce greater equality, more opportunity for advancement for all, and in general to do away with social and racial prejudice and discrimination.

Along with prominent international humanitarians like Albert Schweitzer, Mother Teresa, and Princess Diana, Americans such as Abraham Lincoln, Clara Barton, and Jimmy Carter both publicly and privately, whether as part of a group or individually, helped others without regard to their race, physical appearance, or even health. Over the decades since independence many individual Americans have ignored and challenged social norms and government laws in order to break down discrimination and prejudice in the United States. In the process, they left a legacy of outstanding service to their fellow human beings.

Although not nearly as well known as the public figures just mentioned, Dr. Iner S. Ritchie is similarly worthy of note, examination, commendation, and emulation. A generally self-supporting Seventh-day Adventist medical missionary who often challenged social norms and even government regulations in order to fill obvious needs, he dedicated his life to the service of others through medicine. He treated the poor, taught health principles, and helped create institutions where impoverished people from the United States, Mexico, and other nations could receive medical attention. He also tried to make available to those with whom he came into contact the good news of God's love and the possibility of eternal life for humans. He knew he could not help everyone, but he could make a difference for those close around him. In the process of accomplishing that, Dr. Ritchie left a legacy of humanitarian service that challenges individuals, the entire Seventh-day Adventist community, and progressive people everywhere to dedicate their lives to serve those in need regardless of gender, class, or race. It was not just by chance that he was able to visit the fierce Yaquis without fearing for his own safety.

He was a visionary who dreamed not only about helping those he personally could, but also about instructing others so that they might provide similar service when he was unavailable. Moreover, he possessed the ability to communicate his dream to others and, with their help, to carry it forward to reality. Only constraints of health and time could hold him back.

His friend and fellow medical missionary, Clarence E. Nelson, wrote of him, "the influence of his humble Christian life remains an inspiration to all who knew him." It is the sincere hope of the author of this biography that through its pages others will come to know Dr. Iner S. Ritchie and be inspired to dedicate themselves to a life of service to those in need.

Iner Sheld Ritchie, M.D.

Childhood Dislocation and Hard Work

A symbol of freedom, it had welcomed thousands before them, and it would greet additional thousands—in fact, many millions—in the decades to come. Now, in 1888, the recently erected Statue of Liberty[1] welcomed Leander Sköld and his family to America. Aside from those who were too young to care much one way or the other, immigrants to the United States generally arrived hoping to improve their lives in some fashion. Many desired a freer political climate than existed in their previous homes. Others yearned to be allowed to worship more freely. There were as many different reasons as there were immigrants, but probably the great majority—if not all—anticipated using American economic freedom to improve their financial status in some way. The just arriving Sköld family, whose relatives already living in America had regaled them with tales of successful immigrants in the Dallas, Texas, area where they lived, were principally interested in expanded economic opportunities.

---

[1] The Statute of Liberty, a gift of international friendship from the French people to Americans, and prominently located on an island in New York Harbor, had been dedicated only two years earlier, in 1886.

1

The Skölds were five. Leander, a blacksmith by trade, whose folks came from a long line of Swedish iron workers, hoped to establish a successful blacksmith shop someplace in America, much like his brother, Otto, had already done in Dallas. Leander's wife, Eva, had her hands full with their three young children: Jenny, age seven; Sten, age five; and Einar, age three.[2] They had left their home on a hill, and the blacksmith shop down below by the church, for nothing more tangible than the promise of America.[3]

Also like many immigrants who arrived both before and after them, the Skölds had to go through the sometimes harrowing experience of Castle Clinton, or Castle Gardens, the precursor to

---

[2] Leander Johansson Sköld was born in the parish of Hillared, Province of Älvsborg, Sweden, apparently on July 8, 1858. Two dates exist for his birth. Two documents state July 8, 1858: the Excerpt from Birth and Baptismal Book, and the Certificate of Emigration, both provided and certified by the Royal Consulate General of Sweden at San Francisco, California. However, the Application for Certificate of Derivative Citizenship states August 7, 1858. Because the two older documents are in agreement, and in the absence of convincing statements to the contrary, it seems probable that he was born on July 8. Leander's wife, Eva Charlotte, nee Cederberg, Sköld, was born in the parish of Vessige, Province of Halland, Sweden, on July 28, 1852. They married on October 23, 1880, in the parish of Rolfstorp, Province of Halland, Sweden. Excerpt from Birth and Baptismal Book, certified 6 February 1947 and provided on 21 March 1947, Ritchie Papers, Stahl Center for World Service, La Sierra University, Riverside, California (cited hereafter as Ritchie Papers, SCLSU); Certificate of Emigration, certified and provided 21 March 1947, Ritchie Papers, SCLSU; and Application for Certificate of Derivative Citizenship, no date (ca. 1946); Ritchie Papers, SCLSU.

[3] Hilda Hegland to Anna [Ritchie Nickel], 23 December 1956, Ritchie, Iner S., file, Archives and Special Collections, Del E. Webb Library, Loma Linda University, Loma Linda California (cited hereafter as WebbLLU).

Ellis Island.[4] That, however, was a formality generally easily survived by most skilled and apparently healthy new arrivals.

While their encounter with immigration officials at Castle Clinton may not have been particularly time consuming or difficult, the Skölds emerged from it changed in at least one detail. Their name had been slightly altered. Aside from translators, it was fairly unusual for an American immigration officer to speak, read, or write any foreign language, and those who might have known Swedish were rare indeed. Therefore, when the newly arrived Skölds were asked their name, officials simply wrote what they heard: "Sheld."[5]

Because of this practice, many immigrants were "renamed" upon their arrival in the United States. It mattered little whether their port of entry was New York City,[6] as was the Shelds', or whether it was a different one. While to some such a change might have been anything from amusing to severely distressing, depending on each individual viewpoint, to many it was quite acceptable. If they came to America to stay—and most planned just that—a change of name was a step toward becoming American. They did not necessarily plan to give up any significant part of their

---

[4] While family tradition has them entering the United States via Ellis Island, that facility did not open until 1892. Exactly how long it may have taken them to go through the process at Castle Clinton is unknown. Inelda May Christianson, daughter of Dr. Iner S. Ritchie, telephone interview by Delmer G. Ross, 8 May 2003, Norco, California.

[5] Inelda May Christianson, daughter of Dr. Iner S. Ritchie, interview by Delmer G. Ross, 13 May 2003, Riverside, California.

[6] App. for Cert. of Derivative Citizenship.

heritage—except for hard times. They just wanted to be an integral part of their new country. They wanted to fit in. Like so many other newcomers chasing the so-called "American Dream," they wanted to be American.

Had the Shelds been better acquainted with the English language, had they been in America a longer period of time prior to the name change, and had they known exactly what was happening, it seems probable that their chosen new name would have sounded even more "American." Leander's brother—the one who operated a blacksmith shop in Texas—had changed his surname to "Shields."[7]

Einar, the youngest of the newly renamed Sheld family, had been born in the parish of Rolfstorp, near Varburg, in the province of Halland, Sweden, on October 6, 1885.[8] He doubtless was the least anxious of the newly arrived family. His main concern was keeping track of his mother. Assisting him in that task were his two slightly older siblings, Jenny and Sten.

In addition to giving the family a new surname, immigration authorities changed the given names of the two boys. Sten became "Stin." Einar became "Iner."[9] Iner Sheld would undergo yet another alteration of his name, but that would take place some two decades later.

---

[7] I.M. Christianson, interview by D.G. Ross, 13 May 2003.

[8] Excerpt from Birth and Baptismal Book.

[9] I.M. Christianson, interview by D.G. Ross, 13 May 2003.

The family did not remain long in New York, but traveled to Texas almost immediately. There, as might have been expected, Leander worked briefly in his brother's blacksmith shop.

Whether Leander's original plans included only a short stay in Dallas, or whether something occurred to alter those plans, is unclear. For one reason or another, though, the Shelds soon moved from northern Texas to southern California, where they established permanent residence in Los Angeles. There Leander began working as a blacksmith for Elias Jackson "Lucky" Baldwin. According to family tradition, he rode in Lucky Baldwin's ornately decorated buggy in the very first Tournament of Roses Parade that was staged in Pasadena in 1890 by the Valley Hunt Club. While living in Los Angeles the Sheld family increased by one when Dan was born early in 1890 in a house that stood where City Hall is located today.[10]

Just what caused Leander to start working for Richard Gird is not known, but it is possible that Baldwin's dwindling fortune during the 1890s may have prompted the change. It seems probable that the fact that both Baldwin and Gird owned trotting horses may have led to an initial introduction.[11] While he did not—indeed, considering his youth at the time, probably could

[10]   Sheld family records, 224, Ritchie Papers, SCLSU; [Inelda May Christianson], "Iner Sheld Ritchie, M.D." [brief chronology], Ritchie Papers, SCLSU; Pasadena Tournament of Roses, "Rose Parade History," http://www.tournamentofroses.com/photogallery/timeline/TL-1890s.htm; and I.M. Christianson, interview by D.G. Ross, 13 May 2003.

[11]   "E.J. 'Lucky' Baldwin," http://www.socalhistory.org/Biographies /baldwin.htm; and I.M. Christianson, interview by D.G. Ross, 20 May 2003.

not—clarify the reasons for moving, many years later Dr. Ritchie wrote,

> My earliest recollections all center around childhood experiences on the old "Rancho del Chino" in San Bernardino County, California. My father had left Texas in the late eighties and with his wife and small children had moved westward, finally settling in the beautiful virgin [Chino] valley, in those early days considered the finest of Western cattle ranges.[12]

He recalled his father, Leander, and the rest of his family working for Richard "Dick" Gird, on his Chino Ranch. They lived in a small wooden house in a row of similar homes occupied by ranch employees and their families. Leander, hired mainly to keep his employer's trotting horses properly shod and his buggies in good condition, became something of a general handyman who worked for Gird on quite a variety of projects. These included shoeing other horses, iron working of various kinds, and doing just about anything mechanical.[13] Leander later operated his own blacksmith shop in Chino. He did well enough that he eventually brought his brother, Otto, from Texas, to southern California to help him.[14]

---

[12] "Sheld, Iner," folder item 13, Ritchie Papers, SCLSU.

[13] [Inelda May Christianson], "Iner Sheld-Ritchie, October 6, 1885 - October 24, 1949," [undated chronology], 1, Ritchie Papers, SCLSU; and "Sheld, Iner," folder item 13.

[14] Otto later operated a blacksmith shop in Burbank, California. He eventually became a preacher in the Holiness Church. I.M. Christianson, interview by D.G. Ross, 13 May 2003.

The Sheld family in Chino in 1891, from left to right, back row, Leander Johansson Sheld, Stin, Eva Charlotte Cederberg Sheld, Jenny; front row, Iner, Dan, and Helen.

While living and working on the large, 47,000-acre Chino Ranch, the Sheld family again grew by one member. Helen was born to Leander and Eva in 1891.[15]

---

[15] John Brown, Jr., and James Boyd, eds., *History of San Bernardino and Riverside Counties* (The Western Historical Association, 1922), Vol. 1, 238-239; I.M. Christianson, interview by D.G. Ross, 20 May 2003; and [I.M. Christianson], "Iner Sheld Ritchie, M.D." [brief chronology], Ritchie Papers, SCLSU.

When he was only five years old, Iner went to work alongside his father on the Chino Ranch. Although he was far too small and young for most ranch work, he was helped aboard a tall horse—at least it seemed tall to him—and told to herd the milk cows into the barn twice a day. He actually started milking them at age seven, and soon was doing so on a regular basis, milking forty cows every morning and evening.[16] There were no child labor laws to prohibit such activity on California ranches back then. There were no applicable minimum wage laws either, so his pay was like that of most other ranch children his age: in addition to room and board, as needed, a new pair of overalls every six to twelve months.[17]

Richard Gird, a successful miner and engineer, had bought the Chino Ranch in 1881. Already its various different owners had contributed to the rich history of southern California. Originally known as the Rancho Santa Ana del Chino, it at first belonged to a group of ranches managed by the San Gabriel Mission and was used for grazing its livestock—mainly cattle and horses. After the secularization of the missions, the Mexican government granted the ranch to Antonio María Lugo. Subsequently, Lugo deeded it to his son-in-law, Colonel Isaac Williams. After Williams' death in 1856, his daughter, Francisca, and her husband, Robert Carlisle, owned it. From 1858 to 1861 it served as a stop on the most

---

[16]   I.M. Christianson, interview by D.G. Ross, 17 July 2000; [Christianson], "Iner Sheld-Ritchie, 1885 - 1949," 1-2; and Christina Cicchetti, "El Doctór [sic]," *Journal of the Riverside Historical Society,* Vol. 2, (February 1998).

[17]   Inelda Ruth Sheld-Ritchie, widow of Dr. Iner S. Ritchie, interviewed by her granddaughter, Cheryl Nickel Leathers, 2 March 1986, [La Jolla, California], 23, [9], transcript, Ritchie Papers, SCLSU.

commonly used route of the Butterfield stages. Trustees for Francisca began managing the estate when Carlisle died in 1865, then later sold the ranch to Gird for an estimated $3 to $4 million, paid from part of the proceeds of Gird's sale of his mines in Tombstone, Arizona. The new owner enlarged it from about 35,000 acres through the purchase of additional parcels totaling about 12,000 acres. During the early 1890s under Gird, in addition to approximately 900 horses needed for its operations, the ranch carried some 6,000 head of cattle. It was a major operation. Although there had been times when the future of the Chino Ranch had seemed questionable, for the most part, it had prospered. The prosperity continued under Gird's direction, especially after he began growing sugar beets. By 1891 the sugar mill associated with the ranch was refining nearly fifty tons of sugar per day. He subdivided approximately 24,000 acres of the Chino Valley portion of the ranch, setting aside one section for the City of Chino. As a result of financial reverses in other areas, though, Gird had to give up the ranch in the mid-1890s.[18]

After the breakup and sale of the Chino Ranch, Leander worked as a blacksmith on other area spreads, including the

---

[18] Douglas E. Kyle, *Historic Spots in California,* 4th ed. (Stanford, California: Stanford University Press, 1990), 309-10; Chino Chamber of Commerce, "California Resource Guide, City or Community of Chino," http://www.pe.net/~rksnow/cacountychino.htm; Brown and Boyd, eds., *History,* 30, 66-67, 238-40; "Butterfield Stage Route," http://www.ku.edu/heritage /trails/bsroute.html; Edwin Rhodes, *The Break of Day in Chino* (Chino, California: Edwin Rhodes, 1951), 31, 65 - 67; and "Chino and the Sugar Factory," *Riverside Daily Press Annual,* Souvenir ed., Vol. 7, No. 1711 (9 January 1892), 7.

Slaughter[19] and Pioneer ranches. Several years after Leander worked there, Stin Sheld became foreman of the Pioneer Ranch, and he hired his two brothers as cowboys. Thus all three Sheld boys worked at the same ranch at the same time for a while. Located between Corona and Prado on the north bank of the Santa Ana River, over the years the Pioneer Ranch became known as the Fuller Ranch because the Fuller brothers from Los Angeles owned it and the Pioneer Cattle Company which operated it. For a number of years it functioned as a weekend dude ranch called "Fuller Rancho" that was frequented by movie stars and other notables. Eventually it became a boys ranch.[20]

Only a few years after the Sheld family had moved to southern California a tragic event greatly and forever changed Iner's life. His mother died of consumption, a then common and almost incurable disease. Today it is known as tuberculosis. Iner was only seven or eight years old.[21] He later described his mother as having

---

[19] The Slaughter Ranch had been purchased in 1868 by Fenton Slaughter from the Yorba family. The Yorbas had obtained it as a Spanish land grant. "Mrs. J. Fuqua, Pioneer Citizen Dies at Home," [21 August 1957], unidentified newspaper clipping, Ritchie Papers, SCLSU.

[20] The two Fuller brothers involved were Charles and O.B. Fuller. Dan Sheld, "Story of Dan Shelds—1914 Start of Married Life to 1964 Golden Wedding Anniversary," undated scrapbook text transcription, 1, 7-8, Ritchie Papers, SCLSU; and I.M. Christianson, interview by D.G. Ross, 20 May 2003.

[21] Interestingly, there are three possible dates for her death. In the Application for Certificate of Derivative Citizenship it is stated as May 12, 1894. In notes later written by Dr. Ritchie, he recalls it occurring on May 23, 1893. Pomona Valley Genealogical Society, Mary Swank, ed., *Pomona Cemeteries,* Vol. 1 (1973), p. 51, indicates that the date of death was May 12, 1893. The latter probably is correct.

been, "deeply religious," and possessing "Christian graces developed from a rich spirituality."[22] As might be expected of someone so young, his mother's death influenced him greatly—even in ways that probably could not have been foreseen at the time. Later in life, his Christian beliefs, his gentle tenacity, and his desire to serve humanity probably all had root in his mother's caring life and untimely death.[23]

In one way, though, of perhaps even greater consequence were the kind, yet eventually sadly futile, efforts of his mother's physician. Many years after his mother's premature death he explained that,

> This tragic scene of the country doctor struggling through the long hours of that fateful night to save my mother's life left an imperishable impression upon my young mind and unconsciously a seed was sowing and there was born within me a growing desire as I grew older to join the ranks of the men whom he represented, whose lives are dedicated to the unselfish service and self-sacrifice of the medical ministry to suffering humanity.[24]

---

[22] "Sheld, Iner" folder item 13.

[23] Iner's parents belonged to the Lutheran church, the established church of Sweden. I.M. Christianson, interview by D.G. Ross, 17 June 2003.

[24] Iner S. Ritchie, "Preface," Ritchie Papers, SCLSU. This vivid memory effectively contradicts the view apparently held by at least one family member, Helen Sheld Harris (Virginia Stiles' mother), that Eva Charlotte Sheld may have died of an infection following a miscarriage because her physician was more interested "in his sweetheart who accompanied him in his Buggy when he made his House calls." Virginia & Waldo Stiles to Honey [Inelda May

Unfortunately, the Sheld family separated after this devastating event. Just what went through Leander's mind as he attempted to deal with the loss of his wife is not known, but he soon decided that he could not take adequate care of his children. Apparently helping him to reach that conclusion was a new woman in his life, Edla Fors, a Swedish schoolteacher he married late in 1896, and who seemed to dislike all five of Eva's children. Consequently, Jenny went to work on one of the nearby ranches as a housemaid, and Leander sent Helen, the youngest child, to live with a nearby Swedish family, the Sholanders.[25]

Many years later Helen's daughter retold a story her mother had told her about her brother Stin coming to her rescue before the breakup of the family. Stin arrived home to find their new stepmother spanking Helen. Whether there was any conversation or explaining, or even time for any talking, was not recorded. Stin, though, was irate. He picked up a chunk of firewood and threw it with all his might at his sister's tormentor. She dodged, and the wood went clear through the wall. Obviously enough, as head of the household, Leander had a problem![26]

The probably flustered blacksmith had known that much as early as 1894 when he sent the three boys, Iner, Stin, and Dan, to the Methodist Orphans' Home located at Yale and Alpine streets in nearby Los Angeles. As with many others who for whatever

Christianson], 14 March 1994, Ritchie Papers, SCLSU.

[25] Marriage Certificate of Leander Sheld and Edla Fors, 9 November 1896, copy in Ritchie Papers, SCLSU; and I.M. Christianson, interview by D.G. Ross, 20 May 2003.

[26] Stiles to Honey.

reasons had been forced to do the same thing, he may have expected their stay to be brief, lasting only long enough for him to make other arrangements. In Iner's case, though, his stay extended to more than a year. His brother, Dan, called the orphanage—a large, two-story brick building surrounded by a ten-foot-high brick wall—a "prison." Dan was forced to stay there five years, with a short time out when he ran away.[27] Despite what its founders and operators doubtless intended, it was far from being a happy place for its young inhabitants. It was, however, better than nothing at all.

While living at the orphanage the boys attended the Castelar Street School. Records from the Los Angeles Unified School District report that Iner was enrolled at Castelar Street Elementary School for grades A2-A3 from September 11, 1894, to February 2, 1896.[28]

In 1896 Iner left the orphanage. He went to live at Jennie Sholander's home on Central Avenue in Chino, California, where she and her husband owned a ranch. There, if only for a brief while, he was able to become reacquainted with his little sister,

---

[27] Ibid.; and [Christianson], "Iner Sheld-Ritchie, 1885 - 1949," 1. Dan was not released from the orphanage until quite some time after his father remarried and took him home to Chino. After only a year or so there, he overheard his father and stepmother talking about possibly sending him back to the Orphans' Home. Wanting nothing like that again, he ran away from home—permanently. Dan Sheld, "Story of Dan Shelds."

[28] Deposition of Jennie Sholander, 4 June 1947, Ritchie Papers, SCLSU; and Kay F. Deering, Microfilm Supervisor, Pupil Records and Microfilm Unit, for Los Angeles Unified School District, to Whom It May Concern, 11 June 1993, Ritchie Papers, SCLSU.

Helen.[29] Young Iner apparently also completed the third grade while staying at the Sholanders' ranch. At that time three years was considered to be enough schooling to make a youngster eligible to go to work to support himself. In Iner's case, because he had no family or other benefactor to help, he had to start earning his keep.[30]

During his short life Iner had experienced dislocation when he moved from Sweden to the United States, he had endured his mother's death, and then he had suffered abandonment because his father felt he could not take adequate care of him.[31] Now he went to work.

Iner was yet only ten years old when he began working on the ranches and farms around Chino in 1896. From dawn to dusk he milked cows, herded cattle, tended crops, split wood, cared for barnyard animals such as chickens and goats, and helped older hands with whatever tasks they were assigned to do.[32]

---

[29] Helen was later sent to the orphanage. Although never officially adopted by anyone, "sickly, dirty & with head lice," she eventually was taken from the orphanage by the Silvas, a couple from San Francisco, who treated her as a daughter. Stiles to Honey; and I.M. Christianson, interview by D.G. Ross, 20 May 2003.

[30] I.M. Christianson, interview by D.G. Ross, 3 June 2003.

[31] Iner's father remarried within three years of Eva's death, and he and his new wife eventually made their way north, first to Ceres, then to Turlock, California, where he operated blacksmith shops. He died in Turlock in 1917. Iner, by then better known as Dr. Iner Sheld-Ritchie, attended his funeral. [Iner S. Ritchie], "Papa's Funeral Sermon," Turlock, [California], 9 May 1917, Ritchie Papers, SCLSU; [Christianson], "Iner Sheld-Ritchie, 1885 - 1949," 1; and I.M. Christianson, interview by D.G. Ross, 3 June 2003.

[32] Ibid.

Although he tried lumber jacking for a short time and even sailed as a cabin boy on a coastal vessel, for more than a decade he kept returning to the ranches of the Chino Valley and surrounding areas[33]. Ranch work often was dangerous, especially for someone so young. He never knew when an angry cow or bull might turn on him. Even riding horseback was hazardous because of the possibility of falling or being bucked off. After his work was done for the day, he slept in barns—often enough on nothing more than a stack of hay—and in cowboy bunkhouses. Being a ranch hand was hard work, but it enabled him to sleep soundly.

Sometimes even sleeping could be dangerous. While working on one ranch his sleeping quarters happened to be a barn loft directly above some large, powerful horses. If he had somehow rolled off the loft floor, or perhaps stepped off while sleepwalking—either of which easily could have happened because there was no rail nor any other safety device at the edge of the floor—he would have fallen among the horses. He might even have landed on one or more of them. If he survived the fall itself, startled by an unknown object hitting them during the dark of night, those horses easily might have trampled him, conceivably seriously injuring or even killing him. When he told the story later in life he often speculated that they would have killed him because they were so large and there were several of them. He admitted that as long as he worked there, he always had been a little uneasy about sleeping above them.[34]

---

[33] [Christianson], "Iner Sheld Ritchie, M.D."

[34] Inelda Ritchie Christianson, "The Ritchies," 1, Ritchie Papers, SCLSU; and I.M. Christianson, interview by D.G. Ross, 17 July 2000.

Once Iner was a little older, when he was fourteen or fifteen, his employers began putting him with other ranch and farm hands in the bunkhouse. It was then that he learned to play the guitar and the fiddle, which, along with the harmonica, were bunkhouse favorites. Like many other cowboys, as the saying went, he "had a hundred-dollar saddle on a ten-dollar horse" as soon as he could afford them.[35]

At one point, after he had acquired a small amount of money and a horse of his own, Iner decided to tour the country on horseback. He headed eastward, over San Gorgonio Pass. He got as far as the Stewart Ranch, near Banning, when he paused—whether for water, to spend the night, or for some other reason is unclear today. The ranch was run by two sisters, Laura and Clara Stewart, and some hired help. In the conversation that followed his arrival the sisters told Iner that their hired man had died and that they would be delighted if he would consent to stay and work for them, at least until they could make other arrangements. Although he was only a short day's ride from the beginning of his tour, the wage they offered was enticing enough, and the two ladies in sufficiently obvious need of help, that he accepted their invitation. After he put his horse in their corral and made sure that it had all that it might need, he settled into the bunkhouse. One drawback showed right away; the place was infested with bedbugs. More unfortunately, though, the previous hired hand had used the same bunkhouse—where he had died of scarlet fever. Because the sisters had known nothing about disinfecting the

---

[35] [Christianson], "Iner Sheld-Ritchie, 1885 - 1949," 2.

bedding and the bunkhouse itself, it was not long before the new hand came down with the same disease that had killed his predecessor. While it seems highly unlikely that they had him checked by a doctor for any permanent damage caused by the disease—no one knew much about that possibility in those days—the two owners, mortified by the distress they had caused him, did everything they could to nurse Iner back to good health. As soon as he had recovered sufficiently, he rode back to Chino. In all, his nationwide ride had taken him less than one hundred miles.[36]

He used to tell a story about ranch life in the Chino area. At one ranch where he worked the cooks were Chinese while the housemaids were Swedish. One of the cooks, who had not been in the United States for very long, became enamored of one of the housemaids, but he had no idea about how to conduct a courtship on a ranch in California. The smitten cook was resourceful, though. Ever since he had arrived at the ranch he had heard the cowboys bragging about their romantic exploits. Some of their tales seemed rather far-fetched, but others sounded reasonable enough. He decided to ask a cowboy who claimed to know a little Swedish just what he should do to conquer a fair Swedish maiden's heart. At the very least he needed to know how to say something endearing in Swedish. What an opportunity for a fun-

---

[36] The Stewart Ranch later became a senior retirement complex known as "Sun Lakes Country Club." Many ranch artifacts ended up in the Gilman Ranch museum Collections Room. Joan Coombs, Secretary, Gilman Ranch Hands, Inc., to Inelda [Christianson], 28 February 2002, Ritchie Papers, SCLSU; [Christianson], "Iner Sheld-Ritchie, 1885 - 1949, 2; and I.M. Christianson, interview by D.G. Ross, 24 June 2003.

loving cowboy prankster! With a difficult-to-maintain straight face
the gleeful ranch hand went into great detail, telling the cook to do
essentially exactly the opposite of what he really needed to if he
hoped to further his own best interests, and teaching him to say
something he most definitely should not if he hoped to favorably
impress a lady. Needless to say, the results, while spectacular
enough and quite hilarious to the playful cowboys, were not so
satisfactory for the miserable Chinese cook.[37]

Life on a California ranch usually involved a lot of hard work.
And it could be difficult in a number of ways, some not always
expected!

Iner survived, though, and so did his brothers. More than fifty
years later, in a letter to Iner's elder son, Dan Sheld wrote regarding the people of the Chino Valley and Prado Basin, "I can tell you
[of] many of the times your father and I had in them early days.
We would of had a bad time of it hadent [sic] been for the good
People like Mrs. Julia Fuqua [daughter of Fenton Slaughter, of the
Slaughter Ranch] and others."[38] Many of those people regarded
taking in a stray orphan or two, whether for a single night or for
several years, to be nothing more or less than their moral and civic
duties. Some viewed it as a Christian duty, as well. For young Iner
it was good that it was so.

---

[37] I.M. Christianson, interview by D.G. Ross, 17 July 2000.

[38] Uncle Dan Sheld to Iner W. Ritchie, 22 August 1957, and enclosed
unidentified newspaper clipping, "Mrs. J. Fuqua, Pioneer Citizen Dies at
Home," Ritchie Papers, SCLSU.

Joining the Seventh-day Adventist Church

With the main alternatives being an equally unpleasant and unacceptable jail stay or return to the orphanage, then being farmed out to anyone willing to provide room and board in return for work, young Iner Sheld felt forced to get by on his own. He preferred to negotiate his own terms with people of his own choosing rather than to allow it to be done by others whose main objective was to send him on his way so that they would not have to bear the expense of feeding and housing him. Thus, at an age when most youngsters were mainly concerned with school, play, and doing whatever chores had been assigned at home as quickly as possible, Iner began working full time on a cattle ranch. At a very early age he also worked on farms, in dairies and factories, and even in lumber camps.[1] Making his own way was a manly thing to do, yet he still was only a youngster.

Perhaps it was just as well that he needed to spend many hours every day working to support himself. He thus had less time to feel sorry for himself and to miss his family—especially his

---

[1] Iner S. Ritchie, "Preface," Ritchie Papers, SCLSU.

19

mother. He later acknowledged that a very painful void existed during this time period of his life. While he obviously exaggerated some, romantic hyperbole aside, he apparently spent a great deal of time in solitary mourning, yearning for family company that was no longer possible. As he put it, "Most of the days were spent alone out in the orchard crying for mother. I was 'homesick' but homesick for my mother. Had she been there all would have been well."[2]

Such sentiments have been felt and expressed by many who have lost their mothers, but to have lost his at such a tender age made life seem most unfair as young Iner observed other children enjoying the company of and playing with their own mothers. His was gone, though, and he knew that no amount of wishing could bring her back. Never again would she be there for him, to offer motherly advice, to comfort him when things went poorly, and to express her joy when things went well. He would have to do his best without her.

Moreover, his other family members generally were in no position to help—not even his father. Like Iner, each was trying to earn a living. They attempted to keep in touch with each other. Sometimes they helped each other in various ways, and for a time in the late 1890s and early 1900s the brothers worked together on the same spread in the Chino Valley, the Pioneer Ranch. For the Shelds, though, Eva's death brought an end to the family unit. It was a double loss to them all.

---

[2] "Sheld, Iner," folder item 13, Ritchie Papers, SCLSU.

During this often painful time young Iner became acquainted with a considerable number of Mexicans and Mexican Americans. He worked alongside them in the fields and elsewhere. From them he learned Spanish, which was to help him immensely in his medical missionary work. As he later acknowledged, "What knowledge of the Spanish language I possessed was a great asset to me and proved to be a closer bond than flesh and blood."[3] Considering his later dedication to the medical missionary work in Mexico, his assessment doubtless was correct.

About 1902, Iner Sheld at an apiary where his bees produced honey and "California Golden Alpine Queens."

---

[3] Iner S. Ritchie, "Preface."

While he was working on the Pioneer Ranch, and other farms and ranches in the area, Iner noticed bees swarming in the springtime. That gave him an idea. Why not catch those swarms, then sell the honey they produced? Putting thought into action, he caught a number of them. They apparently were satisfactory for he still had bees when there was little bloom. Then, apparently early in 1900, he discovered he had a problem. Perhaps because he had relieved them of too much honey, or possibly he had divided them too much in an effort to have as many hives as possible, or the cause could have been something entirely different, but for some reason the bees needed to be fed or they might die. He decided to buy honey to feed them to tide them over until they could find enough bloom to feed themselves. So, responding to a business advertisement he read in 1902, he bought some honey from the Ritchie family.[4]

The Ritchies lived not far from downtown Corona, California, a little more than one mile southwest of the train station. Today a medium-sized city in an urbanized area, Corona then was a rather modest little town in rural Riverside County. The Ritchies were best known for having developed a method of preserving olives in tin cans, instead of in the usual fragile glass jars. They shipped the canned olives worldwide. Perhaps as a result of advertising in

---

[4] Inelda May Christianson, daughter of Dr. Iner S. Ritchie, telephone interview by Delmer G. Ross, 27 May 2003, Norco, California; Inelda May Christianson, daughter of Dr. Iner S. Ritchie, interview by Chris Johnston and Christine Yoon, 6 April 1994, Riverside, California, transcript, D.G. Ross Collection, Department of History, Politics and Society, La Sierra University, Riverside, California (cited hereafter as Ross Collection, HPSLSU); and Deposition of William S. Ritchie and Anna L. Ritchie, undated fragment, Ritchie Papers, SCLSU.

Seventh-day Adventist periodicals such as the *Pacific Union Recorder* and *Advent Review and Sabbath Herald* they sold many cases to Adventist missionary families. While they had a few olive trees of their own, they bought most of what they canned from local growers. They also sold olive oil, corn oil, and honey, all of which they bought in bulk, then sold in smaller amounts.[5]

William Shannon Ritchie had worked as a kind of general handyman at the Medical and Surgical Sanitarium operated by Dr. John Harvey Kellogg in Battle Creek, Michigan. After completing "farm, garden, plumbing etc. . . , then," as he once described it, "a part of each evening [I] walked the halls to quiet down loud talking and get all to feel as sleepy as possible at an early hour." He also took some nursing courses. In later years he wrote and recited poetry and refined his interpretation of Armageddon, which he not unreasonably viewed as a spiritual rather than physical battle.[6]

William's wife, the former Anna Lula Joseph, was an unusual woman, especially for those days. Before her marriage she had supported herself by selling silverware and linens door-to-door.

---

[5] Inelda Ruth Sheld-Ritchie, widow of Dr. Iner S. Ritchie, interview by her granddaughter, Cheryl Ann Nickel Leathers, 20 November 1985, [La Jolla, California], transcript, 3 - 5, Ritchie Papers, SCLSU; I.M. Christianson, telephone interview by D.G. Ross, 27 May 2003; and [Inelda May Christianson], "Iner Sheld-Ritchie, October 6, 1885 - October 24, 1949," [undated chronology], 3, Ritchie Papers, SCLSU. For examples of the Ritchies' advertising, see the *Pacific Union Recorder,* Vol. 4, No. 12 (14 January 1904), 16, and No. 21 (15 December 1904), 8.

[6] W.S. Ritchie to Lula Joseph, 12 July 1892, Ritchie Papers, SCLSU; and [Inelda May Christianson], My grandparents were "land poor," no date, Ritchie Papers, SCLSU.

She also gave Bible studies to anyone who was willing to listen. Consequently, she had started the company that built the first Adventist church in Riverside, California. Additionally, she functioned as an elder of the San Bernardino Seventh-day Adventist Church, where her duties included planning services and, if no preacher showed up, presiding. After graduating from the Biblical Course offered by Healdsburg College, and upon gaining some experience as a Bible worker, she was sent as a missionary to the Mormons in Utah. Her salary was to have been a less-than-magnificent $20.00 per month—only part of which she received. When she inquired about her missing miserly pay she was told that the funds were needed for men and that she should just "live with families." After some very trying experiences in Utah, including a proposal of marriage by a handsome Mormon who thought she would make an excellent second wife to go along with his already existing one, she returned to her parents' ranch just south of Corona. Around 1911 she homesteaded a section of land at Hinkley, near Barstow, in California's Mojave Desert. She put in fruit orchards and spent some time each year tending them. She also donated land for a school there. She subdivided her land and began selling small parcels, but the Great Depression ended the business. Throughout the depression she managed to hang onto what land she still had, though paying taxes was a major difficulty. Anna Lula also invested in the Doble Steam Car and one of Richfield Oil's fields, neither of which were profitable.[7]

[7] Mrs. W.S. Ritchie to Eld. E.E. Andross, 17 October 1934, 5, Ritchie Papers, SCLSU; [Anna Lula Ritchie] to Our Beloved Children [Iner and Inelda Ruth Ritchie], 17 February 1935, 2, Ritchie Papers, SCLSU; Inelda Ritchie

While it was through his need to feed his bees that Iner met the Ritchie family, they soon offered him more than honey. The Ritchies, William Shannon, his wife, Anna Lula, and their daughter Inelda Ruth, offered him friendship as well. They talked to him about honey and bees and many other topics, including religion. As he got to know them better, something about the family attracted him. The Ritchies, in turn, saw something appealing in him. He was more serious, more thoughtful, and, in general, more mature than most youths of sixteen. He was also far better informed on many topics than most cowboys his age. Consequently, especially after they had discussed religious beliefs, they invited Iner to their home to worship with them on Saturdays, their Sabbath.[8]

The Ritchie home, the construction of which was completed about 1902, was built of used lumber, doors, and windows

---

Christianson, "Anna Lula Joseph: Romance and Responsibility in Early Adventism," *Adventist Heritage,* Vol. 17, No. 2 (1997), 23-29; [Christianson], "Iner Sheld-Ritchie, 1885 - 1949," 2; and [Christianson], My grandparents were "land poor."

[8] I.M. Christianson, telephone interview by D.G. Ross, 9 June 2003. The Adventists meeting in the Ritchie home became one of the earliest organized companies in the Southern California Conference. That conference later split in two, and Corona became part of what is today known as the Southeastern California Conference. I.R. Sheld-Ritchie, interview by C.A.N. Leathers, 20 November 1985, 5; Chris Johnston and Christine Yoon, "The Religious and Educational Influence of the Ritchie Family on Iner Sheld" (term paper presented for HIST 294/494 History Colloquium, 10 May 1994), 2, D.G. Ross Collection, HPSLSU; and I.M. Christianson, interview by D.G. Ross, 10 June 2003.

salvaged from a church in Wildomar.[9] It was large, with a living room and dining room separated by a folding partition. Folding back the partition created a huge front room that could easily accommodate fifty people and therefore was suitable for church services or other meetings—which was just what the Ritchies intended. A sufficient supply of folding chairs on loan from the Conference office was kept handy for that purpose. There also was another room, called the "Dorcas Room," stocked with food, clothing, and other supplies to be distributed to those in need.[10]

The Ritchies, who had met at church in Los Angeles and then had taken classes together at Healdsburg College, had already established a history of opening their family and the warmth of their home to others. In addition to providing a place for church services, after the only child of their own had been stillborn, they had initiated the adoption of their daughter, Inelda Ruth,[11] as a

----

[9] Wildomar was a small community that was dying because it had lost its water supply. [Christianson], "Iner Sheld-Ritchie, 1885 - 1949," 2.

[10] [Christianson], "Iner Sheld-Ritchie, 1885 - 1949," 2; and I.M. Christianson, interview by D.G. Ross, 10 June 2003. Located at 802 Vicentia Street, in Corona, it was torn down either during or just after World War II, when building supplies were rationed or yet in very short supply, and the lumber was used yet again to build five small houses on the southwest corner of Ninth and Vicentia. [Christianson], "Iner Sheld-Ritchie, 1885 - 1949, 3; and Deposition of William S. Ritchie and Anna L.Ritchie, undated fragment.

[11] Born on February 26, 1897, as Annie LeSueur. Because February 26 was the Ritchies' wedding anniversary, it appears that the date may have been a "chosen birth date," rather than the correct one. Nevertheless, it was the one she celebrated as her birthday. The Ritchies at first planned to name the child Ina, but after hearing and liking the name Nelda, they combined the two, thus Inelda. Inelda Ritchie Christianson, "The Ritchie/Joseph Who's Who," (undated typescript), 4, Ritchie Papers, SCLSU; and [Christianson], "Iner

very young girl from Angels Camp in California. They had obtained her through the Seventh-day Adventist Home of the Friendless of Oakland, California, which advertised itself with the phrase "Good homes provided for orphans and homeless children."[12]

Although she was less than three years old at the time, for the remainder of her life Inelda recalled at least something about the trip to her new home in southern California. They took a ship from San Francisco to Long Beach. In those days, in 1900, travel by ship still was viewed by many as the most comfortable way to travel any distance. What she remembered very clearly about that journey was the water. Its tremendous expanse in the Pacific Ocean along the California coast apparently made quite an impression on her.[13]

While she lived with them from that time onward, the Ritchies did not complete the adoption process until her fifteenth birthday.[14] As Inelda facetiously explained many years later, "They

---

Sheld-Ritchie, 1885 - 1949, 3.

[12] Carrie R. King to Dear Sister [Anna Lula Ritchie], 17 August 1900, Ritchie Collection, Women's Resource Center, La Sierra University, Riverside, California; and C[arrie] R. K[ing] to [Anna Lula Ritchie], Sunday Morning [19 August 1900], Ritchie Papers, WebbLLU; Inelda Ritchie Christianson, "The Ritchies," 1, Ritchie Papers, SCLSU; "Obituaries," Ritchie—Anna Lula Joseph, *Pacific Union Recorder,* Vol. 48, No. 8 (September 27, 1948); and I.M. Christianson, telephone interview by D.G. Ross, 9 June 2003.

[13] I.R. Sheld-Ritchie, interview by C.A.N. Leathers, 20 November 1985, 1.

[14] Order of Adoption, Inelda Ruth Ritchie, a minor, 26 February 1912. Superior Court, Riverside, California.

wanted to see how I turned out!"[15] After her brief joke, though, she quickly admitted that the Ritchies treated her well and that she always felt secure with them.[16] Of possible interest to those aware of the modern debates on home schooling, Inelda was taught at home by her parents, both of whom had been school teachers at one time. They did not want her to be exposed to even the theory of evolution, and the only available schools in Corona were public schools where it might be taught. Inelda later admitted, "I've never been inside of a school,"[17] at least not as a student.

Because she did not attend school, her best opportunity to meet and to socialize with other youngsters of her own age was at church meetings. She especially enjoyed camp meetings where, beginning in 1907, she began playing the organ at the meetings for juniors.[18]

The man in young Iner may have been cautious and even somewhat reluctant at first, but he was curious about the Ritchies and their religious beliefs. He began attending the church services that, because of the dearth of other Seventh-day Adventists in the area, were held in their home. During the services little Inelda Ruth Ritchie kept sneaking looks at Iner. She thought he looked especially dashing in the fine, black silk cowboy neckerchief he

---

[15] I.R. Sheld-Ritchie, interview by C.A.N. Leathers, 20 November 1985, 1.

[16] Ibid.

[17] I.R. Sheld-Ritchie, interview by C.N. Leathers, 2 March 1986, [La Jolla, California], 20-21, [6-7], Ritchie Papers, SCLSU.

[18] I.M. Christianson, interview by D.G. Ross, 10 June 2003. The Ritchies owned both a piano and an organ, and Inelda's mother taught her to play them.

wore to church instead of his usual red bandanna. At first he visited only when he had Saturdays off. In time, though, he began arranging his work schedule so as to be able to attend. While he was learning more about Seventh-day Adventist beliefs, the Ritchies' kindness and love reached out to him and welcomed him. Although his two brothers, Stin and Dan, worked with him at the Pioneer Ranch, the Ritchies gave him the closest thing to a real family he had been able to have since before living at the orphanage.[19]

The Ritchies lived their Seventh-day Adventist Christian faith. Iner, for his part, was interested in what made them the way they were. He wondered why they should be in any way concerned about him and his welfare. What made him different from other lanky, six-foot-tall, young cowboys who worked on the ranches of the Chino Valley and Prado Basin? Just who was he to them, anyway? It had been the thought that perhaps their religious beliefs might hold the answer that had led him to begin attending church services with them. Then during the summer of 1904, when he worked for a brief time near Modesto, California, he observed several Adventist meetings there.[20]

At the repeated invitation and almost urgent insistence of the Ritchies he also attended Seventh-day Adventist tent-meeting services held in 1905 in the Chino area. While he was learning to trust the Ritchies, he did not know exactly what to expect at a tent meeting, so he decided not to show up without some friendly

---

[19] I.M. Christianson, telephone interview by D.G. Ross, 9 June 2003.

[20] "Obituary," 1, Iner S. Ritchie file, WebbLLU.

support just in case he needed it. He brought along several of his buddies from the Pioneer Ranch, cowboys whose main interest was "to have some fun." At the first meeting they sat on the very front row and did things such as crossing and recrossing their legs in unison, hoping to distract the speaker. As the service progressed, though, Iner grew interested in the topic being presented. This was the first time he had seen and heard anyone discourse at length on prophecy using text after text read directly from the Bible. He was fascinated by the charts and pictures of the beasts of Revelation the speaker used to illustrate his presentation. These tent meetings were very different from the intimate little gatherings he had been attending in the Ritchie home. Yet everyone seemed friendly, and he could find little evidence of the religious fanaticism about which some friends and acquaintances had warned him. Instead, he was learning more about the Bible and about God's love for his earthly children than he ever had before.[21]

Favorably impressed, he paid close attention to the speakers at the various services. Soon he felt the Holy Spirit urging him to accept the new light he was privileged to be receiving. He made his decision to join the Seventh-day Adventist church and was baptized late in 1905 by Elder Elmer H. Adams shortly before the close of the tent meetings in Chino. Although he was not quite twenty years old, this event came as the result of a careful and prayerful examination of the issues and was the rational determination of a young adult who had largely been on his own for eight years. He knew his decision would please the Ritchies, but of far

[21] I.M. Christianson, interview by D.G. Ross, 3 June 2003.

greater significance was the knowledge that his decision would please God and that it was a major step toward accepting the Creator's offer of eternal life for himself.[22]

His convictions were soon tested. He had recently begun working at the American Beet Sugar Company mill in Chino. It was a good job that paid well for those days. Moreover, his employers liked his attitude and his work so much that they already were planning to send him back east to another facility where he could train to become a foreman. The problem was that the factory did not close on Saturdays. Iner requested to have his Sabbaths off, but the management refused. In keeping with his beliefs that it was better to obey God than man, he quit. It was a difficult time for him, but the Ritchies and other fellow Seventh-day Adventists living in the area offered encouragement.[23]

At about this time, either before or very soon after his baptism, Iner went to live with the Ritchies. It is not known if they had invited him on earlier occasions, but possibly as the result of a dream Mrs. Ritchie had they did now, and he accepted. Except for occasional errands or projects, he did not work for them, but he stayed with them for the greater part of the next four years, until

---

[22] Christianson, "The Ritchies," 1; I.M. Christianson, interview by D.G. Ross, 3 June 2003; G.W. Reaser, "Southern California Items," *Pacific Union Recorder,* Vol. 4, No. 51 (13 July 1905); "Elders Hare and Adams . . . ," *Pacific Union Recorder,* Vol. 5, No. 11 (5 October 1905), 11; "California Items," *Pacific Union Recorder,* Vol. 5, No. 13 (26 October 1905), 7; and "Obituary," 1, Ritchie file, WebbLLU.

[23] I.M. Christianson, interview by D.G. Ross, 10 June 2003.

he left to attend medical school. Even after that, their home remained his home base until his marriage.[24]

**Family worship in the Ritchie home in Corona in 1908.
Left to right, Iner Sheld, and the Ritchies: Anna Lula,
William Shannon, and Inelda Ruth.**

They were thus able to help provide the young man with continuing guidance. So also could Elder Adams and his associate evangelist, for that matter. After closing their effort in Chino they began new tent meetings in Corona.

---

[24] Deposition of William S. Ritchie and Anna L. Ritchie, undated fragment; Mamma and Amma [Anna Lula Ritchie] to Iner and Inelda [Ritchie], 28 August 1935, 7, Ritchie Papers, SCLSU; Mamma [Anna Lula Ritchie] to Our Beloved Son [Iner S. Ritchie], 2 October 1935, Ritchie file, WebbLLU; and Marc Gonzalez and Todd Cooper, "The Romance of Iner and Inelda Sheld-Ritchie" (term paper presented for HIST 294/494 History Colloquium, 6 December 1995), 1, D.G. Ross Collection, HPSLSU.

At their suggestion, Iner consulted with various teachers—mainly from Corona—about books he might study to expand his intellectual horizons. After he had completed a book or series of books, he would return to the teacher to be tested. In this fashion he completed grades four through eight in one year. Then he began doing the same for high school. It was different from the usual method of study, but he ended up with the knowledge he needed to continue.[25]

The main drawback to this self-taught approach was that he would not earn a diploma upon completion. He had learned that medical schools generally required a diploma as proof of having fulfilled the requirements of high school. Because more and more he thought he would like to study medicine, Iner determined to try to obtain a diploma. He would go to a regular school for his junior and senior years in high school. Again at the suggestion of the Ritchies, as well as because of the urging of other church members he had come to know, he decided to attend the Adventist academy in San Fernando, then known as "Fernando Academy" because "San Fernando" sounded "too Catholic." Unfortunately, he had to leave after only one term. At the end of the first semester he went back to the Pioneer Ranch in Chino Valley to sell a team of horses he had left there. He planned to use the money from the sale to pay his tuition and other costs for the next term. His brother, Stin, however, had already sold the horses—and worse, he had spent all the money from the proceeds of the sale. If Iner was to procure the

---

[25] [Christianson], "Iner Sheld-Ritchie, 1885 - 1949," 3.

needed funds in time to continue his studies at Fernando Academy, he would have to find another source.[26]

Working for wages would, of course, generate income. But it would take him months or even years to accumulate what he needed. Selling merchandise on commission, however, might provide a substantial sum in only a short time if he could make a few good sales. Despite being rather shy, Iner decided to try colporteuring, a traditional Adventist method of financing education. Many students did it. He had heard of some who had sold enough books and magazines in one summer to pay tuition for two or more years. Successfully selling religious publications door to door takes a certain kind of person, though, and Iner apparently was not that type. He was just getting started when he entered a store owned by a Jewish man and his family. Iner undoubtedly hoped that here he might make that one big sale that could provide all his immediately needed funds. But it was not to be. When the owner learned of the young man's business, he became irate, jumped over the counter, and chased him out of the building. That was enough. Iner decided that colporteuring was not the best way for him to earn funds.

Lacking funds needed to attend a regular school, he returned to his earlier method of consulting with high school teachers at Corona regarding material to study and then, having done so, returning to be tested. Although he did not receive a diploma, by

---

[26] I.M. Christianson, interview by D.G. Ross, 3 June 2003. Because by the early 1920s Fernando Academy required expensive major repairs, a new academy was built on the outskirts of Arlington, California, to replace the old one. Named "La Sierra Academy," classes got under way in 1922. It still exists.

the end of 1907 he had completed the equivalent of a high school education.[27]

As a result of the counsel of the Ritchies and his own growing desire to become a medical doctor, he had caught up with, and surpassed, many other youths of his own age. Iner could not escape the mental picture he had of the harried physician striving valiantly to save his mother's life, and now that he was in a position to study medicine he was more determined than ever to do so. He was way too late to save his own mother, but there were many other mothers, fathers, and children out there who undoubtedly would need trained medical assistance at some point in their lives. He knew there was no possibility of helping them all, but he might be able to make a difference for the better for a few. Maybe he could help alleviate someone's pain or help somebody breathe more easily. Perhaps he could help save someone's life. In the process, he might be able to point that person to Jesus as well. Those whose physical health he had helped improve probably would be more willing to listen to any spiritual advice he might have to offer than if he just approached them on the street. If he could help point even one person to Jesus, his life would not be in vain, and studying medicine was a worthwhile task. Therefore, late in 1907, as a young man of 22 summers, he enrolled at the relatively nearby Pacific College of Osteopathy in Los Angeles.[28]

---

[27] I.M. Christianson, interview by D.G. Ross, 3 June 2003.

[28] "Deposition of Ritchie, William Shannon and Ritchie, Anna Lula Joseph," no date, Ritchie Papers, SCLSU.

A major attraction was that a high school diploma was not a requirement.[29]

Although he still was young, a lot had taken place since he had lost his mother and his family. As a result of his friendship with the Ritchies he had become a Seventh-day Adventist Christian. He had studied hard and educated himself to a point beyond what the majority of Americans or any other peoples of his day could claim. He had worked at many different tasks, and, among other possibilities, he was becoming a beekeeper. Although at first it had been impossible to predict, and although he had not had an easy time, by now one thing seemed certain: if he had any say in the matter, Iner Sheld was going to be something more than a day laborer or a cowhand working for a dollar a day and room and board.[30] He had ambition, and while he knew that hard work was the price of success, that certainly did not bother him; he had worked hard since he had been ten years old.

---

[29] I.M. Christianson, interview by Delmer G. Ross, 3 June 2003.

[30] If room and board was not included in the wages, skilled laborers such as cabinetmakers in the Corona area might make as much as $2.00 per day. Skilled farm workers would consider themselves fortunate to make about $1.50. I.R. Sheld-Ritchie, interview by C.A.N. Leathers, 20 November 1985, 4.

Gaining a Family and Becoming a Doctor

In the fall of 1908,[1] Iner transferred to the Loma Linda College of Evangelists—soon to be known as the College of Medical Evangelists—eventually to study medicine.[2] The Loma Linda College of Evangelists, located in Loma Linda, California, was a new institution, only recently founded by the Seventh-day Adventist church. According to George R. Knight, the Seventh-day Adventist church during the first decade of the twentieth

---

[1] Three different dates have been given for his original enrollment in the new school at Loma Linda: 1908, 1909, and 1911. It appears that 1909 may be given based on the date when instruction of medical students began at the Loma Linda College of Evangelists. The third date, 1911, is when he returned to his studies after being out for a year as a result of having contracted typhoid fever. According to many unimpeachable sources, including college accounting-department ledgers, however, the correct date for his original enrollment is 1908. At that time he may have started taking science courses required by reputable medical schools, and soon to be required by the new one, or he could have begun taking the one-year gospel workers course which opened in 1908. Then, when it opened for enrollment in 1909, he began the medical course. "Loma Linda University: 'a miracle that should open the eyes of our understanding,'" *Loma Linda University Scope,* Vol. 27, No.1 (January-March 1991), 6-13.

[2] "Deposition of Ritchie, William Shannon and Ritchie, Anna Lula Joseph," no date, Ritchie Papers, SCLSU.

century reorganized "its structures and institutions for a more functional fulfillment of its mission."[3] Among other things, the church expanded its influence in the western part of the United States by establishing sanitariums in different California locations such as Paradise Valley and Glendale. The church institution in Loma Linda was part of that development.

In 1905 John A. Burden, a Seventh-day Adventist pastor, purchased what was to become Loma Linda Sanitarium and, decades later, the Loma Linda University Medical Center, for a bargain price because health resorts in southern California faced economic difficulties.[4] Ellen G. White, one of the founders of the Seventh-day Adventist Church, proposed with its purchase that, among other activities, the denomination should develop the property to train Christian physicians. She apparently was quite enthusiastic about the acquisition of the parcel, announcing, "This is the very property we ought to have."[5] She envisioned a place where Seventh-day Adventists could share their health message with local people and fitness-minded tourists who were visiting

---

[3] George R. Knight, *A Brief History of Seventh-day Adventists* (Hagerstown, MD: Review and Herald Publishing Association, 1999), 126.

[4] Ibid., 121, and "Loma Linda University: 'a miracle.'" Burden was also manager of the St. Helena Sanitarium, an Adventist institution now known as St. Helena Hospital and Health Center, in northern California. Richard A. Schaefer, *Legacy: The Heritage of a Unique International Medical Outreach* (Mountain View, California: Pacific Press Association, 1977), 85-88.

[5] Knight, *History of Seventh-day Adventists*, 122; and Ellen G. White, quoted in G.W. Reaser, "Southern California Items," *Pacific Union Recorder*, Vol. 4, No. 51 (13 July 1905).

California in ever larger numbers.[6] Acting quickly, the church incorporated the sanitarium, and later in the year of purchase it began offering nursing classes. In the following year, 1906, the Loma Linda College of Evangelists opened and the next year graduated its first nursing class.[7] In keeping with its medical emphasis, it opened its medical school and was renamed College of Medical Evangelists (CME) in 1909 when it obtained its charter from the state of California. Five decades later, in 1961, the institution underwent yet another change of name when it became Loma Linda University.[8]

As a new school opening its door to medical students for the first time in 1909, the Loma Linda College of Evangelists could not afford to be as selective as most well established schools. A high school diploma supposedly was required for admission, but its lack was not an insurmountable obstacle, particularly for someone transferring from the Pacific College of Osteopathy.[9]

---

[6] "Loma Linda University: 'a miracle.'"

[7] *The College of Medical Evangelists: Founders Day* (Loma Linda, California: 26 May 1955).

[8] Keld J. Reynolds, *Outreach: Loma Linda University, 1905-1968,* ([Loma Linda, California: LLU], 1968), 87; The Alumni Association, LLU School of Medicine, *Loma Linda School of Medicine 1909-1989 Celebrating 80 Years of Classes,* (ca. 1989), Ritchie Papers, SCLSU; and "Loma Linda University history," http://151.112.2.51/heritage/Collections.htm#LLU.

[9] Inelda Ruth Ritchie indicated on various occasions that she thought the Corona High School had granted her husband a diploma. That does not jibe with Iner's concern about his lack of one. He may have been given some kind of certificate of equivalence, the usefulness and validity of which Iner may have questioned. No diploma or certificate has appeared in his papers, though, and Corona High School records do not go back far enough to reach any conclusion

Students with high school diplomas only, though, were expected to spend their first year studying the basic sciences. A bachelor's degree or a high school diploma plus a transcript showing the satisfactory completion of a number of premedical courses became the basic CME medical school requirement in 1910.[10]

Regardless of the institution, its name, or its track record, attending medical school was, and still is, expensive. Iner, however, had an advantage not enjoyed by all medical students. He had been developing his bees. By the time he enrolled as a student in the Loma Linda College of Evangelists he had many hives of bees on a location near Cajon Pass. They were productive enough that the sale of honey helped finance a significant part, though certainly not all, of his studies.[11] With good reason he mentioned his bees in a poem he wrote, apparently while studying medicine. Titled "Desert Hungry," the pertinent lines read,

Oh, for the sight of the morning light,
  At the bee ranch in "The Cajon,"
Where . . . wild buckwheat yields its golden sweet
  To the claim of industrious bees,
There's a happy ring in the songs they sing,
  As they wing through the desert breeze.[12]

---

today. Inelda May Christianson, daughter of Dr. Iner S. Ritchie, interview by Delmer G. Ross, 24 June 2003, Riverside, California.

[10] Richard H. Utt, *From Vision to Reality, 1905-1980: Loma Linda University* (Loma Linda, California: Loma Linda University, 1980), 37.

[11] Inelda May Christianson, daughter of Dr. Iner S. Ritchie, telephone interview by Delmer G. Ross, 27 May 2003, Norco, California.

[12] Dr. Iner Sheld Ritchie, "Desert Hungry," Ritchie Papers, SCLSU.

He also worked some, both on and off campus, to help pay his way. During the summers of 1909 and 1910, for example, he worked as "bee boy" in the El Casco Apiary at the Singleton ranch in San Timoteo Canyon.[13] After he had contributed what he could, the Ritchies took care of the remaining educational bill, "amounting to," as they put it, "*many* thousands of dollars."[14]

During his junior year he was honored by his fellow medical students by being chosen class president.[15] Life certainly was improving for the young man whose childhood had been shortened by the death of his mother and the difficult times that had followed.

The year 1909 brought a significant and important change in Iner's life. He was twenty-three years old when the Ritchies "adopted" him on January 26, 1909. Because at age twenty-three he was too old for the regular adoption process, this was not a legal adoption. Instead, it involved a legal change of name. He and his adoptive parents sent out announcements sharing their joyful

---

[13] The bee boy was in charge of the bees and extracting their honey. It was a position of responsibility. Iner called it "El Casco Apiary," named after nearby El Casco Lake, but it is unknown if that was its official name, or, for that matter, if it even had an official identity. Peggy Christian's history of San Timoteo Canyon offers two photographs of Iner. The first shows him and Owen Parrett, his roommate at Loma Linda during 1908-09, in a rowboat on El Casco Lake. The second shows him at the apiary. Peggy Christian, *Historic San Timoteo Canyon: A Pictorial Tour, Myths and Legends* (Morongo Valley, California, 2002), 150.

[14] Emphasis theirs. Deposition of William S. Ritchie and Anna L. Ritchie, undated fragment, Ritchie Papers, SCLSU.

[15] I.M. Christianson, interview by D.G. Ross, 3 June 2003.

news with friends and other family members. Short and to-the-point, the notices stated, "Mr. And Mrs. William S. Ritchie of Corona, California, desire to announce the adoption and presentation of their family name to their foster son, Iner Sheld, whose legal name is now Iner Sheld-Ritchie."[16] After January, Iner no longer only used Sheld as his last name but either added "Ritchie" preceded by a hyphen, or, especially in later years, simply used "Sheld"—or the initial, "S."—as his middle name. He now had something he had longed for since his mother's death—a loving family where he belonged and was appreciated.[17]

Iner's plans suffered a serious setback toward the end of the 1910-11 school year. It happened because of a dead coyote miles away in the San Bernardino Mountains. Part of the water used by Loma Linda for domestic purposes came from Big Bear Lake, created by a dam built high in the mountains in the 1880s. Water reached the valley far below through a series of open ditches and sluices. At some point a coyote apparently fell into the water distribution system. Whether it was alive at the time is unknown. If it was, it soon drowned, and its decomposing carcass began to pollute the water below, including some that was used by Loma Linda for drinking water. About a dozen people came down with

[16] Announcement of name change, no date, Ritchie Papers, SCLSU.

[17] Deposition of William S. Ritchie and Anna L. Ritchie, undated fragment; Deposition of Ritchie, William Shannon and Ritchie, Anna Lula Joseph; Deposition, William S. Ritchie and Anna L. Ritchie, 28 July 1947, Ritchie Papers, SCLSU; and Clarence E. Nelson, "Iner S. Ritchie Dies," *The Journal of the Alumni Association, School of Medicine, College of Medical Evangelists,* Vol. 21, No 1 (January 1950), 16.

A formal portrait of the Sheld brothers in 1912. Left to right, Stin and Dan Sheld, and Iner Sheld-Ritchie.

typhoid fever, including Iner and one other medical student at CME. The students were placed in the Loma Linda Sanitarium "quarantine ward," a cottage atop Sanitarium Hill, until they could recover sufficiently to be no possible danger to others. It took months for Iner to regain enough of his strength to be able to handle his classes. As a consequence he lost a full year of medical training.[18]

Back in school during the 1912-13 academic year, Iner grew concerned about the quality of medical instruction that he was receiving at Loma Linda, and he gave some consideration to the possibility of attending George Washington University, in Washington, D.C., for his final two years of study. Although apparently at least one other medical student at Loma Linda planned to attend George Washington, Iner hated the thought of being so far away from his young "adoptive sister," Inelda. So, at least for the time being, he continued his studies at CME.

By May 1914 he was again considering the possibility. In a letter to Inelda he candidly confessed,

I wish now with all my heart I had gone back to G.W. University. I have seen you precious little this year and only another [year of study] and I would have a diploma from there. Now if I go I would be there two years. Lately I have determined to be there next year but as yet my plans are not fully matured and connected. . . . We have had very poor Bible classes this year. None at all for weeks past and that is the very and only thing we are here for. If we do not get it we are entitled to the best of medical classes which we do not have in this school. The boys back at Washington have had much better Bible than we and the medical work has certainly been 10 X [times] as good.[19]

[18] I.M. Christianson, interview by D.G. Ross, 24 June 2003.

[19] Iner [S. Ritchie] to My Darling Precious Little Girl [Inelda Ruth Ritchie], 14-15 May 1914, Ritchie Papers, SCLSU.

Although it appears not to have been intended as such, Iner's letter offers a sobering indictment of the quality of at least some of the classes at the recently established medical school. In keeping with instructions from Ellen G. White that it should be of the "highest order," it sought to offer high standards of training. That was a commendable goal, especially in an age when it was possible to practice medicine after having served as an apprentice to someone who had earned his Doctor of Medicine degree in as little as six months. It was a goal, however, that apparently was not yet fully achieved.[20]

Iner's first roommate was Owen S. Parrett. He, too, was concerned about the quality of instruction at the College of Medical Evangelists, degrees from which were thought by a good many observers to be well nigh worthless. Like Iner, he graduated in 1915. He eventually talked the Iowa State Board into letting him take that state's medical exams. Much to his surprise—and nearly everyone else's, for that matter—he not only passed them, but did so with honors.[21] Perhaps the new medical school was not so bad after all!

After some encouragement from his instructors at the college in Loma Linda, though, Iner decided not to change schools. One, Dr. Thomas J. Evans, wrote him during the summer of 1914 to ask him not to "desert the school."[22] Evans' appeal may have made

---

[20] Schaefer, *Legacy*; 92, 95; and "Loma Linda University: 'a miracle.'"

[21] Carrol S. Small, ed. *Diamond Memories* (Loma Linda, California: Alumni Association, School of Medicine of Loma Linda University, 1984), 50.

[22] T.J. Evans to Iner Shell [*sic*] Ritchie, 21 August 1914, Ritchie Papers, SCLSU.

the difference, though it seems probable that the additional year required to earn a degree elsewhere was the deciding factor. In any event, on June 8, 1915, Iner became a member of only the second class to earn medical degrees from the College of Medical Evangelists.[23] Except for having lost a year as a result of having succumbed to typhoid fever, he would have graduated with the first class. His eventual graduating class of twelve was twice the size of the first one.[24]

As a student, Iner actively participated in the welfare of the community surrounding his medical school. He realized both instinctively and by training that Seventh-day Adventist doctors needed to work outside of the church as well as within it.

In an article titled "'But By My Spirit.' Zech. 4:6" that appeared in a 1914 issue of *The Youth's Instructor,* then the magazine published specifically for Adventist youth, Iner described some of his experiences as an "interne" at the county hospital.[25] He characterized the initial challenge as difficult and discouraging. Among other difficulties, he faced opposition because he did not work on Sabbath. As time went by, however, and he demonstrated his dedicated work ethic and his practical religion, the patients and employees of the hospital realized he had something special to offer. On one occasion, for example, a nurse

[23] Invitation to Iner Sheld-Ritchie's Graduation, 8 June 1915, Ritchie Papers, SCLSU.

[24] Small, ed., *Diamond Memories,* 39.

[25] Considering that he had not yet graduated from medical school, he probably should have been called an "extern" rather than an intern, regardless of spelling.

called him to deal with a particularly difficult patient. The patient, a woman who was known for her hot temper, had asked for him. When he arrived at her room he asked her how she was feeling. The patient told him that she had asked specifically for him because she had heard that he was a Christian—not because she felt she needed his medical ministrations. What she needed was spiritual assistance. She then indicated that she wished for him to pray for her. Moreover, before his visit was over she asked the Adventist medical student to come and teach her about the Bible every day. Among a number of similar experiences, Iner wrote of attending a Sunday evening service at a nearby popular church. There the wife of a local physician confided, "I really believe you have converted Mr. — to your belief. He keeps your Sabbath, and he believes as you people do." Iner, who months earlier had given the man several tracts—religious pamphlets—and had lent him some Adventist books, commented, "the seed sown had sprung up and borne fruit." Throughout his article, the fledgling medical evangelist made it evident that he felt that physicians and other medical workers needed to labor for people who did not know Jesus.[26]

He also wrote about the attitude of hospital personnel. At first he was regarded as "a bother and a nuisance." When introduced to the head nurse, her response was, "We need nurses here, not internes," and at mealtime he "was sent with the helpers to the common 'mess' table." Before long, though, he was invited to eat at the superintendent's table, he was performing surgery, and he

---

[26] Iner Sheld-Ritchie, "'But by my Spirit.' Zech. 4:6," *The Youth's Instructor*, Vol. 62, No. 42 (20 October 1914), 5-8.

was going on outings with the surgeon and his family. When his superiors went on vacation, he was "placed in charge of the institution for about a week." Moreover, he was invited to return. He had a valuable learning experience while interning, and hospital patients and personnel had learned about God's offer of salvation through his example, his conversation, his prayers, and the many dozens of tracts he had distributed.[27]

Partly as a consequence of his internship, early the following year Iner wrote a letter to John A. Burden, business manager for the College of Medical Evangelists and the Loma Linda Sanitarium, in which he expressed a perceived need for medical students to receive more practical experience in hospitals. He also indicated that other students felt as he did. Burden, who doubtless was well acquainted with Iner's article in *The Youth's Instructor*, tried to let him down gently and perhaps to chastise him for his audacity at the same time,

> I think there is a place for a measure of hospital experience that might be helpful to our work in observing methods and broaden [*sic*] our ideas, but generally to drink in the spirit of the work in hospitals would be to lose one's missionary zeal and conscientious endeavor in the Lord's work. . . . The lines of work that, to my mind,

---

[27] Ibid. Although he did not name the hospital in his article, it was the Riverside County Hospital in Arlington, California. That he, a medical student, was placed in charge of the county hospital for a week certainly is an indication of the high regard his superiors had for him. More significantly, though, it also is an indication of the sometimes appalling state of medical practice that prevailed at both private and government hospitals and other medical institutions during the early twentieth century.

are most helpful and beneficial, are to engage in the real field work and labor for souls, or in some of our institutions where the temptations to self-seeking are not so great.[28]

Burden felt sympathetic toward Iner because he willingly engaged in missionary work. Not all students seemed to realize as well as Iner did that people needing medical care probably also needed some spiritual attention, regardless of where they came from, their social standing, or their religious preference. He knew that Iner was acting out of genuine concern for the well being of the medical school and its students. So, after delivering his gentle scolding, Burden promised to meet with him and the other interested students to "talk over matters further."[29] Just what came of that meeting, or even if it was ever held, is not clear. In time, though, the medical students were encouraged to hone their skills in various area hospitals. A one-year internship became a requirement in 1926.[30]

On November 25, 1914, Iner married his adoptive sister, Inelda Ruth, in Corona, California. Marriage of siblings is unwise and illegal, but this case was different. Although apparently adopted into the same family, Iner and Inelda were not related. Moreover, while Inelda had been legally adopted by the Ritchies, Iner had not. He had become a Ritchie through a name change.

---

[28] J.A. Burden to Iner Sheld-Ritchie, 2 February 1915, Ritchie Papers, SCLSU.

[29] Ibid.

[30] Reynolds, *Outreach,* 39.

On a visit at the Pioneer Ranch in 1914, the Sheld brothers. Standing left to right, Stin and Dan Sheld, unknown, and former ranch hand Iner Sheld-Ritchie.

Exactly when they began to be attracted to each other romantically is unclear. Her parents later admitted, "We discouraged an early marriage,"[31] prior to mentioning their encouraging him to study medicine, so it may have been during the summer of 1911, or even before that. There is written evidence of their romance as early as October 1911, when she was fourteen. As Iner

---

[31] Deposition of William S. Ritchie and Anna L. Ritchie, undated fragment.

began the new school year studying medicine at CME he wrote a letter to Inelda in which he called her "my little love drop" and noted conspiratorially that while at a reception the previous night he had shaken the hand of a young lady who was interested in him, "They don't know all about brother yet; do they?" At the end of two pages, his closing was, "With much love, From your Iner."[32] The implication seems clear. Although they apparently had not made it public, the two already had reached some kind of understanding.

Two weeks later, Iner wrote Inelda a three-page letter that he called, "My First Love Letter." In it there is ample evidence of the existence of an understanding, if perhaps not yet an official engagement. Only the day before writing, he had returned to Loma Linda from the Ritchie home in Corona. Although he often rode his Harley-Davidson motorcycle, this time he rode the train. Inelda saw him off at the Santa Fe depot. He wrote "It has now been just twenty-four hours since I left home but it has seemed twenty-four days," and that "It has been a whole day since you gave me the last sweet kiss from your precious lips." In addition to "my little love drop," in this letter he called her "my little princess," "my little white lily," "my own little sweetheart," "my precious," and "sweet lover," among other endearments. He wrote of caresses and kisses and their love for each other.[33]

---

[32] Iner [Ritchie] to Ina [Ritchie], 2 October 1911, Ritchie Papers, CSLSU.

[33] Iner Sheld Ritchie to My Little Precious [Inelda Ruth Ritchie], 16 October 1911, Ritchie Papers, CSLSU.

While, just as Iner had labeled it, this clearly was a love letter, both he and Inelda were sincerely religious, a fact that became very apparent in the second half of the first paragraph:

> I only hope our love for each other will grow stronger and stronger as the years go by. I believe this will be so if we cherish and nurture this love which God has so graciously given us. How beautiful to know that you are loved with a true and pure love, an attribute which is the very essence of God's character. But we cannot hope to increase this love apart from Jesus, the One who is altogether lovely. Unless we seek his face and counsel daily and let him control our hearts and actions unreservedly, we cannot hope to attain that height and depth of love He intends we shall.[34]

Iner obviously hoped to make sure that the new relationship that he had just entered would be as spiritually successful as it possibly could.

At the time he penned these letters, Iner was twenty-six years old. Having been more or less on his own for more than a decade, he was recognized as being a mature man. Inelda, on the other hand, still was only fourteen. Perhaps that is why parts of his letters to her seem almost educational. Consciously or unconsciously, he may have been attempting to educate her in the way he hoped she would go.

---

[34]　Ibid.

The matter of another young lady, though, remained to be resolved. He had courted her for a time, and had been instrumental in convincing her to take nursing at the College of Medical Evangelists. For one reason or another his ardor had cooled, and he had fallen in love with his young adopted sister, Inelda. He then bought a beautiful gold pin-on watch, with a cover decorated with the image of a fountain and birds and flowers in various shades of gold, intending to give it to Inelda at an appropriate time. His nursing-student friend, however, spotted it and asked to hold it. Iner

Inelda Ruth Ritchie and Iner Sheld-Ritchie, with his Harley-Davidson motorcycle. 1914.

complied with her request. After she had admired it, he explained who it was for and asked her to hand it back. Not believing that it was not for her, she thought the idea of giving it to a fourteen-year-old girl was nothing less than comical and she refused. She knew her own ample bosom was just the right spot for such a watch. Iner finally had to tell her that he planned to have it engraved. She then relented and gave it back to him. Of course, he then gave it to Inelda, as he had intended from the time he had purchased it.

The young nursing student was outraged, and the next summer when she saw Inelda at camp meeting she demanded "her" watch! Inelda, who had been wearing it until moments before this encounter, had wisely removed it and slipped it for safekeeping to a girl who was with her. The nursing student was not fully satisfied, but there was nothing she could do. It was obvious that Inelda was not wearing it. After she left, Inelda got it back. Many years later she donated the watch to the Voice of Prophecy as an antique to sell in its fund-raising gift shop.[35]

Exactly when Iner and Inelda were formally engaged to be married is unclear. The couple's intentions, though, became very obvious less than a month after his so-called "first love letter," when on November 14, 1911, he wrote another in which he called Inelda his "precious little wife-to-be." He also offered some commentary on his life as a medical student: "Every moment of my time seems crowded and it rushes me to get all my lessons read over once and this means 4:30 in the morning till 10 -11: [*sic*] at night. My time seems engaged for weeks ahead." Some things do not change, especially lack of study time and insufficient sleep, as modern medical students can attest. As a kind of postscript, Iner added one more page the next day on which, among other things he asked for information on the efficiency of the postal service:

> I wonder if my little Precious Lover will go down to the Post Office tonight and I wonder will she be happy when she gets this from her true lover so far away. . . . This

---

[35] Class photograph and attachment, Ritchie Papers, SCLSU.

leaves on the 3:15 train P.M. [*sic*] I wish you would let me know if you receive it on the 4:25 at Corona.

Same-afternoon delivery for mail going from Loma Linda to Corona, some 35 miles away? Maybe some things do change, and not always for the better! Be that as it may, as he closed his letter he again called Inelda his "Precious little wife-to-be."[36] If they had not yet publicly announced their engagement, it may have been because of her youth.

Because they could not be together on Inelda's fifteenth birthday, on February 26, 1912, Iner thought it appropriate to send her what amounted to two messages. One was a two-page, endearment-filled letter. The other was a poem entitled "Remembrance" he had composed and illustrated for her. Two of the poem's twelve stanzas read,

> Oh! Quiet evening hour divine
>   For thy sweet calm I care
> Thou bringest thoughts of "Precious Mine,"
>   My little "Love Drop" fair,
>   . . .
> Mine to caress, to fondle, love,
>   Forever and for aye,
> Our souls but one, here and above,
>   In Him who is our Way.[37]

---

[36] Iner [S. Ritchie] to My Own Precious Little Sweetheart [Inelda Ruth Ritchie], 14-15 November 1911, Ritchie Papers, SCLSU.

[37] Iner [S. Ritchie], Remembrance, 26 February 1912, Ritchie Papers, SCLSU.

In the letter itself, among the words of affection, he wrote about something that had become at least a minor irritation,

> Today is my little sweetheart's birthday. She is fifteen years old—yes in years—but maybe twenty in character. [B]ecause she is engaged to be married some say she is tied down and robbed of her girlhood. I wonder if she is sorry or even doubtful of the choice. No I believe she is much more happy [*sic*] in her Lover than she would ever be outside his love.[38]

Apparently the couple had heard of some unfavorable comments on their engagement as something serving to tie Inelda down and to rob her of her childhood. Because of her tender age, such comments could have been expected. Iner probably had been teased about "robbing the cradle" by both his fellow medical students and his cowboy friends. Any such comments were undoubtedly keenly felt by him, especially considering that they were not totally inaccurate! But if youth was a problem, time would take care of it. The couple went on with their plans to be married.

About a year after his first love letter to Inelda, by November 4, 1912, Iner was addressing her in his love letters from Loma Linda as, "My Own Precious Little Wife." He continued to call her his "Sweet Little Love Drop," a favorite term of endearment, and he employed several others. He also continued to devote considerable space to spiritual encouragement. Like many of his

---

[38] Iner [S. Ritchie] to My Darling Little Precious [Inelda Ruth Ritchie], 26 February 1912, Ritchie Papers, SCLSU.

**The Riverside County Hospital nursing class, 1914.
Left to right, front, Intern Iner Sheld-Ritchie, Head Nurse,
Matron Addie Pettis, and William W. Roblee, M.D.
Back, six nursing students.**

other available love letters, this one contained no news of a
personal or any other nature unless a postscript written on the
margin of the second and final page, and reading, "Bye, Bye until
Fri. afternoon," might be deemed news. Considering that he tried
to spend as many weekends as he could with the Ritchies in
Corona, that was no longer news. It was more like "so long." He
signed off with "Your own true husband," a phrase he used in the
text, as well.[39]

---

[39] Your own true husband [Iner S. Ritchie] to My Own Precious Little
Wife [Inelda Ruth Ritchie], 4 November 1912, Ritchie Papers, SCLSU.

As time went by and the couple got to know each other better, and as Inelda grew more mature, Iner included more news in his correspondence. For example, in a letter written while he was interning at the Riverside County Hospital during the summer of 1914, he devoted nearly four of its five pages to an account of two motorcycle trips to the Hemet area to help his brother, Dan, who had suffered a shattered bone in his arm, plus related injuries, when kicked by a horse. He also told her that he was going to assist with a surgery. That letter uncharacteristically offered less than a page of "love words," as Iner often termed them.[40]

Some, while studying Iner's love letters, have been struck by how very much space he devotes to what might be termed "baby-talk."[41] For example, in one letter he wrote,

> It does your lover husband's heart so much good to know his little sweet and precious wife is so true and loves him so much. Darling mine you are the sweetest and most precious little girlie in all the wide, wide, world and then to think you are mine, all mine makes me so happy! I am Oh! So happy in your sweet tender love.[42]

---

[40] Iner [S. Ritchie] to My Darling Little Precious {Inelda Ruth Ritchie], 3 August 1914, Ritchie Papers, SCLSU.

[41] Joel R. Garbutt-Quistiano and Leslie Reeves, "Sweethearts Always" (term paper presented for HIST 294/494, History Colloquium, La Sierra University, Riverside, California, 25 April 1994), 2, D.G. Ross Collection.

[42] Iner [Sheld-Ritchie] to My Own Precious Little Sweetheart [Inelda Ruth Ritchie], 29 April 1912, Ritchie Papers, SCLSU.

While it seems doubtful that the happy couple viewed it as baby-talk, it may have been something carried over from when they first met, when Inelda was but seven years old. Be that as it may, considering that most lovers indulge in a bit of baby-talk from time to time, the only truly unusual aspect in this case is the amount, sometimes more than half of the letter.

Even years later, on occasions when they were away from each other, Iner was generous with terms of endearment in his letters to Inelda. In a two-page, news-filled letter he wrote in 1936, for example, he addressed her as "My Darling Precious Sweetheart Inelda," then used "my own sweet precious wifey" only three lines later. The remainder of the initial page dealt mainly with his trip. Five lines down on the second page, though, he called her "My Darling Precious," and other such terms soon follow: "Lover Mine," "My Darling," "Dear one," and simply, "Dear." The context of the last three of these terms is similar to what he wrote in his early love letters as well:

> Wish you were here tonight with me My Darling. I miss you so much but you can be sure that I love you Dear one, truly tenderly and always. *You are ever in my thoughts the one whom the Lord gave to me forever.* Just think, Dear, what a wonderful gift of lovely children the Lord has blessed us with in these after years of our married life.

After a few additional lines dealing with ordinary matters, he closed with "Lots of love & kisses to you. . . . As ever Your loving husband."[43]   He understood that love and marriage had to be cultivated to be successful.

Although there is only occasional evidence of disagreements in their letters, like most lovers, they did not always see things the same way. In a letter written while he was about to complete several months of clinical training at the First Street Clinic[44] in Los Angeles and Inelda had been away from home at Hinkley[45] in the desert near Barstow for several months, Iner reacted dejectedly after she had told him of some of her plans for the immediate future:

> [W]hy come down here and camp . . . at Albert and May's [her uncle and aunt's place] in the wash when I am up at Arlington? Surely you aren't trying to evade me are you Dear? . . . I don't see why you want to spend the time thus away from me. . . . Darling lover I do love you so and wonder if you really love me as you used to. I hate to think Dear that you do not. . . . I would not for any-thing have you feel that you must marry me whether or

---

[43] Iner [S. Ritchie] to My Darling Precious Sweetheart Inelda [Ritchie], 9 March 1936, Ritchie Papers, SCLSU. The emphasis was Dr. Ritchie's.

[44] Located at 941 East First Street, this facility had been acquired by CME in 1913 so as to provide clinical training for its medical students. It evolved into the White Memorial Medical Center. Adventist Health System/West, "From Clinic to Medical Center: White Memorial Celebrates 80 Years of Making a Difference in Los Angeles," *Pacific Union Recorder,* Vol. 93, No. 16 (16 August 1993), 6-7; Utt, *From Vision to Reality,* 34-35, 54-55; and Schaefer, *Legacy,* 99.

[45] By 1912 the Ritchies were subdividing and selling real estate at Hinkley and at the Wildwood Glen subdivision south of Corona. IRC [Inelda Ritchie Christianson] to Delmer Ross, no date, D.G. Ross Collection, HPSLSU.

no. . . . Better speak the truth now than when things cannot be undone.[46]

He also complained, "Lately your letters have been so far apart and so few love words in them. You do not seem to care as much . . . as you did."[47] He often griped about the lack of communication from her, especially when she was at Hinkley. She had three girl friends out there, and was enjoying a more active social life than she was used to back in Corona. Sometimes she did not answer Iner's letters as quickly as he would have liked, and he felt rather neglected.[48] Although phrased more diplomatically, she expressed the same complaint about him: "Your letters have been quite far apart of late, but then, when I know that you love me it is alright [sic] although I do get so lonesome between letters." Then, to prevent him from being too displeased with her for criticizing his lack of communication, she closed with a promise designed to make everything right, "Lots of love and kisses to you and when you come . . . you will receive lots more. Your loving little wife, Inelda."[49] She had barely turned seventeen, but she knew how to handle her man.

In other correspondence, Iner sent Inelda a postcard with his picture on it. For the most part, though, in his letters he declared

---

[46] Iner to My Darling Precious Little Girl, 14-15 May 1914.

[47] Ibid.

[48] I.M. Christianson, interview by D.G. Ross, 24 June 2003.

[49] Inelda [Ruth Ritchie] to My Own Dear Sweet Lover [Iner S. Ritchie], 18 March 1914, Ritchie Papers, SCLSU.

Iner and Inelda Ritchie's wedding picture, 1914.

his love for her. While only a few of her letters to him still exist, in those that survive she expressed her love for him. Interestingly enough, there is almost no discussion of wedding plans in their letters. They must have dealt with such matters face-to-face. Most comments dealing with their upcoming wedding were like Iner's in a letter written six weeks prior to that event: "Darling I am so awfully lonesome for you but Dearie the time is flying by and our glad and happy wedding day is drawing nearer and nearer."[50]

Iner had often said that he hoped he would be married before he turned thirty. He made it. Inelda Ruth was merely seventeen years old when she married a far more mature Iner, who was already past his twenty-ninth birthday, on November 24, 1914. The wedding, which took place at the Ritchie home in Corona, was a small affair attended by relatives and a few close friends.[51] Although there still seemed to be a vast difference in their ages in 1914, as time went by and they both matured together, the difference loomed less and less significant. While Iner had to spend time in Loma Linda and Los Angeles so as to complete his medical studies, the couple made Corona their home base until he graduated in 1915.[52]

---

[50] Iner [S. Ritchie] to My Darling Sweetheart Wifey [Inelda Ruth Ritchie], 21 September 1914, Ritchie Papers, SCLSU.

[51] I.M. Christianson, interview by D.G. Ross, 24 June 2003; and Marriage License, 25 November 1914, Ritchie Papers, SCLSU.

[52] Inelda Ruth Sheld-Ritchie, widow of Dr. Iner S. Ritchie, interview by her granddaughter, Cheryl Ann Nickel Leathers, 20 November 1985, [La Jolla, California], 5, Ritchie Papers, SCLSU.

A few days after their wedding in Corona the couple took a train to Los Angeles. There Iner showed his young wife the First Street Clinic where he would spend a good deal of the remainder of the school year. Perhaps more importantly to both, they also visited a photographic studio where they posed for an "official" wedding photograph.

Early Medical Practice and Teaching

After graduating from the College of Medical Evangelists in 1915, the new physician spent one year with Dr. Elmer H. Thompson at his hospital in Burbank, California. Dr. Thompson was a Seventh-day Adventist who was well known to the new physician. He had been the family doctor for Iner's Uncle Otto Shields and his family, and he had been one of those who, nearly a decade earlier, had encouraged him to go into medicine.[1]

Although the just graduated medical doctor was eager to serve in some foreign field—Africa and India seemed to attract him in 1915—several of his relatives pointed out to him that having only recently recovered from both typhoid and scarlet fevers, he should perhaps wait until his body had more fully mended. He recognized the wisdom of their advice.[2] He was chosen by the General Conference of Seventh-day Adventists to go to China only a year

---

[1] Inelda May Christianson, daughter of Dr. Iner S. Ritchie, interview by Delmer G. Ross, 24 June 2003, Riverside, California.

[2] [Inelda May Christianson], "Iner Sheld-Ritchie, October 6, 1885 - October 24, 1949," [undated chronology], 5, Ritchie Papers, SCLSU.

later, but financial obligations kept him from doing so. Two years later, in 1918, he hoped for a call to Africa, but nothing materialized.[3]

In 1916, going by the title and name, Dr. Iner Sheld-Ritchie, he began his own private practice with Dr. Edward H. Wood in Arlington, California. Dr. Wood was the superintendent of the Riverside County Hospital, then located in Arlington, where as a medical student Iner had externed—although he was called an "interne"—during the summers of 1913 and 1914. Arlington, sometimes called Arlington Station, was a small community located part way between Riverside and Corona. Today it is part of Riverside.

Over the years, from 1915 to 1927, Iner and Inelda had four children, Iner William, Anna Virginia, Inelda May, and Robert Lorraine. All of the Ritchies' children were born at home. With a doctor in the family there seemed to be no need for hospitalization for normal childbirth.[4]

As a matter of fact, from the very beginning of his practice of medicine and for as long as he lived, Dr. Ritchie offered childbirth in the home for all his patients who requested it. He would have family members get out buckets, boil water, and have clean sheets and newspapers ready. Then he would help the mother bring the new family member into the world.[5]

---

[3] Iner Sheld-Ritchie to Orno Follette [*sic*], 14 August 1919, Ritchie Papers, SCLSU.

[4] Inelda May Christianson, brief chronology, no date, Ritchie Papers, SCLSU.

[5] I.M. Christianson, interview by D.G. Ross, 8 July 2003.

Dr. Ritchie was very busy with his practice, with the position he came to hold at the College of Medical Evangelists, and with his various mission and other medical service projects. Consequently, a few years after the birth of their first children, Iner William, who was born on July 23, 1915, and Anna Virginia, who

In 1916 Dr. Ritchie and young Iner William pose with their first touring car, a 1914 Hupmobile.

arrived on February 23, 1917, Inelda Ruth became concerned that they were not able to spend enough time together. They then lived in Loma Linda and Dr. Ritchie was extremely busy preparing for and teaching classes at CME while still handling a number of patients from his former practice in Arlington. After giving the problem some thought, she came up with a possible solution. Those were the days when doctors made house calls, and Inelda decided that the travel time between patient visits might make good family time. She first told her husband of her uneasiness, then gave him what she viewed as a feasible answer for the family of a busy physician. As someone who could never forget that he had once lost his family, he was as eager as she to spend quality time with family members. He thought over her plan, and decided it just might work. Consequently, they put it into effect. It worked well enough that they continued to do it for the next fifteen years or more. Many years later, Inelda May, their second daughter, remembered that while living in Calexico, California, her mother often cleaned them up, helped them put on their pajamas, and then they all joined their father as he took care of his evening house calls on both sides of the international border. The family remained outside, in the car. If the call was a lengthy one, the children might be allowed to get out, though they had to remain nearby. Dr. Ritchie apparently did not record exactly how his patients reacted to this kind of attention from their physician, but if they knew about those waiting outside they could not fail to see how highly he regarded his family.[6]

A year or so after he began his private practice in Arlington, Dr. Ritchie had to deal with an onslaught of sufferers from the great Spanish flu epidemic of 1918.[7] Although millions of victims

[6] Christina Cicchetti, "El Doctór [sic]," *Journal of the Riverside Historical Society*, Vol. 2 (February 1998), 4; and Inelda Ritchie Christianson, daughter of Dr. Iner S. Ritchie, interview by Maritza Durán, 13 May 2000, Riverside, California.

[7] Estimates of fatalities range from 21 to 50 million people worldwide, with as many as 700,000 of those in the United States. While termed the "Spanish flu," this particular strain of influenza appears to have originated in the United States where it may have developed in pigs. It then spread

succumbed worldwide, as did a large number locally—especially those hospitalized at nearby March Field—none of Dr. Ritchie's patients did. Dr. Ritchie attributed his success to the different advice he gave his patients. In order to make room for new patients, at the March Field hospital recovering influenza sufferers were rotated out of bed as soon as each one's temperature had returned to normal. Then, however, some seemed to suffer recurrences that were as bad or worse than the original bout. Altogether too often such relapses ended in death, usually from pneumonia. Dr. Ritchie, on the other hand, insisted that his patients stay in bed and that they remain well covered for a full three days after they were over their fever. He became famous locally as the one truly successful flu doctor, and there was considerable demand for his services. So much contact with often seriously ill influenza patients had a predictable downside—he too caught the disease. As he began to recover it took his wife and mother-in-law together to keep him from getting out of bed and going back to work too soon, but they succeeded in forcing him to heed his own advice. Like his patients, he recovered.[8]

Those who plan to go into medicine no doubt dream of effecting miracle cures for desperate patients. That is a noble goal, but practicing physicians are very aware of the other side of the

---

throughout the world, hastened by the deployment of infected American troops during World War I. Paul Recer, "Flu that Killed 20 Million Traced," *The Riverside (California) Press-Enterprise,* 21 March 1997, A-17.

[8] I.M. Christianson, interview by D.G. Ross, 17 June 2003. According to family tradition, while none of Dr. Ritchie's influenza patients died, for whatever reason, he was less successful when he helped to treat another physician's patient. See "Obituary," 2, Iner S.Ritchie file, WebbLLU.

coin. They do not always succeed in saving lives. One such incident involved Dr. Ritchie late in 1917. He and another physician were summoned to help an Arlington merchant and his elderly parents who had become violently ill from ingesting some kind of poison. Apparently the mother had mistakenly used a poison that looked like baking powder instead of the real article when she made some pancakes that all three later ate. The two doctors did all they could, but their three poisoned patients died.[9]

For a time Dr. Ritchie was connected with the Sherman Indian School. Located between Arlington and Riverside, it enrolled between 700 and 800 students from many different tribes. There was a small hospital on campus where he often treated acute cases of tuberculosis and trachoma. The latter, which is also known as granular conjunctivitis, and which he described as "a granular disease of the eyelids," was a common student malady. Untreated trachoma was thought to have been at least partly responsible for the high incidence of blindness among Navajo and other Indians of the American Southwest.[10]

He was also the official surgeon of the Orange Growers and Lemon Growers associations and the American Beet Sugar Company. He treated their injured on an insurance basis. His knowledge of Spanish came in handy while acting in that capacity because most of their employees were Mexicans.[11]

---

[9] "Whole Family Dead," *Arlington (California) Times*, 2 November 1917.

[10] I.S. Ritchie to O. Follette [*sic*], 14 August 1919.

[11] Ibid.

Many of Dr. Ritchie's patients came from Riverside's Chinatown, where he was known as the "God Doctor." What really impressed his minority patients, whether they were Chinese, Japanese, Mexican, or something else, was that, aside from obvious emergencies, he saw all his patients in the order that they arrived. Race, money or the lack of it, color, or inability to speak English did not matter to him—except that the last made communication difficult unless he had a good and trustworthy translator. He never deliberately saw Caucasian patients first, the way so many other physicians did. No wonder Chinese patients from as faraway as Los Angeles sometimes car pooled to see him rather than someone nearby.[12]

At the beginning of American involvement in World War I, Dr. Ritchie became a member of the Volunteer Medical Service Corps. His main duty was to examine volunteers and draftees to determine if they were physically fit to serve in the armed forces. For this public service he was awarded a certificate signed by the Secretary of War, among others.[13]

As previously seen with his work as an intern at the county hospital, Dr. Ritchie believed in offering service to others. Beginning about 1918 and continuing for the better part of a decade he also contributed his medical services to the Lake Grove Indian Mission, a church institution only recently begun and

---

[12] [Christianson], "Iner Sheld-Ritchie, 1885 - 1949," 5.

[13] I.M. Christianson, interview by D.G. Ross, 13 May 2003; and Certificate No. 28341, Volunteer Medical Service Corps, 9 November 1918, Ritchie Papers, SCLSU.

developed by Mr. and Mrs. Orno Follett.[14] Located on a section of land at Smith's Lake, about fourteen miles northeast of Thoreau, New Mexico, Lake Grove grew to a sizable mission compound situated just 43 miles south of the present-day La Vida Mission. Among other buildings was a sixteen-bed hospital, a church, and a cafeteria.[15]

Ira and Lorraine Follett, son and daughter-in-law of the founder of the Lake Grove Indian Mission, later wrote about Dr. Ritchie going to the mission and helping Ira's father with major medical problems[16]. Inelda sometimes traveled with him, and they might stay as much as a week. When a medical problem surfaced that was too much for Dr. Ritchie to deal with, he sought help from experts, sometimes taking them with him on his trips to the Lake Grove Mission. For example, in 1917 he convinced Dr. William W. Roblee, at that time probably the most prominent

[14] Minutes of the Meeting of the Indian Work Advisory Committee, Lake Grove Mission, near Thoreau, New Mexico, 4 December 1917, Ritchie Papers, SCLSU; and Inelda Christianson to Monty Andress, 2 March 1994, Ritchie Papers, SCLSU.

[15] Ira and Lorraine Follett to Anna Nickel, 12 May 1994, Ritchie Papers, SCLSU. The ancient Indian name for the site was *Tsin-naz-bans-sa-a,* or Lake Grove, hence the modern name. Minutes of the Meeting of the Indian Work Advisory Committee, 4 December 1917. The approximately 640 acres of land comprising the section on which Lake Grove was located was the only privately owned land in the area. The remainder became part of the Navajo Indian Reservation. [Orno Follett] to R.B. Coberly, 14 January 1918, Ritchie Papers, SCLSU.

[16] I. and L. Follett to A.. Nickel, 12 May 1994.

surgeon in Riverside, to accompany him to Thoreau to do some particularly delicate surgery on a patient at the mission hospital.[17]

Dr. Ritchie did not limit his work at the Lake Grove Indian Mission to what he might accomplish at the hospital. In the 1920s at his home in Loma Linda[18] the den often was stacked with clothes he and Inelda had collected to take to the mission for the Folletts to distribute to needy Indians. Sometimes they took food.[19]

---

[17] I. Christianson to M. Andress, 2 March 1994; and I.M. Christianson, interview by D.G. Ross, 3 June 2003.

[18] They lived at the present address of 25058 East Prospect Street in a redwood bungalow they had built on a lot given to them by William S. and Anna L. Ritchie. It was located adjacent to the 24-room "Ritchie Mansion," then at 365 Prospect—today its address is 11170 Ritchie Circle—which had been designed and built in 1895 by Col. J.T. Ritchie for a retired British sea captain named Lewis Smith Davis. Calling it "Snug Harbor," Davis lived there before it was sold to one of the colonel's nephews, William Shannon Ritchie, in 1916. The Ritchies promptly moved from Corona to Loma Linda and occupied the house until the death of Anna Lula Ritchie, Inelda Ruth's mother, in 1948. Although it had been transferred to the Seventh-day Adventist church, in 1950 Iner William Ritchie, the elder son of Iner and Inelda Ritchie, upon learning of the subdivision of the 8.5 acres on which it stood and of plans to demolish the mansion, promptly bought it to keep it from being razed. He did major remodeling and reconstruction work on it. In 1992 it was acquired by Loma Linda University which, after more reconstruction, uses it to house ambulatory cancer patients receiving proton treatment and their families. Deposition of William S. Ritchie and Anna L. Ritchie, undated fragment, Ritchie Papers, SCLSU; Keld J. Reynolds, *Sunshine, Citrus and Science: Loma Linda from Indian Village to Charter City, An Informal History* (Loma Linda, California: City of Loma Linda, 1985), 34-35, 44-45; Jennifer M. Dobbs, "A Safe Harbor," *The San Bernardino County Sun,* 24 December 2001, D1, D5; and Loma Linda University Medical Center, *Ritchie Mansion,* invitation to grand opening, 12 December 2002, Ritchie Papers, SCLSU.

[19] Inelda [Ritchie Christianson] to Lorraine and Ira [Follett], 5 October 1994, Ritchie Papers, SCLSU; and I. Christianson to M. Andress, 2 March 1994.

Even when they were only passing through on their way to some other destination, they remembered the mission. In 1919 when Dr. and Mrs. Ritchie went back east for him to do some postgraduate work in New Orleans, Chicago, and New York City, they dropped off a large, dome-lidded, steamer trunk filled with oranges when their train went through Thoreau. The Indian children at the mission were in for a nutritious treat. Mrs. Ritchie later commented that, "the Indians would eat them with all the peeling on . . . everything . . . just like you'd eat an apple. . . ." Then, as an afterthought, she added, "I suppose they got some good out of the peelings."[20]

Incidentally, that was the first long trip Inelda Ritchie took, and she found it both interesting and profitable. It became profitable when she took a job in Chicago while Dr. Ritchie was completing his studies there. As she later explained,

> The little hotel that we were staying in . . . had a dining room, and we ate there. . . . I didn't like the waiter, and I told the manager. I said I could do a better job than that waiter. . . .
> He said, "Do you want a job? I just fired him."
> I said, "Yes, I do." So I worked there . . . during that time we were there. . . . I got my board and I got my tips. And he wouldn't let me write anything down. I had to

---

[20] Ibid.; and Inelda Ruth Sheld-Ritchie, widow of Dr. Iner S. Ritchie, transcript of interview by her granddaughter, Cheryl Nickel Leathers, 2 March 1986, [La Jolla, California], 17 [3], Ritchie Papers, SCLSU.

memorize everything, and you were supposed to give it to the right person.[21]

The job doubtless cut into time for sightseeing and window shopping—while admitting that she did not buy anything, she fondly recalled the Marshall Fields department store[22]—but it provided a useful, albeit small, financial windfall.

Inelda also had at least one somewhat disturbing experience—enough so that she still remembered it vividly more than 65 years later. It happened while they were in New Orleans. While Dr. Ritchie took his classes and studied, she explained,

> I just wandered around and looked in the stores. One time . . . I went to a little movie theater. I thought, well I'll go in there and sit down. I was tired, I'd been walking around town. . . . I sat down in one of the seats on the side. Pretty soon a man came in and sat on the aisle. Then he moved over into the seat next to me, and he kept crowding me over all the time. I had a big hat on, which I'd taken off because you were supposed to take it off in a movie. And I had a big hatpin. I put the hatpin down . . . and the next time he crowded me over, I gave it a nudge, and he swore and left.[23]

---

[21] I.R. Sheld-Ritchie, transcript of interview by C.N. Leathers, 2 March 1986, 18 [4].

[22] Ibid., 19-20 [5-6].

[23] Ibid., 18 [4].

The trip was an eye-opening experience for someone from rural Corona, but she handled herself well.

Later in 1919 Dr. Ritchie wrote a letter to Orno Follett in which he wondered if it would be "practical for a medical missionary to enter the field with you and work as such for the Indians." Noting that "I much prefer the outdoor work along with the indoor work and especially in a good wide missionary field," he offered to move to Lake Grove to help the Indians with their medical needs. He indicated that he had accumulated quite a bit of medical equipment that he could take with him, plus two automobiles, a Ford and a Buick, although with their successful use by General John J. "Black Jack" Pershing's troops in their futile attempt to capture Pancho Villa in northern Mexico he wondered if a Dodge might be better.

He went on to indicate "my heart is in this message and I believe somewhere there is a place for me in it." Then he outlined how he thought he might contribute to the Lake Grove Mission:

> I would like to have a kind of center where I could have an office or dispensary and teach at the school and then go out on itinerating tours and teach amongst the Indians on the reservations, not only healing their physical ills but their spiritual also and thus combine the two as did our Master when He was here on earth. I don't believe we will ever reach the ideal until we do this.

He concluded by reiterating that his heart was in the work and stating that "If I cannot help in person I surely can by sending something."[24]

Alluding to his service on the Local Military Exemption Board #1 and commenting that he had "an excellent recommendation from the Governor of our State" may have raised a few eyebrows. Or perhaps Dr. Ritchie's mention that he had made $13,500 in 1918 led to concern on the part of the North American Division of the General Conference of Seventh-day Adventists, which operated the Lake Grove Indian Mission, or there may have been some other reason, but his offer was not accepted. It was not that his service was unwelcome. At the time there simply was not enough money to hire additional personnel. Orno Follett wondered if some local government position might be suitable until such time as means to hire him were available. Although he did not join the staff at Lake Grove, he became a frequent visitor, contributing funds, equipment, and among other things, many days of personal service.[25]

Although aside from the expectation of a profit it is not entirely clear why, at about this time Dr. Ritchie became involved in the Lake Grove area in another way, as well. Along with a local

---

[24] I.S. Ritchie to O. Follette [sic], 14 August 1919.

[25] Ibid.; and Orno Follett to Inner-Sheld Richie [sic], 27 November 1921, Ritchie Papers, SCLSU. In addition to the trunk filled with oranges, and many other items already donated, well before his offer to join the staff of the Lake Grove Indian Mission he had interested others in offering help as well. For example, William S. Ritchie offered to donate, as Follett put it, "three dozen folding chairs, a fairly good surrey, several of our denominational books, and some school books." Orno Follett to W.S. Richey [sic], 2 May 1918.

partner who had been a patient, he invested in a herd of goats. World War I had caused a scarcity of meat in the area, and the partners hoped to fill the vacuum. Before they had been able to make any significant amount of money, though, the war ended—and so did their prospects.[26]

While telegraph and telephone communication was common-place in 1919, carrying letters of introduction and recommendation still was *de rigueur* for those traveling from place to place any significant distance from home where one was known. A letter from a cashier at the Citizens Bank of Arlington presents the traveling physician by stating that, "Dr. Ritchie contemplates visiting the Middle West and eastern states in the near future and we recommend him to be an honest and straightforward young man."[27]   Such a letter may have been helpful as Dr. and Mrs. Ritchie traveled to New Orleans, New York City, and Chicago where he took postgraduate courses to hone his medical skills and to prepare for a teaching position at CME, but the Folletts and the Indians at the Lake Grove Indian Mission needed no such presentation.

Early in his career, though, Dr. Ritchie made it a practice to obtain letters of introduction or recommendation from people in positions of responsibility. He placed them in a notebook. Then,

[26] Inelda May Christianson, daughter of Dr. Iner S. Ritchie, telephone interview by Delmer G. Ross, Norco, California, 15 January 2004; Orno Follett to W.S. Ritchie, 23 July 1918, Ritchie Papers, SCLSU; and I.R. Sheld-Ritchie, transcript of interview by C.N. Leathers, 2 March 1986, 25 [11].

[27] J.W. Wells, Cashier, Citizens Bank of Arlington to Whom it may concern, 14 April 1919, Ritchie Papers, SCLSU.

especially in Mexico, when he arrived someplace where he was unknown he would visit the highest placed local official he could—usually the mayor, military commandant, or political chief—and show him the recommendations in the notebook. Before the visit was over, he would ask whoever he was visiting for a letter of introduction or recommendation which, when received, he would add to the others. Eventually he carried an impressively large notebook filled with such letters.[28]

In addition to his general practice of medicine in Arlington, beginning in 1918, at the request of President Percy Magan of the College of Medical Evangelists, Dr. Ritchie became an anatomy instructor at his alma mater. For the first two years he taught part time. By September of 1920, however, he had given up his office in Arlington and had begun working full time as a regular faculty member at CME. Above average in height and rather stern appearing, it was said that as a professor Dr. Ritchie could "look holes through you" when he felt the need. Consequently his well organized classes proceeded in orderly fashion. Although he had become a member of the teaching faculty, he did not stop taking care of patients. He continued to assist those he had come to know in his practice and who preferred to continue with him rather than go to some other physician for their medical needs. He even took time to serve new patients who were in need.[29]

---

[28] I.M. Christianson, interview by D.G. Ross, 1 July 2003.

[29] "New Notes," *The Medical Evangelist,* Vol.6, No. 4 (March 1920), 27; [O.R. Staines, ed.] "Our Graduates in Medicine—Where are they?" *The Medical Evangelist,* Vol. 7, No.1 (June 1920), 6-7; [O.R. Staines, ed.] "College News," *The Medical Evangelist,* Vol. 7, No. 2 (September 1920), 19; Carrol

By 1920 Dr. Ritchie had become interested in the formation of a College of Medical Evangelists alumni association. Already, in the six years since the first class had graduated, 68 students had received doctor of medicine degrees, and another 14 would in 1920. He had more in mind than occasional get-togethers for the purpose of rehashing school days, though. He explained,

> With the present number of graduates, we feel that we have now come to the time when we can organize into a successful alumni association. . . . It should necessarily be organized upon a sound and proper financial basis, having the support of all its members. Such benefits as a poor students' fund and the establishment or aid of medical missionary work, both at home and in foreign fields are worthy of our attention.
> The hearty co-operation of every graduate is earnestly solicited in this matter.[30]

After soliciting input from all the graduates, Dr. Ritchie also indicated that he believed *The Medical Evangelist* should "be the official organ of the association, and as such should receive the proper support and aid from all the members."[31]

The initial organizational meeting took place on May 26, 1920, at a banquet held during commencement ceremonies. Other

---

S. Small, ed., *Diamond Memories,* (Loma Linda, California: Alumni Association, School of Medicine of Loma Linda University, 1984), 51; and I.M. Christianson, telephone interview by D.G. Ross, 11 June 2003.

[30] Iner Sheld-Ritchie, "The Alumni," *The Medical Evangelist*, Vol. 7, No. 5 (March 1921), 9-10.

[31] Ibid.

meetings followed, and in 1923 the new Alumni Association elected its first president and other officers.[32]

When Dr. Ritchie was not in the classroom he involved himself in a number of activities. One was the presentation of community lectures on health. On October 25, 1921, for example, he took part in a medical evangelism campaign started by the College of Medical Evangelists and the Southeastern California Conference in Redlands, California. Dr. Ritchie gave a lecture about kidney diseases and how to prevent them.[33] He also conducted similar meetings farther from home in the Baja California area. A handbill written in Spanish, and distributed on January 30, 1924, announced that on February 1 Dr. Ritchie would offer the first in a series of illustrated lectures on the causes and effects of diseases and on ways to avoid them. To be presented in Mexicali, all lectures in the series would be free of charge for everyone.[34] A short while later a health lecture he offered in Colton attracted more than 700 listeners.[35]

As Dr. Ritchie's community involvement grew and his supposedly nonexistent practice expanded to include indigents, he

---

[32] Small, ed., *Diamond Memories*, 251.

[33] J.G. White, "The Redlands Campaign," *The Medical Evangelist*, Vol. 8, No. 4 (January-February 1922), 8-9, 12-14.

[34] La Comisión, *Al Público*, a handbill, Mexicali, Baja California, 30 January 1924, Ritchie Papers, SCLSU. Reports on a number of the meetings can be found in "A Mission Field at Our Door," *The Medical Evangelist*, Vol. 10, No. 32 (31 January 1924), 1-2; and Iner Sheld-Ritchie, "The Stranger At Our Gates," *The Medical Evangelist*, Vol. 10, No. 34 (14 February 1924), 1-2.

[35] C.F. Innis, "The Loma Linda Dispensary," *The Medical Evangelist*, Vol. 11, No. 52 (25 June 1925), 2-3.

became busier and the amount of time he had to spend with his growing family dwindled noticeably. As mentioned earlier, the Ritchies decided that the travel time between patient visits might make good family time. Accordingly, when he made his evening house calls, his wife and children often accompanied him in their car. On one such occasion, on May 18, 1924, when Inelda was in an advanced stage of pregnancy, she felt the first contractions and knew that the baby was on the way.

Dr. Ritchie generally was in charge of his own life as well as those of his family members. "Everything revolved around him," was the way his younger daughter put it many years later.[36] But this was one night the spotlight was on someone else.

Mrs. Ritchie's cousin, Lillian Joseph, happened to be along with them that particular evening. Upon Inelda's instruction, she ran to the door, knocked, and when her rapping was answered, explained briefly that the doctor was urgently needed. He quickly returned to the car. He started it up and drove as fast as he could toward home, where all of their children were and would be born. They were traveling way too fast down Magnolia Avenue, then the main route of travel between Arlington and Riverside, when a motorcycle policeman pulled them over. Hoping to avoid a ticket, Dr. Ritchie explained the situation. The cop was more than understanding; he wanted to help. So, after ascertaining the address of the Ritchie home in Loma Linda, he told the worried doctor, "Follow me." Then he got back on his motorcycle and took off, lights blinking and siren blaring. Try as he might, though,

---

[36] I.M. Christianson, interview by D.G. Ross, 9 September 2003.

Dr. Ritchie discovered that he simply could not keep up with that motorcycle! It was frustrating, especially for a man who enjoyed fast cars!

Fortunately, they made it home safely and well before the arrival of the baby. The next morning, following the birth of a healthy daughter they named Inelda May, Dr. Ritchie went out and bought a new car, a Marmon that he hoped could go fast enough to keep up with helpful motorcycle policemen![37]

Several years later the family was along when Dr. Ritchie had to make an afternoon call at a house off of La Cadena Drive, between Riverside and Loma Linda. Young Inelda May and her little brother, Bob, got out of the car to walk up and down

Iner and Inelda with their two daughters, Anna Virginia and Inelda May, 1924.

the long drive to the house. Suddenly the two children were confronted by a hissing, wing-flapping goose that was certain its territory was being invaded. As Inelda May later explained, "I was so scared my feet wouldn't move at first, then I flew to the car."[38]

---

[37] I.M. Christianson, interview by D.G. Ross, 10 June 2003.

[38] I.M. Christianson, interview by D.G. Ross, 24 June 2003.

Bob could run faster, though, and made it to safety first. While they were being comforted in the car by their mother, the goose no doubt considered the results to be quite satisfactory!

From the beginning of his medical career, Dr. Ritchie advocated serving people in need. The life experience of his mother's untimely death and her spiritual encouragement impressed his heart to dedicate his life to helping others and speaking out to encourage others to do the same. In reference to the College of Medical Evangelists, probably as notes for a speech or speeches he would give later, he wrote,

> Do you suppose God would have estab[lished] a school here under the most diff[icult] circ[cumstances] and written volumes about it and the training and ed[ucation] of nurses and physicians and all about med[ical] work if He did not intend us to study hard to get knowledge and then go out and practice[,] work and use that knowledge[?] Where are those who say—Lord send me—Do miracles—no need for all this waste of time, money and work[?] If we get out and do our utmost, God commends us—and He will work with us and do for us where we are unable for His namesake.[39]

Dr. Ritchie employed such appeals to interest his and other students at the College of Medical Evangelists in volunteering for unpaid service to the needy.

He continually challenged others to participate in medical missionary work, and not only in speeches. In an article, "Medical

---

[39] Iner S. Ritchie, note, no date, Ritchie Papers, SCLSU.

Missionary Work in the Homeland," written for *The Medical Evangelist* late in 1923, he once again demonstrated his commitment to and advocacy of medical missionary work.[40] In it he encouraged physicians to be instruments of God. In the process he wrote about a miraculous healing he and another graduate from CME at Loma Linda had personally witnessed. The two physicians had been called to the bedside of a young man who was having a pulmonary hemorrhage. Dr. Ritchie had previously treated him for tuberculosis, a possible aftereffect of phosgene gas with which he had been poisoned while in the army in France during World War I. "As I beheld the pitiful appeal in his face while the lifeblood poured in clots from his mouth," he wrote, "I sent up an appeal to God to stop the fatal flow." He explained that they then took pieces of cord and tied one firmly around each extremity near the man's trunk. They thus kept blood in their patient's arms and legs, saving them, while at the same time, because of the bleeding, reducing blood pressure in his trunk. They gave him a sedative to help prevent coughing, then propped him up on pillows and had him lie with his hemorrhaging lung down. His good lung was then uppermost and gravity would be less likely to carry blood into it and possibly strangle him. They then placed an icebag over the lung area affected and applied heat to the man's extremities. By so doing they hoped to encourage the formation of a clot that would halt the bleeding. In short, they did all they could think of to help their patient, but they knew it might not be enough, and so

---

[40] I.S. Ritchie, "Medical Missionary Work in the Homeland," *The Medical Evangelist*, Vol. 10, No. 26 (December 20, 1923), 1-4.

did his loved ones. Ritchie continued his account, emotionally setting the scene,

> Reader, can you imagine the anxiety of the young wife during this terrible experience? Can you picture the father and mother wringing their hands as they watch the lifeblood flow from their son, their only child? Can you hear them crying in anguish of soul, "Oh doctor save our boy, save our boy." If we are familiar with God's messages to us for this time there will not be a circumstance arise or condition present itself but what we may by the eye of faith see in it an opportunity or blessed privilege of service for Him. It is in such an experience as this that these messages have individual worth and meaning and these experiences will become more frequent in the future.[41]

To those present Dr. Ritchie then explained that while "all had been done that human skill could do . . . God had promised that He would do what we were unable to do." He then opened his Bible and read a number of comforting promises.

To add to his appeal for his readers to become involved in selfless service to others he offered a quotation from Ellen G. White, one of the founders of the Seventh-day Adventist Church:

> The physician can do a noble work if he is connected with the Great Physician. To the relatives of the sick, whose hearts are full of sympathy for the sufferer, he may find opportunity to speak the words of life; and he can

---

[41] Ibid.

soothe and uplift the mind of the sufferer by leading him to look to the One who can save to the uttermost all who come to Him for salvation.[42]

Getting back to his story, he explained what followed:

We knelt down by the bedside and in the presence of all acknowledged God as our Maker and redeemer asking God for his namesake to bless what had been done, and true to His great heart of love, he kept His promise. The sweet presence of God filled the room, our patient became restful and quiet and the hemorrhage ceased. What a wonderful God we serve! Surely He loves us with an everlasting love![43]

The physician continued to check on his patient, doing his utmost to help him heal physically, praying with him, and sharing with him God's tremendous love. All the members of the family accepted God as their personal Savior. Thereafter they welcomed Dr. Ritchie into their home as often as he wished to visit.[44]

The missionary physician encouraged institutions as well as individuals to get involved in medical missionary work. In another article published in *The Medical Evangelist,* Dr. Ritchie encouraged the establishment of a department in the Loma Linda Sanitarium to help those in real need even though they could not

---

[42] Ellen G. White, *Testimonies for the Church*, Vol. 6 (Oakland, California: Pacific Press, 1901), 231.

[43] I.S. Ritchie, "Medical Missionary Work in the Homeland."

[44] Ibid.

pay. He challenged it, and all Seventh-day Adventist sanitariums, to practice what the church preached. The social activist argued,

> Let us consider the need of a dispensary in connection with our sanitariums where the poor from the surrounding country may come and obtain treatment. Whenever a sanitarium is established in a community every one far and near is informed as to the character and purpose of the institution. They are told that it is a Christian institution and therefore a missionary enterprise. How natural then for the unfortunate needy sufferers to turn to the institution for treatment or advice. Those in distress, and unable to meet the sanitarium rates, are sent to us. Should they be turned away without treatment or advice, or should a department be maintained to care for this class? It is my firm belief that every sanitarium should operate a place where the poor, needy, unfortunate sufferers could come for relief. When these are turned away from our institutions because of prohibitive prices it causes unfavorable comment and we are branded as not representing the true spirit for which we stand, but rather belonging to the priest and the Levite class who passed by the helpless, suffering victim, leaving the work for the Good Samaritan to do. We surely need to provide a department of this kind in connection with our larger institutions for both the Bible and the Testimonies speak of our duty to the poor.[45]

Perhaps Dr. Ritchie's appeal had the desired affect because a year later the same publication reported that Loma Linda Sanitar-

---

[45] Iner Sheld-Ritchie, "Work for All Classes," *The Medical Evangelist,* Vol. 11, No. 32 (February 5, 1925), 1-2.

ium once more had a small dispensary for those in need. Work quickly spread resulting in twice as many patients seen in January 1925 as had been in December 1924.[46]

Dr. Ritchie took seriously his commitment to assist the less fortunate in the immediate community as well as those farther away. In 1923 he established a small dispensary for members of the Mexican American community who lived near the College of Medical Evangelists, including those who were indigent. Using his own funds, he even hired a Spanish-speaking Bible worker to assist patients with their spiritual needs. Although he had help, he also did what he could to care for them in person between his class appointments.[47]

Moreover, during the academic spring break in April 1925, as chairperson of the field missionary work committee, he took three sophomore medical students to Calexico, California, and its Mexican counterpart, Mexicali, Baja California, to engage in medical missionary work among the Chinese and Japanese living along the border line between the United States and Mexico. They visited quite a number of Chinese merchants and reported they sold subscriptions to the Chinese *Signs of the Times* to virtually every one.[48]

---

[46] I.S. Ritchie and C.F. Innis, "Loma Linda Dispensary," *The Medical Evangelist,* Vol. 11, No. 35 (February 26, 1925), 4.

[47] I.M. Christianson, interview by D.G. Ross, 17 July 2000.

[48] O.R. Staines, ed., "Loma Linda Dispensary," *The Medical Evangelist,* Vol. 12, No. 11 (September 10, 1925), 1; and [O.R. Staines, ed.], untitled news items, *The Medical Evangelist,* Vol. 11, No. 43 (April 23, 1925).

The medical missionary's service among people of Mexican, Chinese, and Japanese extraction is significant because of the social and political arrangements that were commonplace at that time. Although there were notable exceptions, in general in the United States these three groups did not participate in mainstream American culture, but instead kept to themselves. They often lived in desperate circumstances, and without modern medical care. Although in some areas they were at the heart of the labor force, because of prejudice and poor pay they could not participate in the results of their labor. Much the same was true of people of Chinese and Japanese extraction living in Mexico, where prejudice was often based on religious as well as racial differences.

While he realized that helping such minorities could result in repercussions from those in higher positions in society, or possibly even from government officials, Dr. Ritchie also understood the importance of serving others, no matter what their race, gender, or class might happen to be. It was his Christian duty, as taught through precept and example by Jesus himself.

To the Mexican Border

Even before earning his medical degree, Iner S. Ritchie had been interested in foreign medical missionary service. Once he had the degree and was licensed to practice, he hoped it would not be long before he would be serving God and humanity in some far-off corner of the world. He received a call to China in 1916, but could not go. Later he received another call, this time to India, a place to which he had always hoped to be called to serve. After thinking it over very carefully, he regretfully turned it down because, as Inelda Ruth put it later, "Mamma made such a fuss about it," pointing out that she and her husband "were old and he hadn't ought to go off so far away." That was not the only problem: "there wasn't anything prepared for them, and they didn't have a house to live in or anything else. They just had to scrape it up someway after they got there." Doing that with a wife and two children along, and not knowing the language or native customs, was sobering enough that he regretfully decided against going.[1] Not being able to go to a far-away place did not mean he could not

---

[1] Inelda Ruth Sheld-Ritchie, widow of Dr. Iner S. Ritchie, interview by her granddaughter, Cheryl Ann Nickel Leathers, 20 November 1985, [La Jolla, California], 6, Ritchie Papers, SCLSU.

serve closer to home, but his offer to help as a church employee at the Lake Grove Indian Mission was not accepted. He therefore determined to try the area of the border between the United States and Mexico—on his own. He decided on Calexico, California. It was on the Mexican border, but it was not very far from Loma Linda, and he already knew Spanish.

Dr. Ritchie's work for the Mexican community started with short trips to Calexico, and from there just south of the border into Mexico during the early 1920s. He offered a home nursing course in Calexico in 1923, and it was well enough received that he later offered others on both sides of the international boundary. His first major involvement in the Baja California Norte[2] area occurred in 1924, though, when he joined Dr. Ralph M. Smith in his pioneer medical work in Calexico, California, for the summer.[3]

Dr. Smith had earned a medical degree from the College of Medical Evangelists in 1916, one year after Dr. Ritchie had earned his. After service as a medical officer in World War I, in 1919 he and his family moved to Mexico City where he became known as an excellent surgeon. He even performed major surgery on Pancho Villa. The unrest and violence that accompanied the Mexican Revolution, though, made his and his family's safety uncertain. Then, when the Mexican government enacted a law prohibiting foreign physicians from practicing medicine in Mexico, he moved

---

[2] The Territory of Baja California Norte became the State of Baja California in 1952.

[3] Iner Sheld-Ritchie, "Parting Tribute From Dr. Iner Ritchie, Lifelong Friend and Chum of Dr. Ralph Smith," *The Medical Evangelist,* Vol. 31, No.12 (15 December 1944), 2, Ritchie Papers, SCLSU.

+ o

Library Gift Slip

Date 3 / 5 / 09

<u>Call Number</u>

11214399

per
MC-9

KEEP: Rivera   Science
Music SpCol   Eaton
Cage   Edserv./Juv Ref.
       Maps   Media
       Palm Desert

Scotty:

Checked Out - Due ___/___/___

Missing   On Search   Lost

Usage:

Not On Shelf ___/___/___

Same Date   Y   N
Same Publ   Y   N

Copy 1

Used___ _____times

From _____ to _____

EXCELLENT   GOOD   FAIR POOR

COVERUP CLOTH VINYL PAMB PAPER

Copy 2

Used___ _____times
From _____ to _____

EXCELLENT GOOD FAIR POOR

COVERUP CLOTH VINYL PAMB PAPER

Other Editions: Yes____ No____

Melvyl: B D I LA SB
SC SD SF NRLF SRLF

ADDALL:
Titles _____
Price_____

Replace Stack Copy _____
Withdraw Stack Copy _____
Library Copies Needed _____

TRANSFER DATE DUE SLIP _____

Binding Decisions
Vinyl_____
Pambind_____
Fullbind_____
LC Bind_____
Cover Up_____

DISCARD
Booksale _____
Alibris _____
Toss _____

earch by: _____
sage by: _____

out of that country. A number of incidents on the trip back to the United States seemed to confirm the wisdom of the decision to leave. Soldiers often got off their train and went ahead to inspect the tracks to make certain no dynamite or bombs had been put in place. When they pulled into San Luis Potosí they discovered the train station still burning after an attack. It definitely was time to leave.[4]

Smith still wished to help Mexicans, though, so he developed a general practice at Calexico, California, not just coincidentally right on the Mexican border. He established that community's first hospital—an emergency hospital located at 305 Third Street—in 1922. Because of the excellent reputation he had earned for himself and his hospital, many of his patients came from Mexico. Some of them were Mexican government officials who, as a reward for tending to their own medical needs, carefully looked the other way when he called on other patients south of the border.[5]

---

[4] Inelda May Christianson, daughter of Dr. Iner S. Ritchie, interviews by Delmer G. Ross, 17 July 2000 and 15 July 2003, Riverside, California; and Arthur N. Donaldson, ed., "News Notes," *The Medical Evangelist,* Vol. 7, No. 1 (June 1920): 24.

[5] O.R. Staines, ed., Untitled news items, *The Medical Evangelist,* Vol. 11, No. 23 (4 December 1924), 4; Inelda May Christianson, daughter of Dr. Iner S. Ritchie, telephone interview by Delmer G. Ross, 29 June 2003, Norco, California; Inelda May Christianson, brief chronology, no date, Ritchie Papers, SCLSU; and I.M. Burke, "Dr. Ralph M. Smith," *The Medical Evangelist,* Vol. 31, No. 12 (15 December 1944). Interestingly, Smith became known as "Mexico's leading marksman and sharpshooter" during his stay in Mexico City. More significantly, he later was instrumental in obtaining the land for what eventually became the University of Montemorelos, in the state of Nuevo León, Mexico. "Jean Dunber Smith Hankins, Eulogy & Life Sketch," no date, Ritchie

Dr. Smith was a surgeon, and he wanted to disassociate himself from general practice so that he could concentrate more on his main field of expertise. He had managed to interest his medical-school chum and good friend, Dr. Ritchie, by pointing out the missionary possibilities of the area, then enticing him into making a number of short visits to Calexico and Mexicali. The capital of the Mexican territory of Baja California Norte, Mexicali was much larger than Calexico and was served by a number of Mexican physicians, but they had their hands full with upper and middle-class patients—those who could pay—and devoted relatively little time to lower-class Mexicans, and almost none at all to the Asian and Asian-Mexican minorities living in and around Mexicali.

It did not require many visits for Dr. Ritchie to become aware of the need for medical missionary work in the region, so sometime in 1924 he tentatively agreed to buy Dr. Smith's practice and hospital for $3,000. After spending the summer in Calexico as Dr. Smith's partner, he decided to go ahead with the purchase, the terms of which were agreed upon in July 1925 when he again was working in Calexico. Dr. Ritchie would make an initial payment of $2,000. The remainder of the purchase price would be paid in monthly installments. The purchaser was to be in sole charge of the practice during the summer of 1925. Because Dr. Ritchie had obligations at the College of Medical Evangelists, though, Dr. Smith would take charge again in the fall. During the time of alternating service the two physicians would share equally the proceeds of the practice.[6]

As a consequence of all of this, and to become acquainted with Dr. Smith's patients and to allow them to become acquainted with him, Dr. Ritchie and his family spent the summers of 1924 and 1925 in Calexico. It must have been difficult for them. Winter weather in Calexico may be mild compared with that of most other regions of the United States, but there is nothing mild about summers. High temperatures ranging from 110 to 120 degrees in the shade can last for days—occasionally even weeks—on end. In a letter to her parents Inelda Ruth indicated that

Partners Iner S. Ritchie and Ralph M. Smith, 1925.

it had been 122 degrees and that five field workers had died of sunstroke. It seemed far worse than today because back then people did not have evaporative coolers, let alone air conditioning, in their homes. People on both sides of the border used electric

---

[6] Agreement for the sale of real estate and medical practice (rough draft), July 1925, 1-2, Ritchie Papers, SCLSU.

fans, which with some preparation, could at least help them sleep at night.[7]

Inelda May was only three weeks old when they moved to Calexico for that first summer. As daytime temperatures soared into triple digits, and stayed in the 80s and 90s at night, making the baby almost continually restless, her mother devised a solution:

> There was a little back bedroom that was just a screened porch. And I put her [Inelda May] on a bed on that, and I put an old chair that I found there that belonged to the Smiths, and I wet a towel and put it over the back of the chair and put a fan behind it, and that was my air conditioning for her.[8]

The others just had to tough it out, though, like their neighbors they sprinkled water on their sheets and bedclothes and used electric fans. Even if the fans only put the hot air into motion, it had a cooling effect as it sped the evaporation of the sprinkled water and perspiration.

At first they used an icebox to keep their food from spoiling. The ice house was just across the street, so they did not have to worry about running out even on the hottest days. After refrigerators appeared on the market, though, they bought a large, two-door Frigidaire. It cost $500, which was a small fortune back then, but

[7] I.R. Sheld-Ritchie, interview by C.A.N. Leathers, 20 November 1985, 6-7; and Inelda [Ruth Ritchie] to Precious Mamma and Papa [Anna Lula and William S. Ritchie, 1 August 1924, Ritchie Papers, SCLSU.

[8] I.R. Sheld-Ritchie, interview by C.A.N. Leathers, 20 November 1985, 7.

it was worth it. It was kept in the hospital and was intended for hospital use, but there was enough room in it that the Ritchies used it, too. They had a lady come in and clean the place for them one day a week. One time when they got back from going somewhere, they discovered her sitting on a chair in front of the refrigerator. Both doors were open, and she was fanning herself, trying to cool herself off. As Inelda Ruth put it, that refrigerator "was a real luxury."[9]

Although the exact date is unknown, the Ritchies appear to have moved into their new home at 329 Third Street in Calexico sometime in December 1925. They were less than a block away from their hospital. On January 28, 1926, *The Medical Evangelist*, reported that Dr. Ritchie had relocated to Calexico, California, and was very busy. In less than one 24-hour period he reported he had dealt with "three obstetrical cases . . . , an appendix case, a double fracture of the forearm, . . . numerous office cases and calls . . . [and] a poisoning case where I washed out the stomach." In the same sketch he indicated, "We have a nice little Sabbath School started on the Mexican side—fifteen were present last Sabbath, and I gave them a little talk."[10] He viewed himself as a medical evangelist, and he was not about to forget the evangelistic part of that combination. In a matter of weeks Dr. Orley Van Eman, who had earned his medical degree from CME in 1924, and who had

---

[9] Ibid.

[10] Iner S. Ritchie, quoted in O.R. Staines, ed., "From Here and There," *The Medical Evangelist,* Vol. 12, No. 31 (28 January 1926).

begun a private practice in Arlington, joined him in an association that was to last two years.[11]

Because the practice became quite large he hired a number of other physicians to help him, paying them $300 to $400 per month for their services. Unlike Van Eman who was a partner, these other doctors were employees. The two physicians who eventually bought his practice, Drs. Truman E. Bartholomew and Oran Lamar Webster, started out as his employees, each making $350 per month.[12]

The little emergency hospital Dr. Ritchie acquired from Dr. Smith was way too small for the number of patients the practice soon was attempting to handle. So, after borrowing some money from the local bank, they bought two houses on a corner, then built an addition between them, joining them togther into one larger structure. Offices and examining rooms took one house, x-ray and other services occupied the new part, and the other old home became the new hospital. Even so, the emergency hospital in Calexico was not large. It still could only handle a handful of patients at the same time. On one occasion, when the hospital was already completely full, there was an automobile accident and seven additional patients were brought in. Some had compound fractures with the ends of bones protruding through the flesh, but

---

[11] O.R. Staines, ed., "Dr. Orley Van Eman, Class of '24," *The Medical Evangelist,* Vol. 11, No. 43 (23 April 1925); and O.R. Staines, ed., "News in Brief," *The Medical Evangelist,* Vol. 12, No. 36 (4 March 1926).

[12] Mrs. W.S. Ritchie to Eld. E.E. Andross, 17 October 1934, Ritchie Papers, SCLSU; and Mamma and Amma [Anna L. Ritchie] to Iner and Inelda [Ritchie], 28 August 1935, Ritchie Papers, SCLSU.

no matter how desperate, they were in better shape than some of those already hospitalized. The accident victims had to make do with sheets laid on the lawn.[13]

Dr. Ritchie faced many difficulties in Calexico, from summer heat to border problems. Some he just had to put up with. Others, however, he could deal with. One of the latter variety was caused by a druggist in Calexico who often failed to fill prescriptions as exactly as they had been written, nor did he determine what substitutions might be acceptable. That endangered his patients, and the border physician would not allow such acts to continue. He simply stocked a small pharmacy of his own, then sold the proper medications to his patients. Some, of course, were unable to pay, neither for treatment nor for medications; they were asked to pay token amounts or were not charged at all. Some, whose circumstances might improve, were offered credit.[14]

Once they had moved to Calexico, Dr. Ritchie sent the children back to Loma Linda each summer where they could enjoy relatively "cool" weather, with highs often ranging between 100 and 105 degrees. To most people, that would be hot enough, but it was ten to twenty degrees cooler than it was in Calexico. They stayed with Inelda Ruth Ritchie's adoptive parents, who had plenty of room for them in the Ritchie Mansion. Sometimes they stayed briefly with other relatives, as well.[15]

---

[13] [Iner S. Ritchie], untitled 14-page manuscript with internal title, "God's Vast Design," at top of page 12, no date, 8-9, Ritchie Papers, SCLSU.

[14] I.M. Christianson, interview by D.G. Ross, 17 July 2000.

[15] Inelda May Christianson, telephone interview by Delmer G. Ross, 29 June 2003, Norco, California.

Summer heat in the Imperial Valley was a problem for virtually everyone living there, not just recent arrivals. One of the hospital bathrooms had a large porcelain bathtub where seriously overheated patients could be cooled until their temperatures returned to normal. When needed, the tub was filled with water to which was added ice from the ice house conveniently located across the street from the hospital, then the patient was immersed in the cold water. That tub saw a lot of use every summer.[16]

The oppressive summer heat was especially hard on pregnant women. Although not quantified scientifically, it sometimes was blamed for miscarriages, spontaneous abortions, and related problems. Dr. Ritchie delivered hundreds of perfectly healthy babies during the time he practiced medicine along the border, but he also had to treat women who were not so fortunate. His daughter, Inelda May, later explained one of the results:

> Always the teacher, he preserved a set of embryos in all stages of development, a two-headed baby, and an ancephalic baby. These moved with us wherever we went and finally were donated to the Medical School at Loma Linda University by my brother Iner Wm. Ritchie when, after Daddy's death, he moved into Daddy's Monterrey Medical Building. Pre-meds going to Loma Linda for a tour used to . . . talk to me about them.[17]

---

[16] The America Legion clubhouse was located directly across the street from the hospital, and the ice house was next to it. Inelda May recalls watching the Legion's outdoor movies from the roof of the hospital. I.M. Christianson, interview by D.G. Ross, 1 July 2003.

[17] I.M. Christianson, interview by D.G. Ross, 17 July 2000.

This amply illustrates Dr. Ritchie's way of thinking. Even terrible tragedies could be used to advantage. Along with his faith in God and his work ethic, it was a major reason for his success.

The heat may have been responsible for the breakup of the partnership of Drs. Ritchie and Van Eman. They were supposed to receive equal shares of the proceeds, but after two years of working togther it appeared that Dr. Ritchie had more to show for his share than did Dr. Van Eman. This led to Van Eman or someone close to him suggesting that Dr. Ritchie might have been taking more than his rightful share of the proceeds of the business.

When the word reached Dr. Ritchie, he confronted his partner, denied any wrongdoing, and demanded a thorough accounting. Once the accounts had been checked, it became apparent that the partners had taken only their proper shares, but it was discovered that Dr. Ritchie had done $4,000 more work than his associate. Dr. Ritchie was disgusted with the whole episode, and demanded the dissolution of the partnership. Unfortunately, the accusation also ended their friendship.[18]

In 1927, usually accompanied by a railroad supervisor, Dr. Ritchie traveled over Southern Pacific Railroad lines in northern Mexico as a railroad District Surgeon. Being a physician for an important American company operating in Mexico offered a way to practice medicine there without a Mexican license—as long as he did not stray too far from areas served by the railroad. It also provided a way to travel free. Upon his arrival at some town or

---

[18] Mrs. W.S. Ritchie to Dr. Ralph M. Smith, 6 August 1935, 5, Ritchie Papers, SCLSU.

village along the line, he might treat a railroad employee or two, and a few others, before proceeding to some other place. It was also a good way to learn the lay of the land and about the people living along the line. It allowed him to do missionary work in communities he otherwise might never have visited, all at little expense to himself. Whether he had any other motives for such travel is unclear. Eventually, though, the contacts he made helped the spread of the gospel, not only to areas of Baja California, but also to Hermosillo, Ciudad Obregón, Navojoa, and other places he visited in the large north Mexican state of Sonora.[19]

He did not forget the home front along the border. When he first arrived there was a single family of believers in Mexicali, but by March 1927 he was pleased to be able to report the establishment of a Mexican church with thirty members. It grew rapidly, and by the beginning of June counted more than fifty members. By then it also had its own pastor. Such advances no doubt would have come without Dr. Ritchie's border practice, but his presence in Calexico, his willingness to serve in Mexicali, and his evangelistic zeal stimulated far more rapid growth than might otherwise have been possible.[20]

It was at this time that the Ritchies became acquainted with Clarence and Jessie Moon. Clarence was a Seventh-day Adventist

[19] [Iner S. Ritchie], untitled 14-page manuscript with internal title, "God's Vast Design," 9; and Earl and Hazel Meyer, La Obra Adventista en la Frontera, no date, 1, Ritchie Papers, SCLSU.

[20] [Iner S. Ritchie], "Working in Old Mexico," *The Medical Evangelist,* Vol. 13, No. 47 (19 May 1927), 1-3; and Carrol S. Small, ed. *Diamond Memories* (Loma Linda, California: Alumni Association, School of Medicine of Loma Linda University, 1984), 51.

missionary nurse whose assigned field was northern Mexico, including the Baja California peninsula. Having already served for more than six years in Puerto Rico, the Moons were experienced medical missionaries. As the Ritchies and Moons helped each other in various ways they became good friends. Clarence later was instrumental in convincing Dr. Ritchie to accept the position of Medical Director of the Mexican Union.[21]

Dr. Ritchie in the examination room of the Calexico Hospital, about 1924.

---

[21] Inelda Ritchie Christianson, "Ritchie Family Life in Riverside," 7, Ritchie Papers, SCLSU; and "College News," *The Medical Evangelist,* Vol. 8, No. 1 (July 1921), 26. Clarence Earl Moon, had trained as a nurse at the St. Helena Sanitarium and Hospital in today's Deer Park, California, where Orno Follett had been his roommate. [Inelda May Christianson], "In 1920 the territory . . . ," no date, Ritchie Papers, SCLSU.

In the fall of 1926, when Iner William and Anna Ritchie were ready to go to school, they at first attended the New River Church School. It was located a few miles northwest of Calexico. Their teacher was Jeanne Middleton. She had been Iner William's teacher at church school in Loma Linda before they moved to Calexico, so she helped to provide continuity for the youngster. She was a physical therapist who lived at the hospital.[22]

A year later, though, the children began staying with their grandparents and went to school in Loma Linda. Because Dr. Ritchie worked as a physician for the Southern Pacific Railroad, he had a pass that was good for him and the members of his family. Therefore, when the children traveled between home and school, they took the train. It was a long trip, at least in time—if not miles—so they made it only when they would be able to spend more than just a two-day weekend at home. Depending on the direction of their travel, either their parents or their grandparents made them peanut-butter-and-jelly sandwiches to eat as they rode along.

One time, though, sandwiches were left behind. Inelda May accompanied her mother, Inelda Ruth, as she traveled to San Bernardino to handle a real estate matter. When they got on at Calexico, they boarded a Pullman coach that stood alone on a siding. They then went to bed. During the night the coach was attached to a northbound train. After getting up in the morning

[22] [Inelda May Christianson], Iner Sheld-Ritchie, October 6, 1885 - October 24, 1949, an undated chronology, 6, Ritchie Papers, SCLSU. Jeanne Middleton later returned to Loma Linda and took nursing at CME. She then taught physical and occupational therapy to nursing students there for many years. I.M. Christianson, interview by D.G. Ross, 15 July 2003.

they had breakfast in the dining car. Years later Inelda May recalled a black waiter serving her steaming hot cream of wheat cereal with cream at a table set with white linen and gleaming silver. They got off when the train paused at Colton.[23]

On one memorable occasion the Imperial Valley was struck by an earthquake, not one of the minor ones that are fairly common in the area, but a major shaker. It was nighttime and, to add to the general confusion and consternation, it was followed fairly quickly by several strong aftershocks. For safety, just in case the largest tremor was only the forerunner of an even stronger earthquake, Inelda Ruth and the children spent the rest of the night in the ambulance—really a Lincoln limousine—that was parked in front of the hospital. Inelda May recalls being amused as they watched patrons of bars, brothels, and gambling halls running and stumbling across the line into Calexico as if ghosts or wild animals were after them. Some were kneeling and praying right in the street as they felt each aftershock.[24]

For recreation they sometimes went for drives to places other than Dr. Ritchie's patients' homes. Among the places they visited were the "sand hills," or Imperial Sand Dunes, off to the east of Calexico, where the famous movable "plank road" built in 1916 had been replaced by a paved road in 1926. They drove to the petrified oyster beds and the prehistoric animal tracks in a canyon near Kane Springs in the Chocolate Mountains to the northeast. They also visited the dinosaur tracks in Split Mountain Canyon, to

[23] I.M. Christianson, interview by D.G. Ross, 1 July 2003.

[24] I.M. Christianson, interview by D.G. Ross, 8 July 2003.

the northwest of Calexico. After church on Sabbath they sometimes ate lunch in the park. Because Dr. Ritchie was busy during
the week, most such activities took place on weekends. At home
they often played phonograph records, including one called *The
Three Black Crows,* a vaudeville act. Of evenings they would
listen to the radio—along with many other Americans, *Amos 'n'
Andy* was one of their favorite programs.[25]

Although Dr. Ritchie was licensed to practice medicine in
California, he had no such license for Baja California or any other
part of Mexico. Government officials in Mexico, though, quickly
learned of his good reputation as a doctor, and they soon were
calling on him for help when they were ill or had suffered an
accident of some variety. They promised that as long as he did not
stray too far from Mexicali he would suffer no trouble for
practicing on their side of the border.[26] They needed him, after all.
So, with the help of a Mrs. Webb, a black practical nurse with a
very pleasant, accommodating bedside manner who nursed almost

[25] Inelda Ruth Ritchie to Precious Mamma and Papa [Anna Lula and
William S. Ritchie], 12 December 1926, Ritchie Papers, SCLSU; Nelda Mae
[Inelda May Ritchie] to Iner William [Ritchie], 18 November 1931, Ritchie
Papers, SCLSU; Daddy [Iner S. Ritchie] to Iner William [Ritchie], 28 March
1932, Ritchie Papers, SCLSU; Anna [Ritchie] to Iner William [Ritchie], 28
November 1932, Ritchie Papers, SCLSU; and I.M. Christianson, interview by
D.G. Ross, 15 August 2004.

[26] In reality, there were many unlicenced individuals, both foreign and
Mexican, practicing medicine in Mexico. Apparently this could be done legally
as long as the practitioners did not call themselves doctors. Often, therefore,
they called themselves "specialists in all diseases," or something similar. Once
they were licenced as medical doctors, however, they were considered to be
practicing at a higher level. Henry F. Brown, "The Medical Situation in
Mexico," *The Medical Evangelist,* Vol. 10, No. 19 (1 November 1923), 1-2.

all highly placed government employees throughout the city when they became ill, Dr. Ritchie became the physician of preference for many Mexican officials. Included among them were General Abelardo L. Rodríguez, governor of Baja California Norte, and his family, and various members of the Peralta family. Francisco Peralta, who became a good friend, was Inspector General of Police for Baja California Norte—the chief of police for the territory.[27]

While he appears to have done nothing that was particularly spectacular—like starting a riot or finding a cure for cancer—during his stay in the Calexico and Mexicali area, Dr. Ritchie established a cordial relationship with government officials through his sound and very successful practice of medicine. Moreover, despite many difficulties, with the assistance of Governor Rodríguez, he eventually obtained a license to practice medicine in Mexico.

As previously mentioned, Dr. Ritchie had started out by offering public health lectures for the general public. By way of preparation, in addition to organizing lecture notes and appropriate material for illustrations, he contacted the governor's office and asked for official permission. He was authorized to give the classes, but he still faced occasional opposition and harassment

---

[27] I.R. Sheld-Ritchie, interview by C.A.N. Leathers, 20 November 1985, 8; and Fco. S. Peralta to Jose [sic] Ma. Tapia, 14 January 1929, in Ritchie, Iner S., File, WebbLLU. "He and Mrs. Peralta had several beautiful daughters, all married to important men. The oldest girl's husband was the army general for Baja California. There was one son. He owned a nightclub in Mexicali. The girls came to see Daddy in his office in Riverside." I.M. Christianson, interview by D.G. Ross, 8 July 2003.

from some lower-level officials who thought he should have a license to practice medicine in Mexico before offering any lectures or classes. If one adhered to a very strict interpretation of the law, such individuals may have been technically correct. The governor and many other officials, however, realized that such a rigid view would not be best for the people. Dr. Ritchie was trying to help them enjoy better health. Unless one had a political agenda of some variety, it did not make sense to oppose that.

The problem was that there was such a political agenda, one that was held by many Mexicans of the day. The Mexican Revolution was still in progress. The most violent phase had been over for a dozen years or more, but the slogan, "Mexico for Mexicans," which had been fashionable during the early violence was as popular as ever, and would remain so for another two decades. It was a natural reaction to some of the excesses, or perceived excesses, of the earlier Porfirio Díaz administration. It took men with a certain amount of strength and the ability to think clearly to act contrary to what was politically popular, and apparently legal, as well. Consequently, despite official permission from the governor, Dr. Ritchie faced occasional harassment from lower-level functionaries.

While he was preparing for and praying about the health classes, he was summoned to the Governor's Palace in Mexicali. It was the day when, as the self-supporting missionary physician later remarked, "the angel pinched the baby." The governor's baby had been crying for two whole days, and its mother was becoming frantic. Mexican doctors had been called already, but they had not been able to help. They could not find anything wrong, but neither could they stop it from crying. Maybe Dr.

Ritchie, from across the line in Calexico could help. The worried mother had heard about the miraculous recovery of a woman living right next door who had been dying of puerperal sepsis. Her Mexican doctor had given up and even had refused to see her any more. Although her temperature was 107 degrees and she was delirious when Dr. Ritchie had been called, he had quickly diagnosed the problem and he had operated immediately, right there in her own home. After further treatment, the woman had recuperated.[28]

So the American physician was called. Like his Mexican counterparts, Dr. Ritchie could not determine the cause of the baby's whimpering and wailing, but he decided to give the little tyke some water treatments. He knew they could not hurt, and perhaps they would help. The baby calmed right down. When Mrs. Rodríguez told her husband what had happened he invited the good doctor into his office. Dr. Ritchie went in and politely introduced himself: "Doctor Iner S. Ritchie, a sus órdenes,"— "Doctor Iner S. Ritchie, at your service."

They shook hands and Governor Rodríguez offered his congratulations and some of his best whiskey.

"Thank you very much, but I don't drink alcoholic beverages."

"Oh! Then please accept these fine Havana cigars."

"I thank you again, but neither do I smoke."

---

[28] [Iner S. Ritchie], untitled 14-page manuscript with internal title, "God's Vast Design," 5.

The governor seemed momentarily perplexed, then responded, "In that case, what can I offer you? Maybe there is something you need."

Of course, there was! Dr. Ritchie explained the situation to him. He added that he could really use a good place to hold his classes.

**Home nursing class graduation in the
Mexicali high school, 1932.**

The governor thought for a moment, then responded, "No problem. How about the high school auditorium? It should be big enough."[29]

According to the grateful missionary physician, Governor Rodríguez also "promised no more harassment from local

---

[29] [Inelda May Christianson], Iner Sheld-Ritchie, 1885 - 1949; and I.M. Christianson, interview by D.G. Ross, 17 July 2000.

authorities and offered help providing beds, equipment, linen or anything that could be provided at the municipal hospital" that might be useful for demonstration purposes as he presented his lectures.[30] He even ordered all teachers and other government employees to attend the lectures and saw to it that the military band was available to provide music for special occasions.[31]

The governor's help did not stop there. Realizing that the obstructionism faced by the missionary doctor could not be halted permanently unless certain laws were changed—a nearly impossible task given the political situation—or unless he was given a license to practice medicine in Mexico, Rodríguez recommended to the national government in Mexico City that such a license be granted. The governor was not a political light-weight, as some of his detractors have attempted to portray him. In addition to being the appointed governor of northern Baja California from 1923 to 1929, he was interim president of Mexico from 1932 to 1934. After all of that, he was elected governor of Sonora for a term that extended from 1943 to 1948. His personal recommendation, therefore, was a prelude to action.[32]

---

[30] Iner S. Ritchie, Notes in folder, "Calexico: 1926-29; 1931-32," no date, 4, Ritchie Papers, SCLSU.

[31] [Iner S. Ritchie], untitled 14-page manuscript with internal title, "God's Vast Design," 4.

[32] Iner S. Ritchie, Notes in folder, "Calexico: 1926-29; 1931-32," 4. Those who question Governor Rodríguez's political ability point to the fact that he was appointed governor of Baja California Norte, and Congress, following the guidance of former president Plutarco Elías Calles, named him interim president of Mexico. Those who view him as able, though, note that he was more successful in those positions than many others.

So also was the apparent healing of the governor's crying baby. Dr. Ritchie became the first family's personal physician, and, as the story of the crying baby made the rounds, other government officials from all ranks began to see him for their own medical needs.[33] The good will thus generated opened many an otherwise closed door.

[33] I.M. Christianson, interview by D.G. Ross, 17 July 2000.

Self-supporting Medical Evangelist

After several documents had been prepared and sent to the proper authorities in Mexico City so that Dr. Ritchie could obtain a license to practice medicine in Mexico, he and Mrs. Ritchie made plans to travel to the Mexican capital. Whether they intended to try to expedite matters, to take required examinations, or to go for some other purpose, appears not to be known today. There are quite a number of possibilities, including simply to get to know church officials stationed there—and letting them become acquainted with him. It seems likely that there were several reasons for the trip, and while we do not know exactly what they were, its results were significant, both for the short and long terms.

Using his position as District Surgeon for the Southern Pacific Railroad, Dr. Ritchie obtained railway passes for their travel. A Dr. Thomas, colonizing agent for the Southern Pacific of Mexico, would accompany them.[1]

---

[1] [Iner S. Ritchie], untitled 14-page manuscript with internal title, "God's Vast Design," at top of page 12, no date, 12, Ritchie Papers, SCLSU. A colonizing agent was in charge of the profitable disposal of undeveloped railroad land, usually land the railroad company had earned as the result of construction.

Early on their expected date of departure, though, Dr. Ritchie was called to the home of the Territorial Secretary and Chief of Staff of the Governor. The secretary's wife was about to have a baby, and she all but demanded that he stay until after she had been delivered. Knowing that much might depend on his answer, his response was, "Very well, I shall stay until it is over and you tell me I can go. I am here at your service."[2]

The baby arrived within a few days, and about a week later Dr. Ritchie was informed that, having carried out his duty, he was free to leave the area. Wasting little time, he and Inelda Ruth began their planned trip to Mexico City.[3]

Traveling with Dr. Thomas, the Ritchies started southward along the Pacific side of Mexico. They had stopovers at Hermosillo, the capital of the state of Sonora, and at Guaymas, a port on the Gulf of California, also known as the Sea of Cortés. Their next stop was Ciudad Obregón. There they spent several days visiting fertile rice and wheat farms in the Yaqui River Valley. They were amazed to see heads of wheat measuring as much as eleven inches long and containing as many as seventy grains each. A single pile of 15,000 tons of rice was equally astounding. They observed lakes full of wildfowl and ducks so fat from eating grain that they could not fly. Dr. Ritchie was reminded of the Chino Ranch during his childhood.[4]

---

[2] Quoted in Ibid.

[3] Ibid., 12-13.

[4] Ibid., 13.

The Ritchies then continued their trip to Mexico City. According to the diary of James G. Pettey, long-time treasurer of the Mexican Union of Seventh-day Adventists, they arrived by train on February 1, 1929. Pettey went to the Colonia Station in Mexico City to meet them. As usual, the train was late.

At first Pettey seems to have felt rather noncommital toward Dr. Ritchie, but by February 9 Pettey appeared to see the medical evangelist in a somewhat different light. "Dr. Richey [sic]," he wrote in his diary, "seems to have a burden for Mexico and has several good recommendations from influential men. He wants to start a San[itarium] in the City here and get other doctors in for different centers."[5] He noted that the Ritchies did some sightseeing over the next few days, visiting the National Palace and National Pawn Shop, buying some stuffed animals[6] at the Thieves' Market, and inspecting "the pyramids"—probably those at Teotihuacán. On Sabbath the 16th they ate dinner together after church services, and he commented, "Had a pleasant time with the Ritchies. It seems he will get his permit to practice in Mexico."[7]

According to a telegram sent to General Rodríguez two days earlier, on February 14, all that still was needed for Dr. Ritchie to receive the desired authorization was a document certifying his

---

[5] J[ames] G. Pettey, "Diary, Aug.25, 1927 — ," 104, Ritchie Papers, SCLSU.

[6] He bought a stuffed alligator and a little black monkey. About 18 inches long, tail included, the monkey was like a puppet. Its head could be manipulated by putting one's hand inside an opening at the back. Dr. Ritchie occasionally used it to illustrate his lectures. The two animals are in the Stahl Center Museum at La Sierra University, Riverside, California.

[7] Pettey, "Diary," 104-109.

medical service in Mexicali during a minimum of five years. The sender did not realize that such a certification had already been drawn up and signed only the day before.[8]

On February 19 Pettey noted, "Dr. and Mrs. Richie [*sic*] are still here. He expects to get his permit soon." At prayer meeting the next evening Dr. Ritchie offered a health lecture which he illustrated "with stereopticon." His entry for the 21st ended with, "Dr. & Mrs. Richie [*sic*] . . . left tonight for the States. The Richies [*sic*] will likely return, as he has been promised his permit to practice here."[9]

The Ritchie's return trip to Calexico was fraught with danger. Rebels were attacking government positions and, among other things, were burning railroad bridges. Fortunately for the medical missionary and his wife, although sometimes the danger was very close, the burnt bridges were all behind their train.[10] Upon arriving home Dr. Ritchie again had to wait for his license to practice medicine in Mexico.

Government bureaucracy generally moves slowly, when it moves at all, and the desired permit was not issued until April 22, 1929. It stated that Dr. Ritchie's course work at the College of Medical Evangelists had been examined and approved as comparable to that which was required for the degree of Doctor of

---

[8] Trinidad Sánchez Benítez to Gral. Abelardo Rodríguez, telegram, 14 February 1929, Ritchie Papers, SCLSU; and H.M. López to Antonio Castro Leal, 13 February 1929, Ritchie Papers, SCLSU.

[9] Pettey, "Diary," 110-113.

[10] [Iner S. Ritchie], "Border experiences," 2-page outline, undated, 1, Ritchie Papers, SCLSU.

Medicine at the Universidad Nacional de México—the National University of Mexico.[11] Exactly when Dr. Ritchie received his equivalency certificate which would allow him to practice medicine in Mexico is a matter of conjecture. It is known that his former partner in Calexico, Dr. Ralph M. Smith, collected his own permit to practice medicine in Mexico in Mexicali late in the fall of 1929, and, considering that his and Dr. Ritchie's apparently were applied for together, it seems reasonable to assume that they were both issued, and then later picked up at the same time. What is known is that only a tiny handful of foreigners were licensed to practice medicine in Mexico at that time, and two of those were self-supporting Seventh-day Adventist missionaries who had graduated from the College of Medical Evangelists, Iner S. Ritchie and Ralph M. Smith.[12]

In 1930 Mexico's Departamento De Salubridad Pública, its national Department of Public Health, published a booklet recording the names of newly registered health professionals as an addendum to its officially sanctioned list. As might be expected, it contained Dr. Ritchie's name. Interestingly, though, it does not

---

[11] Jefe del Estado Mayor to Antonio Castro Leal, 13 February 1929, Ritchie Papers, SCLSU; Sánchez Benítez to Rodríguez, telegram, 14 February 1929; and Universidad Nacional de México, Certificate of equivalency, 22 April 1929, Ritchie Papers, SCLSU.

[12] Dunbar W. Smith, *The Travels, Triumphs & Vicissitudes of Dunbar W. Smith, M.D.* (Loma Linda, California: Dunbar W. Smith, 1994), 72-73; Inelda May Christianson, daughter of Dr. Iner S. Ritchie, interview by Delmer G. Ross, 1 July 2003, Riverside, California.

list Dr. Smith's.[13] It may be that because Dr. Ritchie's former partner no longer was actively practicing medicine in Mexico, even though he was at last officially qualified, he saw no reason to register to do so.

In addition to serving paying patients, including Mexican government officials, on both sides of the border, Dr. Ritchie helped those who could pay only part of his regular fee, or perhaps nothing at all. Most of the destitute or nearly destitute patients were Mexicans or Mexican Americans. But there were others, as well.

Mexicali was the home of quite a number of Asian and Asian-Mexican people. The largest group, numbering 8,000 or more, were of Chinese extraction, but large numbers of immigrants from Japan and India existed, as well. Virtually all were discriminated against because of their racial and, especially, their religious differences. The fact that these minorities often lived as tightly knit groups in their own *barrios* or neighborhoods did not help matters.

Because of the general public prejudice against them, when they became ill or suffered an injury, very much like Mexicans in the United States, they tended to seek assistance from their own health practitioners, sometimes with devastating effects. But what else could they do? Mexican physicians often refused to treat

---

[13] Mexico, Departamento De Salubridad Pública, *Lista de los Médicos Cirujanos, Homeópatas, Veterinarios, Cirujanos Dentistas, Farmacéuticos, Parteras y Enfermeras que han registrado su título profesional en este Departamento durante el año de 1929, Suplemento al Directorio General* (México, D.F.: Imprenta del Departamento de Salubridad Pública, 1930), 14-15.

them, not because they could not pay, but for fear of losing their regular patients. Dr. Ritchie, however, treated them. If he feared a loss of other patients, he never showed it. It seems probable that, as busy as he was, he was not particularly concerned about the possible loss of a racist patient or two.

Moreover, because during his youth he had picked up a little Chinese from the Chinese cooks while working on ranches in the Chino area, he could converse at a basic level with many of his Chinese patients. That he would even try amazed and delighted them. Of course, most of his communication with his Chinese patients was accomplished with the assistance of an interpreter.[14]

One time Dr. Ritchie went to see one of his Chinese patients in Mexicali. After determining that all was well, he returned across the border to Calexico. He had barely reached his emergency hospital in the United States, though, when the phone rang and the Chinese people he had just left on the Mexican side asked for him to return immediately. He was urgently needed. It turned out that a tong war was in progress, and while the fighters had politely waited until he had finished seeing his patient, just as soon as he was safely out of the way, bullets had started flying. In the melee his patient had been quite deliberately shot to death, and a number of others had been injured, several critically.[15]

---

[14] "Obituary," 1, Ritchie file, WebbLLU; and Inelda May Christianson, daughter of Dr. Iner S. Ritchie, telephone interview by Delmer G. Ross, 24 November 2003.

[15] Inelda Ruth Sheld-Ritchie, widow of Dr. Iner S. Ritchie, by her granddaughter, Cheryl Ann Nickel Leathers, 20 November 1985, [La Jolla, California], 8-9, transcript, Ritchie Papers, SCLSU.

Many had been arrested, including most of those who had been injured. The physician explained to them that it was useless to call for him because they were prisoners of the Mexican government and he could not treat their injuries without the express permission of the territorial chief of police. The chief, however, called almost immediately and said, "Come on over and I will help you."[16] With that kind of a plea for help it was not difficult to guess that the problem was a major one.

When Dr. Ritchie returned to Mexicali he discovered the bullet-riddled body of his former patient plus 26 additional victims. All were taken to the emergency hospital in Mexicali, a large building with about fifty cots in it, where an attendant placed gauze and adhesive over the bullet wounds of those yet alive. Then, as Dr. Ritchie put it,

> The Chief helped me load as many as possible into the back of my vehicle like cordwood and we rushed them over to our little hospital. We were all night opening up abdomens and sewing up holes in the intestines. The newspaper comment was "They took them over to the hospital but they will all die." However just the opposite was the result. Not one died. They all lived.[17]

On another occasion an elderly Chinese card dealer who worked in one of the gambling operations in Mexicali had been shot a number of times in the abdomen. With bullet holes perforat-

---

[16] Quoted in [Iner S. Ritchie], untitled 14-page manuscript with internal title, "God's Vast Design," 7.

[17] Ibid.

ing his intestines, he needed surgery right away. Dr. Ritchie's emergency hospital was only three blocks from the border, but to get him into the United States he had to put up a bond to guarantee that his patient would leave the country once he had recovered sufficiently to do so. He also had to obtain the permission of the Mexican government to take the man out of Mexico—not a particularly difficult task considering that the officials in charge were Dr. Ritchie's patients, too. All the paperwork took time, and time was of the essence in those days before the development of penicillin and other antibiotics. Infection spreading from the perforations in his intestine could easily kill him. Mrs. Ritchie called the patient "a hard looking critter," and he must have been tough because only hours after surgery he exposed himself to one of the nurses. Dr. Ritchie then laid down the law, "You do that once more," he warned, "and we'll take you right back across the line, and you can die over there."[18] He had to do it through an interpreter because the invalid only spoke Chinese, but the man understood and behaved after that.[19]

The Chinese in Mexicali often lived in underground rooms where the temperature was cool compared with that in above-ground buildings. They might work all day in the hot sun picking cotton or cultivating some other crop, but at night they disappeared into their den-like quarters where they slept on narrow bunks surrounded by naturally cool air. Often when Dr. Ritchie had gone into one of those dens to see a patient, one of the occupants would

---

[18] Quoted in I.R. Sheld-Ritchie, interview by C.A.N. Leathers, 20 November 1985, 9.

[19] Ibid., 9-10.

sidle over to him and say "I guess I'd better have a shot today."
Then another would come over and say, "I guess I'd better have a
shot, too." That was their way of asking for Salversan for syphilis.
Sometimes Dr. Ritchie gave as many as a dozen shots of Salversan
before he was through. He charged a steep ten dollars per shot, but
they always seemed to be able to pay.[20]

The great majority of Chinese patients, of course, were
nothing like the tong warriors, the gambling-parlor worker, or the
men suffering from venereal disease. For example, on another
occasion, one evening when the family was together as Dr. Ritchie
visited patients in Mexicali, he stopped in front of the home of a
Chinese grocer. Leaving the children in their Lincoln limousine—the one they often used as an ambulance—the physician and
his wife went inside to visit the invalid. Moments later the
patient's young daughter came out of the house. She knocked on
the window of the car, showed the children a doll she had brought
along, and asked if Inelda May would like to play with her.
Because the Ritchie children had instructions to remain inside the
vehicle, Inelda invited her inside, where they played together until
the house call was over. On another occasion a Japanese patient,
grateful for what Dr. Ritchie had done for him and for the
Japanese community in Mexicali, gave Anna Ritchie a valuable
presentation doll.[21]

Incidentally, although they often were poor enough, Dr.
Ritchie's Chinese patients generally paid their medical bills right

[20] Ibid., 9.

[21] I.M. Christianson, interview by D.G. Ross, 30 September 2003.

away—usually at the time of service. To do otherwise would have meant "losing face" with their peers, something to be avoided at almost all costs. That brought its own problems, though, because on many occasions they opted to go without needed medical attention because they knew they did not have funds in hand to pay the doctor. Their healthy companions often "helped" them. On more than one occasion when Dr. Ritchie approached an obviously ill person in a Chinese bunkhouse his house mates would hasten to warn him, "Don't bother to treat him! He doesn't have any money."[22] If allowed to, Dr. Ritchie treated them anyway, but no one knows how many may have died while trying to avoid losing face.

In fact, his second Chinese patient in Mexico was one such. Dr. Ritchie was called to a Chinese laundry that operated under a *ramada,* a simple structure of poles with straw, palm fronds, or something similar laid across the top to provide shade. Upon his arrival, he found about fifty men and women washing and ironing clothes. The boss escorted him to the rear where there were some small huts. On the way they passed a semiconscious Chinese man lying on the ground. Dr. Ritchie quickly turned about, set his medical bag on the ground, and bent over to try to help him.

With a note of alarm in his voice, the boss protested, "He not sick boy. You no see him. He no got money." He then took the doctor's arm and guided him to one of the huts. Inside, sitting up, was his patient, a Chinese man whose ailment was "only a slight cold." After a few comfort measures, the doctor was through.

---

[22] Ibid., 1 July 2003.

On his way back, he went by the very sick man again. This time, despite the protests of the work supervisor who kept repeating "He got no money," Dr. Ritchie paused to examine the man. He indicated that it did not matter if the man could not pay; he needed help. Later Dr. Ritchie wrote about the experience:

> I rolled him over and found he was toxic and cyanotic, almost choking from the pressure of a large pharyngeal abscess on his trachea. . . . I opened the abscess and held him up head downward and let this drain out to keep him from strangling, then cleaned out the cavity with swabs and disinfectant and left him medicines with directions for use. "Now, I am coming back to see you this afternoon and every day until you are well," I told him. As I passed through the crowd again in the "ramada" there was a fearful silence for sometimes terrible punishment or death was inflicted on those who did not pay their debts to their foreign doctors.[23]

This time, though, all turned out well. Dr. Ritchie explained that his service would be gratis this time, so there would be no debt. When the boss translated that news the fifty workers responded with a loud and enthusiastic cheer.[24] The patient recovered.

---

[23] [Iner S. Ritchie], untitled 14-page manuscript with internal title, "God's Vast Design," 6.

[24] Ibid.; and Deborah Nassimian and Roxana Maddalena, "Dr. Ritchie and His Patients" (term paper presented for HIST 294/494, History Colloquium, La Sierra University, Riverside, California, 5 December 1995), 2, D.G. Ross Collection, LSU.

Moreover, as news of what he had done spread rapidly throughout the Chinese community, Dr. Ritchie was appointed official physician of a number of Chinese organizations in northern Baja California, including the Chinese Women's Society. Thus an act of service to a sick man who could not pay led to a large and lucrative practice among the Chinese of the area. It also led to the spread of the gospel because no matter how miraculous appearing the cure, Dr. Ritchie always gave God the credit. One of his Chinese patients told him "All China boys call you God's doctor."[25] Not only was he a good doctor, his was an effective witness for God.

The Japanese Association of Central Imperial Valley, with headquarters in El Centro, California, expressed the appreciation of their members for Dr. Ritchie's service and racial blindness by presenting him with a beautifully inscribed certificate. The president of the Association wrote:

> During all the time that you have been in [the] Imperial Valley you have been very considerate of my countrymen, treating them with kindness without regard to racial differences.
> We all look up to your noble character and appreciate your benevolence. I want to thank you on behalf of all members of the Japanese Association. . . .[26]

---

[25] [Iner S. Ritchie], untitled 14-page manuscript with internal title, "God's Vast Design," 6-7.

[26] The Japanese Association of Central Imperial Valley, certificate; and Kiyokichi Umezawa to I.S. Ritchie, 18 May 1929; Ritchie Papers, SCLSU.

A few years later, during World War II, government agents seized the certificate. Even that did not keep the racially and politically oblivious physician from traveling to the wartime Japanese internment camp at Manzanar, California, to treat his patients.[27] His fellow doctors may have wondered about the fierce loyalty of some of his patients, but there was a reason.

In those days most people paid with cash. At the Calexico hospital patients made payment at a large desk in the reception area. One of Inelda May's earliest memories of the hospital is the clinking sound made by silver dollars, pesos, and other coins as Office Manager C.F. Innis dropped them into a drawer of that desk. Some patients did not have any money, so they paid what they could. Several of his Japanese patients paid with produce.[28]

And if they could, why should they not pay? Most of his Mexican and Asian patients were proud to be going to the physician with the best reputation in the region. Many felt that it was an honor—as well as good common sense—to be attended by Dr. Ritchie. They did not want that to change for failure to pay a medical bill.

His reputation as an outstanding healer began when he was called to see a woman with a severe toxemia. The cause was an infected knee joint. This was before there were any so-called "wonder drugs" such as penicillin or streptomycin, so her case had

---

[27] Christina Cicchetti, "El Doctór [sic]," *Journal of the Riverside Historical Society,* Vol. 2 (February 1998), 1-9.

[28] In addition to being office manager, Innis was a Bible worker who gave Bible studies in Spanish to interested parties in Mexicali and the surrounding area. I.M. Christianson, interviews by D.G. Ross, 1 and 15 July 2003.

been given up as hopeless except by a surgeon who told her that she might possibly live if her leg was amputated. Living with one leg was better than not living at all, but she hoped there might be a way to recover without any loss. She appealed to Dr. Ritchie. He realized there was little hope of saving her leg, but he quickly started "using the methods God has blessed and instructed us to use"—although he did not elaborate, probably hot and cold hydrotherapy and much fervent prayer. The patient began to improve, and soon recovered completely.[29]

On a later occasion it was the little daughter of the Inspector General of Police in Baja California Norte who needed help. Inspector Francisco Peralta, one of Dr. Ritchie's good friends in Mexicali, phoned one day and asked that he drop by to examine his baby girl. When the doctor called he discovered the girl had an advanced case of pneumonia. Having earlier lost a son to the same disease, when he heard the diagnosis the inspector became very concerned and distraught. But he did not give up, and neither did Dr. Ritchie nor his nurse, Mrs. Webb. They called in a specialist from quite a distance away, but nothing seemed to work. One morning, at about three o'clock, Dr. Ritchie and his friend went outside to talk. The physician told him honestly that he had done everything he knew to do. He could do no more for one of his own children. Did he wish to try someone else? The sorrowful father replied, "No, doctor, I have seen enough. We want no other. In your hands she lives or in your hands she dies."[30]

---

[29] [Iner S. Ritchie], untitled 14-page manuscript with internal title, "God's Vast Design," 4.

[30] Ibid., 10.

That statement was not a threat; it was a declaration of confidence and faith. The two men went back inside to discover Mrs. Webb on her knees, praying for her little charge, just as she had done many times already. But this time the results were different, and from that time onward the girl improved. Within only a few more days it was possible to invite family members to a meeting of rejoicing. Dr. Ritchie and nurse Webb were there, as pleased as any over the outcome.[31]

With miraculous recoveries like that, it is no wonder that Dr. Ritchie gained an outstanding reputation as a physician. He was always careful, though, to give credit where he felt credit was due. "The secret of these recoveries is found in the following from the pen of Inspiration,"[32] he wrote, and then he quoted Ellen G. White:

> My brother, as a surgeon you have had the most critical cases to handle, and at times a dread has come upon you. To perform these difficult duties you knew that rapid work must be done and that no false moves must be made. . . . Who has been by your side as you have performed these critical operations? Who has kept you calm and self-possessed in the crisis, giving you quick, sharp discernment, clear eyesight, steady nerves, and skillful precision? The Lord Jesus has sent his angel to your side to tell you what to do. A hand has been laid

---

[31] Ibid.

[32] Ibid., 5.

upon your hand, Jesus and not you has guided the movements of your instrument.[33]

Take for example the case of the lady with pneumonia. Two men approached Dr. Ritchie one evening. They requested that he hasten to the home of the one whose wife was ill and appeared to be dying. The good doctor later wrote about the case:

> I immediately hurried to the house and after opening the door entered and approached her bedside. She appeared to be in coma and after examining her found she was expiring from double pneumonia. My nurse applied treatments and with a prayer that God would spare her life to her husband and little children we continued our efforts in her behalf. Imagine my surprise [the] next day when she reached for my hand and said, "Dr. I am so glad you came. When I was dying yesterday the devil came in the door just before you did. He had a coffin with him and came over to me and began putting me into it. He was tugging and pushing me into it and my breath was gone. Just then you came in the door and came to my side. He began to back away and as he reached the door to back out he made a terrible face and put out his tongue at me.

It was an amazing account, but his patient was not yet through. After pausing as if to gain courage following the story of her

---

[33] Ellen G. White, *Testimonies for the Church,* Vol. 8 (Kansas City, Missouri: Pacific Press Publishing Co., 1904), 187-88.

frightening visitation, she inquired, "Who was the other person who came in with you?"[34]

The woman's Christian physician may have been surprised, but he felt certain he knew the proper response to her question. As he often did, for an answer Dr. Ritchie turned to Ellen G. White who had written, "The Great Physician in Chief is at the side of every true earnest God fearing practitioner [he substituted the word "physician" for "practitioner"] who works with his acquired knowledge to relieve the sufferings of the human body."[35]

While practicing in Calexico and Mexicali Dr. Ritchie developed a particularly eclectic clientele. It included the governor of Baja California and his family as well as members of the two rival Chinese tongs. It included generals and indigent Mexican laborers. Also included were local officials such as the chief of police as well as Japanese store owners. It even included many of the so-called "working girls" and "soiled doves" from the gambling casinos and saloons in Mexicali. Moreover, while it certainly mattered whether or not they could pay him for his services, he treated them all.[36]

Dr. and Mrs. Ritchie lived in the Calexico area from late 1925 until 1929 and then again during 1931 and 1932. They made many trips back to the Loma Linda area during that time. Even when the

---

[34] [Iner S. Ritchie], untitled 14-page manuscript with internal title, "God's Vast Design," 5.

[35] Ibid.; and Ellen G. White, *Counsels on Health and Instruction to Medical Missionary Workers* (Mountain View, California: Pacific Press Publishing Association, 1923), 536.

[36] I.M. Christianson, interview by D.G. Ross, 17 July 2000.

main purpose was to visit loved ones, Dr. Ritchie often combined business and pleasure. A good number of such trips were for the purpose of trying to recruit physicians he could hire to help him with his thriving practice. His visits were anywhere from a few hours to several days long, depending on the object. A visit such as that of May 1926 when he was reported as having visited CME for a few days probably had several purposes, not the least of which was to acquaint various people with the medical, material, and spiritual requirements of those living along the border.[37] Such needs became one of his major concerns.

Even when the demands of his busy practice prevented personal appeals to those who might provide assistance, Dr. Ritchie continued to plead for those in need through the journal published by the College of Medical Evangelists, *The Medical Evangelist*. After he had worked in the Calexico-Mexicali area for several years, he was keenly aware of the need for more help. In one article he wrote,

> Do you know that Mexico needs medical missionaries today as much as any country on the face of this old earth? Yet to date, brethren, there is neither doctor nor nurse, sanitarium, hospital, dispensary or treatment room in all Mexico to represent the right arm phase of the message.

He did not limit his appeal to medicine:

---

[37] O.R. Staines, ed., "News Notes," *The Medical Evangelist,* Vol. 12, No. 48 (27 May 1926), 1.

There are great opportunities down here to establish schools for the Indians, also dispensaries and by all means a school farm where agriculture and the trades could be taught. I have been praying that the Lord would raise up some David Livingstones among our medical people and put His spirit into them so they might determine to come down here to the neediest, nearest, most neglected field in all the world.

He also suggested the construction of a sanitarium in Mexico City and the establishment of some kind of Seventh-day Adventist medical presence in Guadalajara.[38]

In the same article, he mentioned one of the practical methods he used to reach others. The medical missionary advocated listening for people's needs and providing for them. He wrote, "the possibility of winning them will come more quickly through our ministrations of helpfulness and kindness in a material way than by any other method."[39] Dr. Ritchie understood what psychologist Abraham Maslow proposed in the 1970s: that people have basic needs. Before concepts of faith and religion could be introduced to people, their physical needs should be met. The humanitarian self-supporting missionary realized this through his personal experience and advocated the method without the complexities of Maslow's hierarchy of needs, which included physical safety, love and belonging, esteem, and self-

[38] I.S. Ritchie, "Another Appeal From Mexico," *The Medical Evangelist,* Vol. 15, No. 38 (21 March 1929).

[39] Ibid.

actualization.[40] It was very much the same approach employed by Jesus Christ nearly two thousand years earlier.

Summertime in 1928 brought the usual almost suffocating heat, and this time Dr. Ritchie himself was a victim. He often had to treat patients in their overheated homes. Delivering babies, sometimes in small rooms where there was little or no air circulation, was particularly hazardous. Exactly how it happened is not clear, but this time the missionary physician suffered heat hyperpyrexia, commonly called heat stroke, while attending his patient. Fortunately, it did not result in his death, but once was quite enough. The Ritchies decided to sell his now thriving practice and the enlarged emergency hospital, and to return to the Loma Linda area where summers were cooler.[41]

The close call may also have influenced his making arrangements for the continued care of the children should something happen to him and Inelda Ruth. Like all good parents, Dr. and Mrs. Ritchie were concerned about their children's well being. Moreover, they realized that either one or both of them might succumb to disease or suffer a fatal accident while in their chosen mission field. Dr. Ritchie's recollection of his own childhood experience of his mother's death, then being placed in an orphanage, probably also greatly influenced his concern. He did not want his own family separated as his father's had been during his childhood. Therefore, on January 23, 1929, as Dr. and Mrs. Ritchie were making plans for their trip to Mexico City, they sent

---

[40] Spencer A. Rathus, *Psychology in the New Millennium*, 6th ed. (Fort Worth, Texas: Harcourt Brace College Publishers, 1996), 359.

[41] I.M. Christianson, interview by D.G. Ross, 1 July 2003.

a document to their mother, Anna Lula Ritchie, certifying that if they died, whether by accident or in some other manner, she should have custody of their four children, Iner William, Anna Virginia, Inelda May, and Robert Lorraine. In addition, they appointed her to administer their estate.[42]

---

[42] Certification and power of attorney signed by Dr. Iner Sheld-Ritchie and Inelda Sheld-Ritchie, 23 January 1929, Ritchie Papers, SCLSU.

From Colton to Pomona Via Calexico

Once the Ritchies had decided to leave Calexico, they needed to determine where they should go. Their first choice was Riverside because so many of the physician's friends and former patients lived there. One of the friends was Dr. Ralph M. Smith, with whom Dr. Ritchie formerly had been associated in Calexico. The two physicians apparently favored renewing their partnership, but Dr. Smith's wife opposed. She had her way, and the two doctors abandoned the idea. Dr. Ritchie then decided they should settle in Colton where they would be near members of their family, but would not be in direct competition with his former partner.[1]

While Dr. Ritchie tried to find someone interested in buying his practice, Mrs. Ritchie got busy trying to find an office and living quarters for them in Colton. She found a large two-story house. It was old fashioned, but she thought it would make a good office as well as an adequate place for them to live. The people in it were willing to sell, if they could find another place they liked better and could afford. She then found a nice modern house in a

---

[1] Mrs. W.S. Ritchie to Dr. Ralph M. Smith, 6 August 1935, 4, Ritchie Papers, SCLSU.

135

good neighborhood in San Bernardino that the Colton people liked. The owners of the house in San Bernardino were willing to take some desert land in the Hinkley area in exchange for their home. Thus, after considerable effort, Inelda Ruth had put together a double trade that gave them not only a place to live, but also an office.[2]

The home and office building was well located, only a block or two from downtown Colton. Moreover, across the alley in back was a two-story hospital. The garage, spacious enough for two cars, was on the alley. Their cars were a Durant sedan and the Lincoln limousine Dr. Ritchie had used as an ambulance in Calexico. In front of the house, wide steps led up to a porch. The children, but especially Inelda May, liked to sit on those steps and watch the world go by. Entrance was by way of either of two doors, one leading to the living room and the other to Dr. Ritchie's office. Mrs. Ritchie's efforts to obtain a home and office without much expense had been markedly successful.[3]

For his part, Dr. Ritchie located a possible buyer for the hospital, their home, and his practice in Calexico. Although it is not entirely clear today who the buyers may have been, one of them was Fred C. Gregg, a physician from San Diego. Gregg's brother was involved, and possibly one additional associate, a Dr.

---

[2] Inelda Ruth Sheld-Ritchie, widow of Dr. Iner S. Ritchie, interview by her granddaughter, Cheryl Ann Nickel Leathers, 20 November 1985, [La Jolla, California], 7, transcript, Ritchie Papers, SCLSU; and Inelda May Christianson, daughter of Dr. Iner S. Ritchie, telephone interview by Delmer G. Ross, 29 June 2003, Norco, California.

[3] Inelda May Christianson, daughter of Dr. Iner S. Ritchie, interview by Delmer G. Ross, 1 July 2003, Riverside, California.

E.G. Colby, also from San Diego. Gregg wanted the negotiations to be kept secret so as not to upset anyone already associated with him. Dr. Ritchie wanted $35,000 for his interest in the properties and his practice. Considering that $5,000 remained to be paid on the home, the total asking price was $40,000. Exactly when negotiations began is not known, but on April 2, 1928, Gregg offered to pay $25,000 for his interest, or $30,000 all told. That was twenty-five percent less than he was asking, and Dr. Ritchie apparently felt that he should do better. He had invested a total of $34,000 in the property and practice, and he thought he should receive at least that much. Therefore, the hoped-for sale to Dr. Gregg did not materialize.[4]

Dr. Ritchie then found two additional buyers, Truman E. Bartholomew and Oran Lamar Webster. Both earned medical degrees from the College of Medical Evangelists in 1928, so it seems possible that he had earlier taught them anatomy. While the sale price was said to have been $34,000—probably including what Dr. Ritchie owed. That was significantly more than the earlier offer, but there was a drawback. The buyers did not have that kind of money, so they were to make periodic payments. By the end of January 1929, a new partnership was in operation, Drs.

---

[4] Fred C. Gregg, M.D. to Dr. Iner Sheld-Ritchie, 2 April 1928, Ritchie Papers, SCLSU; and Anna L. Ritchie to C.E. Wood, 14 February 1935, 1, Ritchie Papers, SCLSU.

Ritchie, Bartholomew & Webster. Dr. Ritchie, of course, was introducing the buyers of his practice.[5]

Although the purchasers could not have known it, 1929 was not the best time to go into debt to buy a medical practice—or anything else, for that matter. The Great Depression that followed the stock crash of that year ruined many well-thought-through plans, and those of Drs. Bartholomew and Webster were among them. With a depression-caused decrease in paying patients and increase in charity cases, it soon became impossible for the two physicians to make the payments on the hospital and practice they had bought. Only six months after Dr. Ritchie had turned it over to them, the two physicians abandoned their purchase.[6]

When asked how he managed to succeed in his border practice, Dr. Ritchie said, "It was my experience that the Mexicans always paid if they could. They were much better than white Americans at paying for my services."[7] Despite that, the world-

---

[5] I.M. Christianson, interview by D.G. Ross, 1 July 2003; Anna L. Ritchie to C.E. Wood, 14 February 1935, 1; and Envelope postmarked 25 January 1929, Ritchie Papers, SCLSU.

[6] I.M. Christianson, interview by D.G. Ross, 1 July 2003; and Anna L. Ritchie to C.E. Wood, 14 February 1935, 1. A number of years later, in a tragedy that took place one Sabbath right after church services were over, Dr. Webster was shot and killed by a patient he had recently diagnosed as having serious mental problems. Apparently the doctor's diagnosis was altogether too accurate. Having murdered the doctor, the murderer turned his gun on himself and committed suicide. Dunbar Smith, the newly assigned pastor, conducted the funerals of both men. Dunbar W. Smith, *The Travels, Triumphs & Vicissitudes of Dunbar W. Smith, M.D.* (Loma Linda, California: Dunbar W. Smith, 1994), 81-82.

[7] Quoted by I.M. Christianson, interview by D.G. Ross, 15 July 2003.

wide economic depression of the 1930s brought deflation and difficult times generally, so the Ritchies returned to Calexico in 1931.

During the depression Anna Lula Ritchie had some advice for her unofficially adopted and often overworked and underpaid son:

> You should work toward [being] an expert diagnostician and charge accordingly. For outstanding work, those who are able to pay should pay an outstanding price. Of course you will have to do charity work but you should not be afraid to charge those who are able to pay. They should be made to understand that by paying well they help and have a part in your charity work. Thus you will be able to support yourselves and meet your obligations as they come.[8]

It may have been good advice, but it was hard to follow when the depression had impoverished so many. People got sick, had accidents, and needed medical help without regard to their pocketbooks. Dr. Ritchie, as did many other physicians, refused to take time to determine each patient's immediate ability to pay.

That, of course, meant that some accounts receivable would have to be written off. Therefore Inelda Ruth admonished Iner William, who was away at school and working to pay at least part of his expenses, to "Work all you can Darling as your Daddy is haveing [sic] an awfully hard time to make both ends meet and

---

[8] Mamma and Amma [Anna L. Ritchie] to Dearly Beloved Children [Iner and Inelda Ritchie], 11 August 1936, 10, Ritchie Papers, SCLSU.

sometimes they don't meet, so do your best."[9] It was not the first time he had received such advice, nor would it be the last.

The Great Depression was yet to come, though, when the Ritchies moved into the big house Inelda Ruth had acquired for them in Colton. Dr. Ritchie immediately became active again in efforts to help people in the Inland Empire region of California.

The children began exploring the area around their new home. Bob, for example, liked to run down to the railroad yard to watch the trains and all the switching of cuts and single cars. Because he sometimes would slip away without letting anyone know, it was necessary to keep a close guard on him. One day Anna was given the task of watching him as he went to sleep during his midday nap. When Inelda Ruth went in to see if he had awakened from the nap she found Anna seated next to his bed, sound asleep. She still held in her hand the little switch which she was supposed to use if he tried to get out of his crib. Bob, on the other hand, was nowhere to be seen. As often happened, he had quietly sneaked away to "see the choo-choos." His fascination with trains and model trains was to last all his life.[10]

For the time being, though, his interest caused problems. He had long, blonde hair. Over and over Colton police caught him at the railroad yard and took him back home, chiding Inelda Ruth for allowing her "pretty little girl" to go to such a dangerous place, full of hobos, bums, and other drifters, not to mention all the locomotives, freight cars, passenger coaches, and other railroad

[9] Mamma [Inelda Ruth Ritchie] to Precious Son [Iner William Ritchie], 28 March 1932, Ritchie Papers, SCLSU.

[10] I.M. Christianson, interview by D.G. Ross, 15 July 2003.

equipment. Tired of explaining that Bob was not a girl, one day she took him to a barber who cut off those beautiful golden curls. Bob looked so different that the next time they went to visit the boy's grandparents in Loma Linda his grandmother failed to recognize him. Instead, after watching him for a few minutes, she asked, "Who is that boy you brought who's running around and getting into everything like he owns the place? He sure is making himself right at home."[11] Upon learning who the youngster was and what had been done, Anna Lula Ritchie, known as "Amma" to her grandchildren, wept.[12]

Inelda May got into some trouble of a different kind. Shortly after they had moved to Colton, some of her teenage cousins were visiting and decided to go downtown—only a block or two away—for some sodas. They didn't want a little five-year-old girl tagging along, so they sneaked out of the house. Inelda May spotted them before they got far, though, and began running after them. She started to dash across a street, but did not make it. There was a horrible squealing of breaks as she was hit by a passing car, and everything went blank. She regained consciousness in their living room, but she was in great pain and it was clear that one of her legs was broken. Dr. Ritchie took her to a nearby hospital to be checked. The break was a bad one, and she had to spend the next three months in bed in traction. The gentleman who had hit her owned an orange grove and sent her a little orange tree in a pot. Jessie Moon and her daughter, Melva, with whom they had

---

[11] Quoted by I.M. Christianson, interview by D.G. Ross, 1 July 2003.

[12] [Inelda May Christianson], "Iner Sheld-Ritchie, October 6, 1885 - October 24, 1949," undated chronology, 8, Ritchie Papers, SCLSU.

become good friends during their stay in Calexico, dropped in to see her and leave her a shopping bag full of surprises to be opened at the rate of one each day. It was a thoughtful gift that Inelda May remembered appreciatively for the rest of her long life.[13]

Having returned to California's Inland Empire in 1929, Dr. Ritchie soon began missionary work among Mexicans, Mexican-Americans, and other hispanics living in the area. Public announcements in Spanish advertised two health conferences organized by Dr. Ritchie in 1929. One of the free conferences was held at the School of Health on Main Street in Corona, California.[14] The other free conference was held at the School of Health in Colton, California.[15] Both symposiums offered information on preventing and fighting diseases. He also spoke at a Colton Kiwanis Club luncheon on October 4, 1929, where he shared his interest in Mexico with the club members.[16] Moreover, as he had done many times throughout the years since he had been a medical student, he participated in evangelistic meetings, often giving a short health lecture before the evangelist presented his sermon. For example, a handbill advertised that he would lecture on "Veneral

---

[13] I.M. Christianson, telephone interview by D.G. Ross, 7 July 2003; [Inelda May Christianson], "Iner Sheld-Ritchie, 1885 - 1949," 8; Inelda Ritchie Christianson, "Ritchie Family Life in Riverside," 7, Ritchie Papers, SCLSU.

[14] Public Announcement, 5 August 1929, Corona, California, Ritchie Papers, SCLSU.

[15] Public Announcement, 12 July 1929, Colton, California, Ritchie Papers, SCLSU.

[16] "Mexico Topic Dr. I.S. Ritchie Able Address," *Rialto (California) Record,* Vol. 21, No. 22 (October 4, 1929), 5.

[*sic*] Diseases or the Results of Adultery" on April 29, 1931, at the "Bible and Health Chautauqua"—a series of tent meetings in San Bernardino. Dr. Ritchie's presentation would be followed by a presentation answering the question "Is it necessary to belong to the Church in order to be saved?"[17]

Dr. Ritchie also engaged in a kind of missionary service to his extended family. Even though the depression made it difficult at times, he sent two of his nieces—his two sisters' youngest girls—through nurses training at the College of Medical Evangelists. One, Virginia Harris, married a medical student there, Waldo Stiles. They later served as medical missionaries to Bolivia and Ecuador, where Waldo was the medical director of the Inca Union of Seventh-day Adventists. They thus helped perpetuate Dr. Ritchie's personal goal of service to mankind.[18]

While helping others reach their educational objectives, Dr. Ritchie continued his own education in southern California. On December 1, 1930, he obtained a diploma in physical therapy from the Southern California School of Physical Therapy in San Gabriel, Los Angeles County.[19] Always interested in helping others as much as he could, and in order to maintain his practice as up-to-date as possible, the physician continued his education

---

[17] "The 'Monkey Question,'" handbill for the week of 26 April through 3 May 1931, in Ritchie Papers, SCLSU.

[18] [Inelda May Christianson], "Iner Sheld-Ritchie, 1885 - 1949," 8. He intended to help a third niece through nursing school, but she got homesick and returned home. I.M. Christianson, telephone interview by D.G Ross, 7 July 2003.

[19] Southern California School of Physical Therapy, Diploma, (San Gabriel, California, 1 December 1930), Ritchie Papers, SCLSU.

throughout the course of his life. He did so even when there were no continuing-education requirements such as those in place for licensed medical doctors today.

As already mentioned, Drs. Bartholomew and Webster, who had purchased Dr. Ritchie's practice and hospital in Calexico, soon ran into financial problems that prevented them from making their promised payments. In order to avoid losing his own interest in the property, Dr. Ritchie had to repossess and begin operating it himself. That meant that whether he wanted to or not, and high summer temperatures notwithstanding, he had to return to Calexico. It appears that he no longer was as concerned about possibly overheating as he previously had been. No doubt he promised himself to be very careful.

Before returning, though, the Ritchies took a vacation trip. On occasion they had driven up to Big Bear in the San Bernardino Mountains when Dr. Ritchie felt the need for a break in his busy work schedule. More than four decades later, Inelda Ruth Ritchie remembered those weekend breaks:

> We . . . went up to Big Bear, camped out, and we could hear the coyotes yowling, and we went to a spring and got water. And we had a little camp stove with us, I think that [it] was a little gasoline stove. . . . We used a tarp on the ground, and then that kept the bedding clean, you see. And then I put cotton blankets for sheets, and I think we had lots of quilts, too.[20]

---

[20] Inelda Ruth Sheld-Ritchie, widow of Dr. Iner S. Ritchie, transcript of interview by her granddaughter, Cheryl Nickel Leathers, 2 March 1986, [La Jolla, California], 16 [2]. Ritchie Papers, SCLSU.

At an elevation of 6,750 feet above sea level, Big Bear could be quite chilly at night, so quilts had been needed. But the vacation the Ritchies now planned would be longer than a single weekend trip. They decided to go to Yosemite National Park where they would enjoy the Independence Day holiday. While they had planned to stay in a hotel, upon their arrival they discovered there were no vacant rooms. Others apparently had made plans for the Fourth of July, as well. Mrs. Ritchie explained what they did:

> We made a camp with some branches from the trees and some tarpaulins, and we had some bedding. . . . I had a little stove thing . . . made . . . out of a five-gallon can . . . as a camping stove. Used it without gasoline. As I remember it, we used it with little chips and things. I had the frying pan and things and we made it over an open fire. . . . We had a lantern, so we had light at night. And we had such a good time. We'd go for long walks and feed the deer. And . . . the bears would come. . . .[21]

They had not brought food with them, so they bought what they needed at the park store. Maybe they had been forced by circumstances to improvise, but they experienced quite a change of pace and scenery, and they had an enjoyable time.

Dr. Ritchie and his family returned to Calexico in 1931. This time they lived in the second story of the hospital. Those were

---

[21] I.R. Sheld-Ritchie, transcript of interview by C.N. Leathers, 2 March 1986, 15-16 [1-2].

difficult times, and, like millions of others, the Ritchies needed to economize wherever they could.

It was hot in that apartment above the hospital, especially during the summer. One time C.F. Innis showed up without previous announcement. Inelda May, in an attempt to stay as cool as possible, had shed all her clothes except her black sateen bloomers. The only convenient place to hide was under the table, so, to avoid embarrassment, she quickly ducked under. The table cloth effectively kept her from being seen, but it also prevented the free circulation of the air. It quickly became oppressively warm under there. Inelda May spent a very uncomfortable hour or more before the office manager left.[22]

Mrs. Ritchie came up with something that helped to make the heat more tolerable, at least temporarily. She kept an electric ice cream maker on the kitchen counter. On hot days she would mash some bananas and make banana ice cream. It always seemed to help. During the summertime they had it almost every evening.[23]

A major share of Dr. Ritchie's—and other Calexico physicians'—income came from practicing medicine across the border in Mexicali. As long as there had been plenty of paying patients to go around, this had not been a problem. But with the Great Depression affecting incomes south of the border as much as it did to the north of it, some looked at Dr. Ritchie's practice with a certain amount of envy. One such was a Dr. Talbot, who at one time had lived next door to the Ritchies. He tried to bribe Mexican

[22] I.M. Christianson, interview by D.G. Ross, 1 July 2003.

[23] Ibid.

border officials into preventing the self-supporting missionary doctor from crossing into their country. He even bragged about how he had "fixed" matters. But Dr. Talbot's arrangements soon unraveled.[24]

As he had done previously, from time to time Dr. Ritchie offered lectures on health topics. In 1931, though, he determined to offer a course of study that would lead to a certificate in practical nursing. He went to the new territorial governor of Baja California Norte, Agustín Olachea Avilés,[25] to determine what the official reaction might be. He requested permission to "conduct public health lectures, organize classes in home nursing and dietetics, distribute efficient literature on health temperance and hygiene," and "also to bring into the country duty free necessary equipment and supplies to carry on said work and to bring in competent nurses and instructors and such help as is necessary in this work.[26] The governor, who was very much aware of Dr. Ritchie's excellent reputation and of his friendship with previous Governor Abelardo Rodríguez, enthusiastically endorsed the plan, not only giving official permission, but also offering equipment, supplies, and even promising to publicize the classes at government expense. Prodded by the governor, the minister of education offered a place for the meetings, the largest auditorium at his

---

[24] Mother [Inelda Ruth Ritchie] to Darling Precious Son [Iner William Ritchie], 19 November 1931, Ritchie Papers, SCLSU.

[25] With the exception of a three-week period in 1932, Olachea served as governor of the territory from 1931 to 1935.

[26] Iner S. Ritchie, handwritten manuscript in folder "Calexico: 1926-29; 1931-32," no date, 2, Ritchie Papers, SCLSU.

command, the "Salón de Actos"—the assembly hall—of the boys' high school in Mexicali.[27]

With several thousand hand bills printed at government expense spread throughout the city and nearby communities, attendance at the initial public lectures was good. When the practical nursing course got under way, 87 students were enrolled. They received instruction from Dr. Ritchie, three nurses, and an evangelist.

All appeared to be going well when, quite suddenly, a major obstacle loomed on the horizon. As Dr. Ritchie explained,

> When things are going too well to suit him, Satan always has his pharaoh to resist and oppose. This was in the person of the chief of the health department. He made a special trip to Mexico City going to the Secretary of the Central Government and to the Department of Public Health where he lodged false charges against me saying I was peddling opium, killing women and committing other crimes.

Although the entire program seemed to be in jeopardy, a way to possibly resolve the difficulty soon presented itself. Dr. Ritchie saw the hand of God in the matter:

> At just this point the Lord sent a patient to us who was to prove a great help to us. It was the governor's wife and she came to us at just the right time. She had spent great sums of money and had consulted many specialists and

---

[27] Ibid.

suffered many things at the hands of many physicians but she was so well pleased with her treatments and her improvement in health that she wanted to be with us and help us in our work.[28]

Dr. Ritchie had been helped by his successful treatment of a previous governor's family member, so he tried again. Based on his false accusations, the chief of the health department had succeeded in obtaining an order prohibiting Dr. Ritchie from entering Mexico. Now the missionary physician explained to his patient what had happened. She promptly arranged for Dr. Ritchie to meet with her husband in their home. He left with a signed document countermanding the prohibition.[29] When he tried to cross the border into Mexico the next morning, though, he was stopped and taken to the chief of Immigration. When he read Dr. Ritchie's document he promised to contact the governor about it, but would not let the missionary continue into Mexicali. When he learned what had happened, Governor Olachea was irate and not only took care of the matter but offered additional help, promising

Anything you need to help you in the way of beds, equipment, linens or supplies or anything at our municipal hospital you shall have it. Just make a list and leave it on my desk and I will order the truck to take it to the

---

[28] Ibid., 3.

[29] Agustín Olachea to Delegado de Migración, 5 December 1931, Ritchie Papers, SCLSU.

place and at the time you say. And if you are too busy [to come to my office] just phone me.[30]

When the minister of education had offered a place in which to hold the meetings and classes he had told Dr. Ritchie that there was to be no proselytizing or teaching of religion, nor was there to be any kind of sales. Such activities were prohibited in public buildings. The missionary doctor was quite aware of the restriction, and he fully intended to abide by the government regulations. He had hoped, however, to use *Ministry of Healing* by Ellen G. White as a textbook. So, he presented a copy each to the governor and the minister of education of the territory and asked that it be approved for use in the class. After reading the book the latter official's comment after granting permission for its use as a text was, "That is a very good book, it goes back to first principles. Sell as many books as you can to the people."[31]   That approval—coupled with what amounted to an order to sell as many as he could—was especially encouraging because Dr. Ritchie had already bought sixty copies of the Spanish translation to distribute to his students.[32]

The director of the territorial health department still hoped to put a halt to Dr. Ritchie's success in Mexicali, though, so he went to Mexico City where he tried to arrange for either a law or

---

[30] Quoted in Iner S. Ritchie, handwritten manuscript in folder "Calexico: 1926-29; 1931-32," 4.

[31] Quoted in Ibid., 5.

[32] Ibid., 4-5; and O.R. Staines, ed., "Dr. Ritchie Working in Mexico," *The Medical Evangelist,* Vol. 18, No. 45 (5 May 1932).

regulation prohibiting anyone who was not a citizen or a naturalized citizen from practicing medicine in Mexico. After a short time he became concerned that even that would not be enough because he feared Dr. Ritchie might decide to become a Mexican citizen. He then began to push for a prohibition that would include naturalized citizens. He must not have been very successful for Dr. Ritchie later summarized the chief's efforts with a terse, "Governor's order stood."[33]

While Dr. Ritchie spoke Spanish and had lectured in Spanish on numerous occasions, he realized that his was colloquial street Spanish. With official eyes on him, he thought it best to use a translator. He therefore lectured in English, and the editor of the local newspaper translated his lecture into Spanish.[34]

Exactly how many of the 87 students who started the course of study in 1931 actually graduated as practical nurses in 1932 is unclear. The governor's wife was helpful right to the end, though, at which time she handed out the diplomas during the graduation ceremony.[35]

The practical nursing course was barely over when, on April 1, 1932, Dr. Ritchie began offering classes in practical hygiene and home nursing every Monday and Friday evening in Mexicali. This time all the active physicians in the city would be joining him. Not only would he be able to introduce the Adventist health

---

[33] [Iner S. Ritchie], "The Medical Missionary Work," 18-page handwritten manuscript dated Sabbath, January 5, 1946, [5], Ritchie Papers, SCLSU.

[34] I.M. Christianson, telephone interview by D.G. Ross, 6 July 2003; and O.R. Staines, ed., "Dr. Ritchie Working in Mexico."

[35] I.M. Christianson, telephone interview by D.G. Ross, 6 July 2003.

message to the members of the general public who attended, but because of their participation he could also present it to every practicing physician in the territorial capital. In addition to the major thrust in Mexicali, Dr. Ritchie and C.F. Innis began a series of health lectures in Calexico.[36]

Although he was very actively engaged in missionary activities in Calexico and Mexicali after he had resumed his practice there, Dr. Ritchie continued to try to find someone to buy it from him. He traveled to Loma Linda to speak at a chapel hour at the College of Medical Evangelists and he advertised in *The Medical Evangelist.*[37]

The Great Depression had spread to Mexico, though, and was bound to have an effect on anyone who worked there, including even the most selfless of medical missionaries. At one of the chapel periods at CME a lecturer on Mexico, a Dr. C.N. Thomas, reported having visited a hospital in Ciudad Obregón, Sonora, that was run by two CME graduates. His comments on the ability of their patients to pay was not encouraging: "On account of the marked depression in Mexico sixty per cent of their work is charity; thirty per cent pay a small fee; and ten per cent of the patients pay a reasonable fee."[38]

---

[36] *Al Público: Clases Prácticas de Higiene,* handbill, 1 April 1932, Mexicali, Baja California; and [Inelda Ruth Ritchie] to Precious Daughter [Anna Ritchie], 23 March 1932; Ritchie Papers, SCLSU.

[37] O.R. Staines, ed., "Dr. Ritchie Working in Mexico." For an example of his advertising see "Wanted," *The Medical Evangelist,* Vol. 18, No. 45 (5 May 1932).

[38] Quoted in "Progress in Mexico," *The Medical Evangelist,* Vol. 19, No. 1 (7 July 1932).

**The Calexico Hospital in 1936 after
Dr. Kortheuer took over.**

Dr. Ritchie's practice and his hospital in Calexico may have shown a higher percentage of paying patients, but the Great Depression meant that the asking price would have to be lower, the terms more generous, and the possibility of default would be greater than before.

Despite the desperate times, he eventually found someone to take his practice and the emergency hospital. It was Dr. Karl Kortheuer, recently graduated from the College of Medical Evangelists. As might be suspected of someone who had just finished school, Dr. Kortheuer had little money. So instead of buying, he rented, paying Dr. Ritchie all of $40 per month. Considering that the taxes alone were nearly $800 per year, the Ritchies were losing about $300 per year. But $480 a year seemed better than nothing, and the world economy would turn around someday. When it did maybe the hospital and practice could be sold for something closer to its true value.[39]

In the meanwhile, the Ritchies could leave Calexico for someplace where summers were not so sweltering hot. Dr. Ritchie's health demanded no less. They would not return to Colton, though, because Dr. Ritchie felt that the dust from the big cement plant there could possibly harm their health. There were times when the dust in the air was visible, and it covered every-thing that was exposed virtually all the time.[40]

Once more, in 1932, he and his family left the Calexico-Mexicali border area. *The Medical Evangelist* journal reported in November that he was practicing medicine in Pomona. He set up his office in their home on East Holt Avenue, next door to the home and office of Drs. Hersel E. and Mabel Butka. Fellow graduates of the College of Medical Evangelists, like Dr. Ritchie, they were interested in mission service; in fact they had only recently returned from serving in Bolivia. When the Montemorelos Sanitarium and Hospital opened in the Mexican state of Nuevo León in 1947, Hersel Butka was its director.[41]

---

[39] [Anna L. Ritchie] to Dear Precious Loved Ones [Iner and Inelda Ritchie], 12 February 1936, 1, Ritchie Papers, SCLSU; and O.R. Staines, ed., "Pencilgrams," *The Medical Evangelist,* Vol. 19, No. 18 (3 November 1932).

[40] I.R. Sheld-Ritchie, transcript of interview by C.A.N. Leathers, 20 November 1985, 7.

[41] O.R. Staines, ed., "Items," *The Medical Evangelist,* Vol. 19, No. 19 (10 November 1932), 4; I.R. Christianson, "Ritchie Family Life in Riverside," 7; and I.M. Christianson, interview by D.G. Ross, 8 July 2003. Hersel Bukta earned his M.D. degree from CME in 1917; Mabel earned hers in 1918. O.R. Staines, ed., "Dr. Hersel E. Butka, Class of '17," *The Medical Evangelist,*

Even though times were difficult economically, as had always been the case previously, Dr. Ritchie soon developed a thriving practice. In his final month of practice in Pomona he performed work valued at $1,447. While he did some of it on credit, and he probably would not have been able to collect all that was owed, for those days that was a princely income.[42]

It was in the summer of 1934, while he was in Pomona, that Dr. Ritchie saw and took a liking to Jadaun, a fine-looking, dappled-gray Arabian stallion that had been ridden by Rudolph Valentino. It happened while he was visiting the W.K. Kelloggs, of Kellogg's Corn Flakes fame, at a horse ranch they had recently acquired in Pomona.[43] Valentino had ridden the horse in the sand dunes near Yuma, Arizona, during the filming of his last film, *The Son of the Sheik,* released in 1926. The film star had abused Jadaun, seriously cutting. its flanks with his spurs. When Dr. Ritchie expressed his admiration of the horse—and his disgust at the way it had been mistreated—Kellogg, sensing a kindred horse lover in the former cowboy, gave the splendid animal to him. He

---

Vol.19, No. 43 (27 April 1933).

[42] Anna L. Ritchie to C.E. Wood, 14 February 1935, 2.

[43] Dr. Ritchie's adoptive father, William S. Ritchie, had known the Kellogg brothers when he lived in Battle Creek, Michigan, and W.K. Kellogg had visited with the W.S. Ritchies in California on a memorable occasion in 1926. It was memorable because Kellogg had driven up in a true motorhome, something of a rarity for the time. [Iner W. Ritchie], two-page untitled manuscript on stationery of Liga México-Pan-Americana Medico [sic] Educacional, Riverside, California, no date but believed to be from the 1980s, Ritchie Papers, SCLSU; and Ron Hotchkiss, "Kelloggs of Battle Creek," *American History,* Vol. 29, No.6 (February 1995), 62-66.

was unable to do much with it, though, because he and his family soon moved to Mexico City. Jadaun stayed behind on the Kellogg horse ranch.[44]

The next time Dr. Ritchie saw W.K. Kellogg both were in Mexico City. Kellogg was seriously ill with pneumonia, and the medical evangelist was able to help because he had accepted a call from the Mexican Union Mission of Seventh-day Adventists to direct the medical endeavors of the church in that country.

---

[44] [Iner William Ritchie], As a young boy, 2-page manuscript, [1980s], 1-2, Ritchie Papers, SCLSU; and I.M. Christianson, interview by D.G. Ross, 8 July 2003.

Beginning Denominational Service in Mexico

During the first half of the twentieth century Seventh-day Adventists became very active in missionary endeavors, with church headquarters sending ordained ministers and other qualified personnel to follow up on leads and opportunities created by self-supporting missionaries. Heeding the example of Jesus, whose short earthly career included miraculous healing as he cared for both physical and spiritual needs of people, the church taught that medical work could be the "right arm" of its ministry. As church leaders often put it, medical work could be the "entering wedge of the gospel" as it sought to reach others with its spiritual message. Therefore, a significant number of church-sponsored missionaries were physicians, nurses, and other health professionals. Hundreds were sent all over the world. Under the overarching objective of spreading the gospel, their immediate goals generally were two: to provide health care through the establishment of clinics and hospitals, and to teach health principles in schools and public meetings. That, of course, is exactly what Dr. Ritchie had been doing on his own. Beginning even before graduating from medical school, because of his faith in Christ and his commitment to helping others, his work and energy had focused on these same two objectives.[1]

Of intense interest to Adventist leaders in Mexico was the fact that Dr. Ritchie had successfully accomplished that type of work on the Mexican border. If possible, of even more interest was the fact that he had done so with the approval and assistance of Mexican government officials despite strict anticlerical laws and the Roman Catholic beliefs held by far the great majority of Mexicans. For nearly a decade, either directly or indirectly, Mexico had been led by General Plutarco Elías Calles, a well known and confirmed anticleric. Laws designed to reduce the political influence of churches passed during his administration regulated most types of missionary work—or outlawed them altogether. For more than a century prior to the enactment of the anticlerical laws the Catholic Church had made it difficult to impossible for other denominations to operate freely. Mexico, therefore, had always been a country in which non-Catholics encountered almost insurmountable obstacles preventing them from easily and openly dealing with the public or even individuals. Because of his experience and success along the border, though, Adventist officials believed Dr. Ritchie could break down barriers and get things done in Mexico despite the apparent obstacles.

The additional fact that he enjoyed the confidence of, and a working relationship with, his friend, General Abelardo L.

---

[1] Elizabeth Vodeb and Andrew Howe, "Dr. Ritchie's Relationship with Mexican Governors" (term paper presented for HIST 494, History Colloquium, La Sierra University, Riverside, California, 29 November 1995). D.G. Ross Collection.

Rodríguez, who had become Interim President of Mexico in 1932, was a major consideration also. Opportunity seemed to be knocking at the door. Moreover, as a result of Dr. and Mrs. Ritchie's trip to Mexico City in February 1929, during which they had met many Adventist church officials who had been impressed by their devotion to Christian principles and their sincere desire to help the church and Mexicans, many church leaders in Mexico viewed Dr. Ritchie as a trusted fellow worker.

Therefore, on July 5, 1933, the Mexican Union Mission Committee of the Seventh-day Adventist Church voted:

> That we place a call with the Inter-American Division for Dr. Ritchie, of California, to connect with the medical work in Mexico City as a regular worker on salary, and that we pay transportation through to Mexico City on such medical equipment as may be arranged by counsel with the Union Committee and that we pay transportation on household goods . . . , and [an] outfitting allowance according to Division policy.[2]

Dr. Ritchie, who had been consulted beforehand, immediately accepted the Mexican Union's offer of employment and began preparations to move to Mexico City. His "adoptive" mother and mother-in-law, Anna Lula Ritchie, however, expressed reservations because his pay would be cut by 90 percent, or more. He had a number of financial obligations of his own, and with the Great Depression serving to impoverish them all, she expected him to

---

[2] Mexican Union Mission Committee, "Minutes," Vote 347, 5 July 1933, [Mexico, D.F.], copy in Ritchie Papers, SCLSU.

help her and her husband as well. Doctor Ritchie's quick acceptance of a church call to a poorly paid position in Mexico became a source of frequent discussion and friction during the following two years. He believed his decision to have been the right one, though, and he refused to change his mind for financial reasons.

As Dr. Ritchie and his family began making preparations for their move, the first order of business was to acquire the necessary permits to enter and live in Mexico. The unsettled and volatile relationship between the United States and Mexico at that time made such paperwork more necessary than usual. In order to avoid possible problems later on, everything had to be in order.

Because the employment of foreigners in many fields of endeavor was legally prohibited in Mexico, an appeal for an exception was made to the Mexican president—Dr. Ritchie's friend, former governor of Baja California Norte, General Abelardo L. Rodríguez. Acting on the orders of the president, the Federal Department of Public Health in Mexico City approved his immigration and sent word to that effect to the Ministry of Government[3] in mid-October 1933.[4] Dr. Ritchie had received immigration papers in February, 1932, but they appear not to have

---

[3] Ministerio de Gobernación, roughly the equivalent of the Department of the Interior in the United States.

[4] Dr. Gastón Melo, Chief, Departamento de Salubridad Pública, to Secretario de Gobernación, 20 October 1933, Ritchie Papers, SCLSU. Dr. Ritchie had received immigration papers in February, 1932, but they appear not to have been exactly what he needed. Mamma [Inelda Ruth Ritchie] to Precious Son [Iner William Ritchie], 16 February 1932, Ritchie Papers, SCLSU.

been exactly what he needed.[5] About three weeks later the Ministry of Government sent word to Dr. Ritchie informing him of the approval and outlining a number of conditions that had to be met both before and after his arrival. The most demanding of the qualifications called for an investment of no less than 10,000 pesos "in the establishment of hospitals, sanitariums and clinics that you propose to found." This was to be accomplished "within the first six months of your stay in the country."[6] A possible reason for this demand could have been the government's first real focus on building a health and sanitation program in the mid-1920s and 1930s. Under the leadership of General Calles, a Department of Public Health had been formed to ensure the establishment of sanitation codes and higher health standards for Mexican citizens. A practical application of such efforts was, for example, the inoculation against smallpox of more than five million Mexicans in a government-sponsored nationwide campaign in 1926.[7]

Mexico had been the first nation outside of the United States to host Seventh-day Adventist medical missionaries, with a beginning made in Guadalajara as early as January 1894 and the

[5] Mamma [Inelda Ruth Ritchie] to Precious Son [Iner William Ritchie], 16 February 1932, Ritchie Papers, SCLSU.

[6] Secretaría de Gobernación to Dr. Inner [sic] Sheld Ritchie, 9 November 1933, Ritchie Papers, SCLSU.

[7] Michael C. Meyer and William L. Sherman. *The Course of Mexican History,* 5th ed. (New York: Oxford University Press, 1995), 584-585.

opening of a sanitarium there early in 1899.[8] While initially successful, much of their work had eventually been abandoned—at least partly because of government-imposed obstacles, if not outright opposition, and as a result of the violent phase of the Mexican Revolution beginning in 1910.[9] Now it almost seemed that the national government of Mexico was demanding that such work not only be reinitiated, but that it be done in a major way almost immediately. Dr. Ritchie certainly did not mind!

Once the paperwork had been completed and the boxcar containing medical equipment and the Ritchies' personal effects had been entrusted to the Southern Pacific Railroad, five Ritchies—Dr. and Mrs. Ritchie and their three younger children, Anna, Inelda May, and Robert—were ready for departure. They left Loma Linda on May 1, 1934, traveling toward Mexico by automobile, a black Oldsmobile with a trunk on a rack behind.[10] Because they had not been able to fit everything they wanted to

---

[8] F.M. Wilcox, "The Opening of Our Work in Mexico," *Advent Review and Sabbath Herald,* Vol. 71, No. 8 (20 February 1894), 116-17; "The Work in Many Lands: Operations in Mexico," *Advent Review and Sabbath Herald,* Vol. 71, No. 28 (10 July 1894), 437; J.H. Kellogg, "An Appeal for Mexico," *Advent Review and Sabbath Herald,* Vol. 74, No. 26 (29 June 1897), 408; and L. Monning, "The Guadalajara Sanitarium," *Advent Review and Sabbath Herald,* Vol. 76, No. 17 (25 April 1899), 269.

[9] The Guadalajara Sanitarium was sold in 1907 to Methodists who used the building as a school. Clarence E. Wood, *In the Land of the Aztecs* (Takoma Park, Washington, D.C.: Review and Herald Publishing Association, 1939), 61.

[10] [O.R. Staines, ed.], "News Flashes," *The Medical Evangelist,* Vol. 20, No. 45 (10 May 1934), 4; and [Inelda May Christianson], "Iner Sheld-Ritchie, October 6, 1885 - October 24, 1949," an undated chronology, Ritchie Papers, SCLSU.

**Ready to leave Loma Linda for Mexico City, May 1, 1934.
Left to right, Inelds May, Inelda Ruth, Robert Lorraine.
Anna Virginia, and Dr. Iner S. Ritchie, and Neff Soto.**

take in the railroad boxcar, they towed a heavily loaded trailer behind their car. Neff Soto, a patient from Pomona who was interested in possibly moving to Mexico, had joined the Ritchies and would help with the driving. After leaving California, they drove through Arizona and New Mexico to Texas. They experienced some excitement and considerable apprehension when they discovered that young Inelda May had been left behind after they had stopped in Benson, Arizona. That mistake, fortunately enough, was quickly rectified. By dint of long hours and steady travel, in less than three days they managed to reach Laredo, Texas, where they left the United States and entered Mexico on May 3.[11]

Although they had covered more than half the distance from Pomona to Mexico City in less than three days, the remainder took a week. They finally reached the Mexican capital on May 10, where Dr. Ritchie and his family did not even have time to unpack before he began his administrative duties as head of Adventist medical work in Mexico, and where he was promptly voted membership on the important Mexican Union Mission Committee.[12] In a short letter to a friend and colleague back in California, Dr. Ritchie briefly described their trip, coincidentally offering a clue as to why the Mexican portion of their trip took twice as much time as did the longer American segment:

> We had a wonderful trip down here by auto over the new Pan American highway via Laredo, Texas—Monterey [sic], Victoria, Valles, etc. Our trailer was quite heavily loaded. Passed through jungles, ferried over rivers infested with alligators, saw flocks of parrotts [sic], gorgeously plumed birds, huge colored butterflies, herds of wild antelope, wild turkeys & pigeons, & wonderful forests and mountains and rivers.[13]

---

[11] Ibid. Dr Ritchie's Conditional Immigration Certificate erroneously states that he entered Mexico via Ciudad Juárez, Chihuahua. Mexico, Servicio de Migración, "Registro de Extranjeros," Mexico, D.F., 3 May 1934.

[12] Mexican Union Mission Committee, "Minutes," 14 May 1934, and Vote 372, 15 May 1934, [Mexico. D.F.], copy in Ritchie Papers, SCLSU.

[13] [Iner S.] Ritchie to Dr. [Benton] Colver, 30 June 1934, Ritchie Papers, SCLSU. Written on the reverse of a family photograph on postcard stock, this brief note may never have been mailed. Dr. Colver had performed a

He then urged his physician friend to make a similar trip in order to experience it all himself, but not until "the road is completed and after the rainy season."[14] That was good advice. Although the Pan American Highway between Laredo and Mexico City had been opened to dry-season traffic, it could become impassable very quickly when it rained. Near Tamazunchale, San Luis Potosí, the Ritchies had been forced to pause several times while the road immediately ahead was made passable for them by workers with picks, shovels, and wheelbarrows. One evening a rainstorm caught them. It rained so hard they could not see the road, so they pulled over for the night. The following morning they discovered they had stopped just in time to avoid going into a river.[15]

Once they reached the capital they stayed with the Clarence E. Moon family until they rented a house. Located in an area known as Colonia del Valle, their spacious, two-story home was called *La Casa de las Botellas* (The House of the Bottles) because of its milk-bottle-shaped windows. There they were able to live comfortably and also had enough room for Dr. Ritchie to set up his private medical practice. Once they had a place of their own, they needed their furniture and other personal items. Because the missionary evangelist had an interview with the Mexican President at the time, James G. Pettey, the Union treasurer, accompanied Inelda Ruth and the children as they shepherded their belongings

---

mastoidectomy on Dr. Ritchie when the latter had been practicing in Pomona.

[14] Ibid.

[15] [Inelda May Christianson], "Iner Sheld-Ritchie, October 6, 1885 - October 24, 1949," an undated chronology, Ritchie Papers, SCLSU.

through Mexican customs. Inelda May later recalled that the customs "inspectors' eyes lighted up when they saw the home canned fruit," and that "some of the *'dulces'* (sweets) were confiscated."[16]

They later moved to a house on the corner of Obregón Street and Insurgentes Avenue in Colonia Roma. That made it easier for some patients to find Dr. Ritchie's office, although it made no difference at all to most of his more prominent ones. Secretary of War General Gilberto R. Limón and his family, for example, did not go to the doctor. Instead, the doctor went to them. That, of course, was not at all unusual in the days when physicians made house calls. On one such occasion Dr. Ritchie took Inelda May with him to play with the general's daughters. It was quite an eye-opening experience for her. "For the first time," she explained, she saw "walls of wardrobes of suits and uniforms and yards of shiny boots and shoes outside those in a store. Mrs. Limón's boudoir was all rose satin and ecru lace with French perfume in pint-sized bottles."[17]

In their haste to enter Mexico and reach the capital before anything might happen to government officials to possibly prevent their legal entry, Dr. and Mrs. Ritchie had left their elder son, Iner William, behind. He was completing his first year of college at San Bernardino Junior College and it had not seemed wise to take him on the trip to Mexico with only weeks to go until the end of the academic year. After school was out, he could follow his folks

---

[16] Ibid.; and Inelda Ritchie Christianson, "Ritchie Family Life in Riverside," 8, Ritchie Papers, SCLSU.

[17] [Inelda May Christianson], "Iner Sheld-Ritchie, 1885 -1949."

and stay with them in Mexico City until the beginning of a new school year made it desirable for him to return to the United States. One of his sisters, Anna, who had hastened to complete high school at Loma Linda Academy so as to be able to travel to Mexico with her family, would return with him.

The plan was for Iner William to follow his parents in a car belonging to a classmate, Jim Lash. That plan underwent major alterations when a stretch of the Pan American Highway between Laredo, Texas, and Mexico City had to be closed, possibly because of washouts.[18] The revised plan was for Iner William to travel by bus or by train—whichever proved less expensive—to El Paso, Texas. After crossing the border into Mexico, he was to take the train to Mexico City.

After mailing him a second-class ticket for the train in Mexico and funds to pay for tickets on the train or the bus from Colton, California, to El Paso, his mother sent Iner William detailed instructions. From the bus depot or train station in El Paso he was to take a taxi or the trolley to the train station in Ciudad Juárez, Chihuahua. The taxi might cost as much as fifty cents, "but bargain for the price before you get in," while the street car fare was a dime. He was to take with him sandwiches, bread or crackers, and a thermos of hot milk. If necessary, he could purchase bread, bananas, and boiled milk on the way. She also instructed him to check his baggage except for one suitcase. With a locked padlock he was to chain that suitcase to his seat and keep

---

[18] Ibid.; and [Iner S.] Ritchie to Dr. [Benton] Colver, 30 June 1934, Ritchie Papers, SCLSU.

it in sight every waking minute, and at night, or if he napped during the day, to "sleep on it."[19]

The young man's trip was long and, especially if he really slept on any part of his luggage, probably rather taxing. Because everything was new to him, he doubtless also found it quite exciting. He joined the rest of the Ritchie family in Mexico City in July 1934.

One of the first items on Dr. Ritchie's agenda once he reached Mexico City was to visit some relatively remote area of Mexican Indian country where there was no medical service. While he was helping those with medical problems, he hoped to photograph Indians who were suffering so as to convince government officials of the need to provide medical assistance to them. News of the arrival of a physician who might dispense free medical care resulted in a small crowd of patients to welcome the doctor and those with him not long after they arrived in the Totonac Indian town of Pantepec after traveling a day by train and automobile, then eleven hours more on horseback. Elder Clarence E. Wood later wrote:

> During the three days we spent in this town there were fifty or more patients waiting their turn to see the doctor every hour he was able to be with them. The scene reminded me of the multitudes of sick people that crowded about the Great Healer. . . .
>
> This visit has emphasized in our minds the need and importance of training our mission workers, under Dr.

---

[19] [Inelda Ruth Ritchie] to Iner William [Ritchie], 4 July 1934, Ritchie Papers, SCLSU.

Ritchie's direction, so they will be able to render medical as well as spiritual help to these poor Indians.[20]

Dr. Ritchie had made his point with Elder Wood, the superintendent of the Mexican Union, and the others members of his party with a single visit and without any need for photographs! The pictures helped considerably, though, because when they were shown around government offices in the capital a number of influential government officials were very favorably impressed with what the American physician and those accompanying him had accomplished at Pantepec and hoped to do elsewhere.[21]

Another of the early tasks of the newly arrived head of medical work was to deal with the matter of a recently closed and greatly missed medical clinic. When Dr. Ritchie had been called to serve in Mexico, the belief of the members of the Union Mission Committee in Dr. Ritchie's ability was so great that they further decided on February 14, 1934, to close the sometimes troublesome Tacubaya Clinic until after his arrival.[22] It was not that the clinic, located in a separately administered suburb of Mexico City, had not attracted patients or that there had been malpractice issues. Most of the time, though, it had experienced a

---

[20] C.E. Wood, "Itinerating with Our Doctor in Mexico," *Inter-American Division Messenger,* Vol. 11, No. 12 (December 1934), 9-10.

[21] Clarence E. Wood, *In the Land of the Aztecs* (Takoma Park, Washington, D.C.: Review and Herald Publishing Association, 1939), 86-88, and Iner W. Ritchie, Jr., "Itinerating with the Doctor," *Youth's Instructor,* Vol. 86, No. 18 (3 May 1938), 5-6, 12.

[22] Mexican Union Mission Committee, "Minutes," Vote 370, 14 February 1934, [Mexico, D.F.], copy in Ritchie Papers, SCLSU.

rather glaring inadequacy of leadership—particularly no permanent physician. Despite that lack, according to a report prepared
several months later by Clarence E. Moon, "Those who have been
treated in the Clinic have been well pleased and have nothing but
a good word for the kind attention they have received." He then
offered an indication of one of the problems, "Some have wanted
to make it their home because of the help they received."[23]
Exactly how recently arrived Dr. Ritchie was expected to resolve
this and other problems at the clinic was not stated, but it was
assumed that he would soon reopen it and operate it so that it
might achieve its goal of helping the church spread the gospel.

As he had done on many previous occasions during his stay
along the border, Dr. Ritchie soon initiated communication with
various government officials to try to gain their participation in the
process of building up the clinic, or at the very least to secure a
promise from them not to oppose its reopening and subsequent
operation. He also worked to convince the membership of the
Union Mission Committee of the wisdom of securing official
recognition of the clinic from the Chamber of Commerce.
Contacts made through such registration could prove invaluable.
After hearing a convincing appeal from their new medical
director—he had not yet been in the capital two weeks—the
committee voted to attempt to secure affiliation.[24] His efforts to
register the clinic, however, did not succeed until March 3, 1937,

---

[23] Mexican Union Mission Committee, "Minutes," 17 May 1934,
[Mexico, D.F.], copy in Ritchie Papers, SCLSU.

[24] Mexican Union Mission Committee, "Minutes," Vote 408, 21 May
1934, [Mexico, D.F.], copy in Ritchie Papers, SCLSU.

when it was granted a membership certificate from the Cámara de Comercio e Industria de Tacubaya y Mixcoac.[25]

While securing the membership certificate from the Chamber of Commerce had taken nearly three years, assistance for the Tacubaya Clinic from other sources materialized more quickly. As already mentioned, Dr. Ritchie believed in the advantageous employment of letters of recommendation. He had accomplished much through their use in the past in Calexico and Mexicali, and he hoped they would be equally helpful in Mexico City. While it is impossible to determine the number of such letters written, it is known that there were many. One apparently penned by a Mexican physician or government official, for example, is a statement of appreciation for Dr. Ritchie's missionary and medical work in Mexico. Addressed to Dr. José Siurob, the director of the Public Health Department, it urges the director to meet with Dr. Ritchie for the benefit of all parties involved, especially the Mexican people.[26] Carefully worded to appeal to the director's humanitarianism, nationalism, patriotism, and sense of duty, such an appeal could not easily be dismissed. It was not long before another such letter, from the Secretary General of the Public Health Department and directed to Dr. Ritchie, offered evidence that the recommended meeting had taken place. Moreover, the second letter thanked the medical evangelist specifically for his work of

---

[25] Cámara de Comercio e Industria de Tacubaya y Mixcoac, "Credencial," Tacubaya, D.F., 31 March 1937, Ritchie Papers, SCLSU. By the time the certificate was granted, Dr. Ritchie had returned to the United States for health reasons.

[26] JMC to José Siurob, 28 October 1935, Ritchie Papers, SCLSU.

combating alcoholism in the state of Oaxaca and throughout southeast Mexico.[27] Such letters were mere words, of course, but they could help influence government officials and others when decisions about more material matters were required. While the letters often praised Dr. Ritchie, the Tacubaya Clinic which he directed was the principal beneficiary.

A few years before Dr. Ritchie's arrival in Mexico City, Clarence E. Moon, director of the Central Mexican Mission, had described the goals of the dispensary as relieving the sick and providing classes in nursing, treatments, cooking, and dietetics. He also described a system used to teach those living in outlying areas. Teachers would go to remote villages for three to six months and conduct classes for children during the day and for adults at night. Such classes were provided in Spanish as well as in several Indian dialects. Elder Moon appealed to his readers to provide monetary support for the work being accomplished.[28]

During his two-year tenure as director of Adventist medical work in Mexico, because of its proximity, most of Dr. Ritchie's efforts naturally concentrated first on the reopening and then the operation of the Tacubaya Clinic, but he did not alter its goals. As he quite accurately understood it, in addition to medical relief the objective of the clinic was "the dissemination of the Gospel of

---

[27] Jesús Díaz Barriga to I.S. Ritchie, 18 April 1936, Ritchie Papers, SCLSU.

[28] C.E. Moon, "Dispensary at Tacubaya, D.F., Mexico," *The Medical Evangelist*, Vol. 18, No. 14 (1 October 1931), 1.

Health and the prevention of disease by education of the people."[29] The means by which to accomplish the second objective he saw as educating leaders, providing public health lectures, distributing literature, writing and voicing one's opinion for the extension of missionary work in Mexico, supporting "the standard of clean morals, of temperance, and of law and order and faithful obedience to the government, and persuading others to do the same."[30] When he genuinely believed in something, Dr. Ritchie could really sermonize!

Located adjacent to Mexico City in the Tacubaya section of the Federal District, once back in business the clinic was open for patients Monday through Friday from eight o'clock in the morning until noon. Health-care classes on topics such as personal hygiene, prenatal care, and midwifery were offered all day long. Evening classes, generally conducted from 7:30 to 9:00, were offered to accommodate those who had to work during the day. If he was to reach the goals set for the clinic, Dr. Ritchie definitely had a heavy work load ahead of him.[31]

In a letter to his friend and former partner, Dr. Ralph M. Smith, who was then living in Glendale, California, the hard

---

[29] [Iner S. Ritchie], "This Chart of Communicable Diseases," Tacubaya, D.F., no date, Ritchie Papers, SCLSU.

[30] Ibid.

[31] Clínica Tacubaya, sheet from note pad, Tacubaya, D.F., no date, Ritchie Papers, SCLSU. Although it appears that relatively little of a documentary nature still exists on the midwifery classes, a photograph of one remains. Probably a graduation photograph, it shows sixteen students with their two instructors, Dr. Ritchie and Alfonso Báez. Photograph of Midwifery Class, Tacubaya Clinic, 1935, Ritchie Papers, SCLSU.

working and committed medical missionary admitted that he had been "terribly busy." He indicated, though, that instead of a heavy load of patients, most of his activity involved class work. He then described his daily routine by first enthusiastically describing his classes and his current enrollment of 40 native ministers, colporteurs, and other church workers participating in a six-week intensive course in practical nursing and health subjects. The medical missionary's day began at six o'clock in the morning with breakfast, followed by worship, then classes until noon. Between two o'clock in the afternoon until nine o'clock in the evening, with a small break for supper at six, he taught seminars dealing with a variety of topics including hydrotherapy, diseases and causes, anatomy and physiology, accidents and emergencies, and dietetics and temperance. He showed them what contaminated water looked like under a microscope, how to set bones, and how to sew up a wound. After their short course of study, he knew they would become the "doctors" in their villages, and he wanted them to be as well prepared as he could make them in the time he had with them. He even had them practice giving health lectures of their own. During prayer meetings and Sabbath services when they were not in class, his students told of their experiences.[32] He acknowledged he was quite impressed by their stories.

My heart was thrilled to the core as I listened to them. . . . They know what it is to bear the cross of Christ. They are no novices, but have a practical knowledge of this

---

[32] Inelda May Christianson, daughter of Dr. Iner S. Ritchie, interview by Delmer G. Ross, Riverside, California, 17 July 2000.

truth. They have suffered persecutions and imprisonment. They have been beaten by mobs, and some have been left for dead. They have been cast into filthy dungeons and have been hailed before magistrates. Nothing that one reads about in the Acts of the Apostles is more wonderful. . . . In fact the Acts of the Apostles is being rewritten right here in Mexico.[33]

Dr. Ritchie had dozens of his students' stories recorded and transcribed. If he intended to publish them, he never got around to doing so.[34] On the other hand, he used several as sermon illustrations. Many were like the experience of José Maciel who told of talking about the evils of tobacco to a small group of men. One of his listeners admitted that he had been trying to stop smoking for three days, but felt terrible, which was to be expected after smoking five packs of cigarettes every day for years. Maciel tried to encourage him. Their conversation got around to religion, which led to an amazing story:

When I told him of the Seventh-day Sabbath, he said with surprise, "Do you keep the Sabbath? I have been anxious to meet a person who observes this day because my grandfather taught us since we were children that the seventh day is the day that should be kept as the Sab-

---

[33] Iner [S. Ritchie] to Ralph M. Smith, 12 May 1935, 2, Ritchie Papers, SCLSU.

[34] There appears to be little doubt that he hoped to publish them eventually. He wrote a rough draft titled "Foreword," a list of possible illustrations, and several drafts of his experiences during his trip to Pantepec in 1936. File folder: Medical Missionary Experiences in Mexico, Ritchie Papers, SCLSU.

bath." He was very pleased to meet me. About two months later he came down from the mountains with a very ancient Bible to show me. It was written in Spanish, and dated 1700. . . . These people in the mountains . . . had been keeping the seventh-day Sabbath from the days of their grandfather.[35]

Maciel apparently did not say if the gentleman was able to give up smoking, but, given the later visit, it seems probable.

As busy as he was with his classes, Dr. Ritchie also had to deal with the day-to-day operation of the clinic and the medical work of the church throughout the country. Perhaps it was just as well that, overall, the medical work in Mexico still was in its infancy!

In his letter to his former partner, Dr. Ritchie also mentioned a problem. Apparently, as meager as it was, his salary was not in the budget. But this did not concern the mission-minded physician for long. He told his friend, "it takes faith to step out and leave a paying practice, move your family and all you have into a field like this—but the Lord has certainly blessed us for our obedience to His call."[36] The recently installed church employee unquestionably believed that the Lord had called him to work in Mexico.

He further shared with Dr. Smith the success he was having in connecting with Mexican officials in the health department. Dr.

<hr>

[35] José Maciel, "Experiences of José Maciel of Sta. Rosalía, Lower Calif.," no date, file folder: Medical Missionary Experiences in Mexico, Ritchie Papers, SCLSU.

[36] Iner [S. Ritchie] to Ralph M. Smith, 12 May 1935, 3, Ritchie Papers, SCLSU.

Ritchie, along with a group of students from the Tacubaya Clinic, visited the local health department and displayed slides on health and temperance, shared health literature, and explained the content of their courses. The health administrators were so impressed by the demonstration that they asked Dr. Ritchie and all his students to become lecturers in the Temperance Department—an invitation they gladly accepted because of the government protection they then would enjoy.[37] For years thereafter, when government officials were preparing antialcoholism initiatives they often contacted Dr. Ritchie—or in his absence, someone else from the church—for ideas, speakers, and other types of assistance. For example, the medical evangelist was asked to provide input for and to attend the major, government sponsored National Antialcoholism Congress of August 1 to 5, 1936.[38]

The missionary closed his letter to Dr. Smith by humbly giving all the credit to God. He explained how he saw the hand of the Almighty in control of the missionary work in Mexico. He was convinced, for example, that God had intervened so that a hostile health department administrator had lost his job and then had put someone in power who would help Dr. Ritchie achieve his Lord's work.[39]

Calling church workers together for health classes at the Tacubaya Clinic was the result of several visits to the tropical regions of southern Mexico for the purpose of determining health

---

[37] Ibid., 4.

[38] Jesús Díaz Barriga to I.S. Ritchie, 18 April 1936.

[39] Iner [S. Ritchie] to Ralph M. Smith, 12 May 1935, 6.

care needs. During the summer of 1934 Dr. Ritchie was delighted to take his elder son, Iner William, on at least one such trip, an excursion to the jungles of Chiapas. Traveling by train, bus, dugout canoe, and on horseback, on each tour Dr. Ritchie treated literally hundreds of people who otherwise had no access to medical care. Although the equipment and supplies he could take with him on such trips were very limited, in addition to pulling countless decayed teeth, he dealt the best he could with almost everything, from tropical sores to broken bones and from diarrhea to leprosy. His assessment was that the church should establish a school and a hospital in each state of Mexico. Because that was impossible at that time, he determined to offer basic health training to existing church workers who then could help those with minor problems. Such assistance might pave the way for spreading the gospel. They would also be in a position to instruct others in principles of healthful living.[40] He announced that he agreed completely with Ellen White who had written "It is the divine plan that we shall work as the disciples worked. Physical healing is bound up with the Gospel Commission."[41] Accordingly the word soon went out to various types of lower echelon denominational employees who began to assemble in Tacubaya. Arriving from

[40] C.E. Moon, "Healing the Paralytic," *Inter-American Division Messenger,* Vol. 12, No. 9 (September 1935), 7.

[41] Ellen G. White, *The Ministry of Healing* (Washington, D.C.: Review & Herald, 1905), 141.

Students doing calisthenics in the physical education class, part of the six-week Medical Assistant course offered by the Tacubaya Clinic in 1935. Drs. Iner S. Ritchie and T. Gordon Reynolds stand at far right.

virtually every state of Mexico, on February 17, 1935, they began studying practical nursing and techniques of evangelism.[42]

After six weeks of intensive courses dealing with health principles, hygiene, and other matters at the Tacubaya Clinic, and armed with government-issued certificates proclaiming them to be public health workers, the students returned to their homes scattered throughout the country. They soon began sending back reports on their work. One, for example, a colporteur named Daniel Landeros, had been called upon to treat a severely injured bandit. The outlaw had been slit open, from chest to groin, by someone with a short temper who wielded a wickedly sharp machete. "Doctor" Landeros was asked to sew him up. The colporteur boiled some water and carefully washed the exposed intestines. Then he sewed the wound closed. There was little left to do but to pray, and Landeros certainly did that! His prayers were answered, too—affirmatively. The bandit lived.[43]

The training that had made Landeros' apparent miracle possible was made available at other times and locations. By the late 1930s Clarence E. Wood, who was in charge of the Mexican Union, could write, "Nearly every worker in the Mexican Union

[42] [Inelda May Christianson], "Iner Sheld-Ritchie, 1885 -1949;" [Iner S. Ritchie], "Following the 'Blueprint' in Old Mexico," 22 March 1935; E.E. Andross, "A Visit to Mexico," *Inter-American Division Messenger,* Vol. 12, No. 6 (June 1935), 9-10; and Gloria Banfield and Ken Kurts, "Dr. Ritchie Paper: His Education and Medical Missionary Work in Mexico" (term paper presented for HIST 294/494, History Colloquium, La Sierra University, Riverside, California, 6 December 1995), 2, D.G. Ross Collection.

[43] Iner S. Ritchie to Brethren, 15 April 1935, Ritchie Papers, SLSU; and [Inelda May Christianson], "Iner Sheld-Ritchie, 1885 - 1949."

carries an official card issued by the Mexican government which authorizes him to give lectures in the interest of temperance,"[44] and, depending on how far the skill and daring of the holder wished to stretch it, by inference possibly to do considerably more. Two years after the classes at the Tacubaya Clinic Elder Wood acknowledged, "This training has been a great asset to our workers in entering new territory and winning the confidence of the people."[45] It was simply amazing what a difference those small cards could make. Dr. Ritchie wrote, "now instead of being persecuted, beaten, cast into prison or even killed, our workers are free to carry on our work on a higher plane than ever before and are rated as officials of the government, even having been given military escorts in some regions."[46] Moreover, the government often provided the Adventist health workers with medicines they needed at no charge.[47] Aside from all being Seventh-day Adventist laborers instead of government employees, the members of this medical work force were just like the later "barefoot doctors" of China for which the communist regime in that country received much public acclaim even in anticommunist nations.

The health workers trained at the Tacubaya Clinic served their church and impoverished Mexicans very well for many years.

---

[44] Clarence E. Wood, *In the Land of the Aztecs* (Takoma Park, Washington, D.C.: Review and Herald Publishing Association, 1939), 69.

[45] C.E. Wood, "Medical Missionary Work in Mexico," *Inter-American Division Messenger,* Vol. 14, No. 17 (15 September 1937), 6.

[46] [Iner S. Ritchie and O.R. Staines], "Itinerating in Old Mexico," *The Medical Evangelist,* Vol. 24, No. 34 (17 February 1938), 1-3.

[47] Wood, *In the Land of the Aztecs,* 88.

Clarence E. Wood wrote in 1939 that the training the workers had received at Tacubaya "has proved to be a great blessing to them in their evangelistic work, and many doors have been opened to them, which otherwise would have remained closed."[48] A quarter century later Horace Kelley, then principal of Colegio Linda Vista in the state of Chiapas, wrote to Dr. Ritchie's son, Dr. Iner William Ritchie, about José Rodríguez, who had spoken with a group of visiting dentists from CME:

> When I accompanied the Dental group to Blanca Rosa, a man came 21 miles on horseback and afoot over the almost impassable trail to be for a few hours with men from the school that years ago sent his teacher down here. He showed me ever so proudly a little leather case made to carry ampoules [sic], and stamped on the front, Iner S. Ritchie, M.D., a graduation present from his teacher so long ago. He showed me the diploma with your father's name, and the official letters from Salubridad, the governor, and from more recent heads of the State Health Departments authorizing him to practice... the healing arts in this state.[49]

Rodríguez's six weeks of classes had led to a lifetime of service to God and to fellow Mexicans who, for lack of available services or

---

[48] C.E. Wood, "Mexican Union Mission: Report of Union Committee Session," *Inter-American Division Messenger,* Vol. 16, No. 9 (1 May 1939), 4.

[49] Horacio [Horace Kelley] to Iner and Marian [Ritchie], 3 September 1959.

lack of funds, needed basic health care. And he was only one of dozens of students.

Enrollment in health classes offered at the Tacubaya Clinic was not limited to church employees. Dr. Ritchie advertised the clinic to the community. Wishing to help as many people as possible, he offered health conferences and short classes to the general public.[50] Classes were offered at different locations, as well. For example, in May 1935, along with a local pastor and various other participants he conducted a week-long seminar focusing on hygiene and prenatal care at the El Mesías Church in Mexico City. As an added incentive, the clinic offered vaccinations for those in attendance who desired them.[51]

With such a program in place, and with Dr. Ritchie's supervision and direct participation in dealing with patients and in class instruction, the activity surrounding the Tacubaya Clinic grew rapidly. Moreover, that activity did not cease when he was forced to leave after two years. The medical missionary's approach of treating the complete person, beginning with the patient's most basic needs and continuing with instruction on how to make lifestyle improvements, became the clinic's aim. As valuable as the instruction it offered was, however, the clinic always maintained its direct involvement with patients. An illustrated brochure issued by the clinic in 1943, several years after Dr. Ritchie's departure, reaffirmed the institution's mission to alleviate the

[50] Julio Gilbert White, *Aprenda cómo estar bien,* trans. A.J. Calderón, [Clínica Tacubaya]: Tacubaya, D.F., no date, copy in Ritchie Papers, SCLSU.

[51] Iglesia "El Mesías," *"Semana de Higiene,"* Iglesia "El Mesías": Mexico, D.F., 6-10 May 1935, copy in Ritchie Papers, SCLSU.

misery and pain of those who were suffering. By then, in addition to examination rooms, the clinic had an operating room, a dental department, and several semi-private rooms for over-night patients.[52]

[52] *Clínica Tacubaya*, 1943, Ritchie Papers, SCLSU.

The Sacrifice of Foreign Service

Dr. Ritchie's accomplishments in the field of improving medical care for the Mexican people were not achieved without considerable personal sacrifice and great faith. His abnegation was not limited to the already mentioned financial losses when he accepted the call to Mexico. He also yielded time with his children, especially the two eldest. They stayed with his parents in Loma Linda, California, while attending college in southern California. Moreover, his move to Mexico City led to strains in his relationship with his own adoptive parents and in-laws.

The latter was no small consideration. From the beginning Dr. Ritchie's adoptive mother and mother-in-law, Anna Lula Ritchie, had opposed his decision to comply when he did with the church's request for him to engage in missionary work in Mexico. Because she was observant and intelligent, she most often was right. That, combined with her questioning of the timing of the call, was serious enough, but the fact that she was not the least timid about expressing her views to others led to occasional embarrassment and other complications. For example, in a letter to Elder Clarence E. Wood, president of the Mexican Union, she explained that she believed her son had prematurely accepted the church's call. As a concerned mother, she wrote, she had advised Dr. Ritchie not to go to Mexico City until God had provided a buyer for property they owned in order to be able to pay off their financial obligations. Disregarding this advice, Dr. Ritchie had accepted the call because of the fear of church leaders—a fear he shared—that if he waited very long to enter Mexico it would become more difficult, if not impossible, to do so. They hoped to take advantage of the fact that a known friend, Abelardo Rodrí-guez, was president of Mexico. In her letter Anna Lula Ritchie described her son's actions as "presumption," and "stepping into the water, as it were, expecting the Jordan to part, before him."[1]

Anna Lula's concerns were not unwarranted. Between the fall of 1934 and the winter of 1935, the family began to experience significant financial difficulties.[2] Dr. Ritchie's financial obliga-tions were many. They included tuition for Iner William and Anna at two different Christian schools; the upkeep and payments on two homes—one in Mexico City for him and three other members of his family, and the other in Loma Linda for his parents and his older daughter, Anna; property taxes and assessments on various parcels, including the emergency hospital in Calexico; and, of

---

[1] Anna L. Ritchie to C.E. Wood, 14 February 1935, Ritchie Papers, SCLSU.

[2] Ibid.; Mrs. W.S. [Anna Lula] Ritchie to E.E. Andross, 17 October 1934, Ritchie Papers, SCLSU; Mamma [Anna Lula Ritchie] to Precious Children [Iner S. and Inelda Ruth Ritchie], 24 January 1935, Ritchie Papers, SCLSU; Mrs. W.S. [Anna Lula] Ritchie to T. Gordon Reynolds, 15 February 1935, Ritchie Papers, SCLSU; Mamma and Amma [Anna Lula Ritchie] to Beloved Children [Iner S. and Inelda Ruth Ritchie], 11 August 1935, Ritchie Papers, SCLSU; and Mamma [Anna Lula Ritchie] to Beloved Children [Iner S. and Inelda Ruth Ritchie], 13-14 November 1935, Ritchie Papers, SCLSU.

course, the normal, every-day expenses that any family encounters. While he had hoped to sell the hospital in Calexico, because of the Great Depression he had been unable to do so. From a financial standpoint, accepting the call to Mexico was ruinous, with the greatest sacrifice resulting from leaving his new, yet economically flourishing, medical practice in Pomona.[3]

Because his call to serve in Mexico had originated with the Mexican Union Mission, all he could depend on was a trifling salary amounting to approximately $100 (U.S.) per month, and even that sometimes did not arrive on time. Had he been called by the General Conference of the church his salary would have been more substantial, if still far short of his previous income. From the outset Mexican church administrators had been aware of the problem and had sought to solve it by allowing Dr. Ritchie to set up his own private practice in the Mexican capital. He had done so, but because of his obligations to the Mexican Union he simply did not have enough time to earn what he and his family required.[4]

After writing a number of letters to church administrators to try to convince them to provide her adopted son with a reasonable salary, all without appreciable immediate result, she came to view ministers with a certain amount of disdain. She commented on those she had contacted, "these preachers are generally both bosses and leaners. I am hard on preachers but they need it." She then added, "Doctors are hard working men but preachers like to wear

---

[3] Anna L. Ritchie to C.E. Wood, 14 February 1935.

[4] Mamma [Anna Lula Ritchie] to Iner and Inelda, Nelda May, and Bobbie [Ritchie], 24 October 1934, 1, Ritchie Papers, SCLSU; and Anna L. Ritchie to C.E. Wood, 14 February 1935, Ritchie Papers, SCLSU.

fine clothes and do nothing themselves but talk and boss." Her advice to Dr. Ritchie concerning Elder Clarence E. Wood was, "I am trying to get you to use good common sense and do what is right and not become subservient to a mind that is evidently short sighted to say the least."[5]

Such sentiments may have been a little premature because the church later provided Dr. Ritchie with "a considerable sum of money" which his mother-in-law admitted "he sent to me to pay taxes." She used the funds to pay other obligations as well. She also admitted that the church in Mexico had encouraged him to develop his private medical practice in Mexico City to supplement what it paid him. Unfortunately, while on occasion he might see as many as "eleven or twelve patients," generally "he had only two or three a day." That helped, but still left him pinching pennies because, as she put it, "After fourteen months his income is most disappointingly small."[6] So was his salary. According to Elder Wood, who responded to Anna Lula in August 1935, Dr. Ritchie had recently been authorized to receive "the highest rate paid to doctors in our organized work," all of "$43.00 gold per week." He pointed out that such pay was considerably more than the president of the Inter-American Division earned, who received "a trifle over $33.00."[7] For someone used to an income of several hundred

[5] Mamma [Anna Lula Ritchie] to Precious Children [Iner S. and Inelda Ruth Ritchie], 24 January 1935, Ritchie Papers, SCLSU.

[6] Mrs. W.S. [Anna Lula] Ritchie to Ralph M. Smith, 6 August 1935, 3-5, Ritchie Papers, SCLSU.

[7] C.E. Wood to Anna L. Ritchie, 17 March 1935, Ritchie file, Archives and Special Collections, WebbLLU.

dollars per week, and who had obligations to match, $43 was a pittance. Dr. Ritchie, though, had always been willing to sacrifice in favor of God's cause.

With the physician and his wife in Mexico City, it fell to Anna Lula to try to hold off local creditors and also to try to raise money. While real estate, of which the Ritchies had a substantial amount, may not have been selling well at all, it is interesting and revealing to note that she was able to raise $40 by selling Iner William's saddle. To save on the expense of paper she sometimes wrote on the backs of letters to her, or in the margins, and to save on postage, instead of mailing her letters, she occasionally sent them with individuals to hand deliver. She kept detailed accounts, reporting everything from the cost of a car for Iner William—$159.88—to handkerchiefs for Robert—they cost ten cents for four—and the increase in sales tax from two percent to three percent. Like millions of others during the Great Depression, Anna Lula had to be frugal. Unlike most others, though, she was trying to keep two households afloat.[8]

Although Anna Lula Ritchie frequently and perhaps annoyingly advised her son to remember his financial responsibilities and to make decisions to comply with them, she was a vital source of encouragement and support to him. She adroitly managed his finances in southern California. More significantly she took care of his eldest children. Periodically, she updated Dr. and Mrs. Ritchie on what and how well they were doing. For example, in

---

[8] [Anna Lula Ritchie] hand carried by Iner William Ritchie to [Iner S. Ritchie], July 1934, Ritchie Papers, SCLSU; and [Anna Lula Ritchie], "Account of expenses," no date, 2, 5-6, Ritchie Papers, SCLSU.

October 1934 she wrote that Iner William was doing well in school, but also indicated that she thought he could be a more zealous student. She further explained that Anna had been quite ill for nearly four weeks, but had improved enough to start back to school.[9] She continued to write such reports as long as her own children lived in Mexico and she felt the information was needed. In one of her last summaries she wrote, "The children are RUSHED now. They are winding up their year of work with much reviewing. . . . They scarce want to be spoken to at all." After mentioning their class picnic she added, "Iner Wm. is working as he has never worked before. For the first time in his life he has got right down to hard study."[10]

She also continually reminded her adopted son of his great skills as a physician, and at least once shortsightedly pressed him to spend more of his time helping people with their medical needs rather than training future medical practitioners.[11] While she might not always agree with what her son-in-law did, she defended him before others. In a letter to one correspondent, she described his patient care as taking "time to make the patient and family understand what he is doing and why and to secure their cooperation and trust and confidence and he . . . works to win and

---

[9] Mamma [Anna Lula Ritchie] to Iner and Inelda, Nelda May, and Bobbie [Ritchie], 24 October 1934, 1, Ritchie Papers, SCLSU; and Mamma [Anna Lula Ritchie] to Our Dearly Beloved Children [Iner S. and Inelda Ruth Ritchie], 27 September 1935; Ritchie Papers, SCLSU.

[10] Mamma [Anna Lula Ritchie] to Iner and Inelda [Ritchie], 29 April 1936, Ritchie Papers,SCLSU.

[11] Mamma [Anna Lula Ritchie] to Iner and Inelda, Nelda May, and Bobbie [Ritchie], 24 October 1934, 4, Ritchie Papers, SCLSU.

permanently establish himself in their affections.[12] He was the kind of doctor who would take the time to get to know his patients and their pain.

Dr. Ritchie missed his older children. Only a few months after they had returned to California to go back to school he took time to see Iner William, Anna, and his own adoptive parents. Despite the distance between Loma Linda and Mexico City, in December 1934 he arranged to spend Christmas with them.[13]

On his way back to Mexico City and the Tacubaya Clinic, however, he visited a colleague, Dr. T. Gordon Reynolds, who had an office in Ciudad Obregón, a small city in southern Sonora until 1928 known as Cajeme, and still called that by many.[14] Along with an associate, Dr. Eugene E. Gloor, Dr. Reynolds also operated a small hospital—the Hospital Buena Esperanza (Good Hope

---

[12] Mrs. W.S. [Anna Lula] Ritchie to E.E. Andross, 17 October 1934, 4, Ritchie Papers, SCLSU.

[13] Mamma [Anna Lula Ritchie] to Our Dear Precious Children [Iner S. and Inelda Ruth Ritchie], 24 January 1935, 1, Ritchie Papers, SCLSU; and Mamma and Amma [Anna Lula Ritchie] to Darling Iner and Inelda [Ritchie], 17 July 1935, 3, Ritchie Papers, SCLSU. By traveling on a second-class coach which cost only half the first-class fare, Dr. Ritchie was able to take his wife and two younger children with him. His family was thus reunited for Christmas. Inelda May later recalled that her father spent a lot of time conferring with teachers at CME and obtaining information from them to use in his classes at the Tacubaya Clinic. She also remembered traveling on the train in Mexico "with Indians taking chickens and piglets to market." Inelda May Christianson, daughter of Dr. Iner S. Ritchie, interview by Delmer G. Ross, Riverside, California, 17 July 2000.

[14] On July 28, 1928, Cajeme was renamed Ciudad Obregón in honor of Mexican President Alvaro Obregón, who had been assassinated one day earlier. Cajeme, "Cajeme: Una Historia de Orgullo, Antecedentes," http://www.cdob1 .com/cajeme/historia/cronologia.php.

Hospital)—and nursing school in Esperanza, a community located a few miles north of Ciudad Obregón.[15] Because of the volume of patients he faced every day, Dr. Reynolds had become fatigued and needed temporary assistance. Additionally, because he was practicing medicine in Mexico without the appropriate Mexican license, he desperately needed that temporary help to come from someone with such a license. That would place his practice on a more "legal" basis. Dr. Ritchie, of course, was one such physician. Moreover, he was in a position in Mexico City where he could use his influence to help Dr. Reynolds obtain his own license to practice medicine in Mexico.[16]

Financial hardships were conspiring to make it difficult for Dr. Ritchie to continue working for the church in any official capacity. The Mexican church could not pay him the salary an American doctor might expect and which, in Dr. Ritchie's case,

---

[15] Anna L. Ritchie to C.E. Wood, 14 February 1935, 3-4. Esperanza was one of several communities within the municipality of Ciudad Obregón. Dr. Reynolds established the first hospital in the area as early as 1929 or as late as 1934, depending on the source used. Cajeme, "Cronología de Hechos Históricos," http://www.cdob1.com/cajeme/historia/cronologia.php; Cajeme, "Cajeme: Una Historia de Orgullo, Antecedentes," http://www.cdob1.com /cajeme/historia/cronologia.php; and Don F. Neufeld, ed., *Seventh-day Adventist Encyclopedia,* Revised ed. (Washington, D.C.: Review & Herald Publishing Association, 1966), s.v. "Mexico, Departmental Work, Medical Work."

[16] Anna L. Ritchie to C.E. Wood, 14 February 1935, 3-4, Ritchie Papers, SCLSU; and Mexican Union Mission Committee, "Minutes," Vote 373, 15 May 1934, [Mexico, D.F.], copy in Ritchie Papers, SCLSU. Exactly how Dr. Reynolds managed to practice medicine in Mexico without a licence is not clear, but it was not unusual for foreign physicians to practice under someone who had the proper credential, at least nominally.

was needed by him to fulfill his financial responsibilities.[17] Now the formerly self-supporting medical missionary used his visit with Dr. Reynolds in Sonora to help his friend and at the same time to earn some extra money. His salary of $280 per month was less than he had paid recent graduates who worked for him in Calexico, but it would help to pay some long overdue bills.[18]

Although Dr. Ritchie returned to Mexico City after helping Dr. Reynolds in Sonora, only a year or so later, by February 1936, he was back working with him.[19] This time his financial affairs did not provide a significant motivating factor in his move. The high altitude of Mexico City, about 7,500 feet above sea level, combined with the effects tropical diseases such as dysentery and the heat of lowland regions where he did much of his traveling, proved to be a significant strain on Dr. Ritchie's health. The tremendous load of work and responsibility and consequent lack of rest and sleep certainly did nothing to help. Anna Lula Ritchie had noticed and wrote later that her son-in-law had "been frail for several years and I never [felt] entirely at ease about him." She added that she had not mentioned it earlier because she had been

---

[17] [Anna Lula Ritchie] to Our Beloved Children [Iner S. and Inelda Ruth Ritchie], 17 February 1935, Ritchie Papers, SCLSU.

[18] Anna L. Ritchie to C.E. Wood, 14 February 1935, 3; and Mrs. W.S. [Anna Lula] Ritchie to T. Gordon Reynolds, 15 February 1935, Ritchie Papers, SCLSU; Mamma and Amma [Anna Lula Ritchie] to Iner and Inelda [Ritchie], 28 August 1935, 1, Ritchie Papers, SCLSU.

[19] Inelda May Christianson, daughter of Dr. Iner S. Ritchie, interview by Maritza Durán, 4 August 2003, Riverside, California.

unwilling to "needlessly worry him."[20] It all climaxed in January 1936, when, while at home in Mexico City, he suffered a mild heart attack. Although it was not serious enough to stop the mission-minded physician from doing his work, it did cause him to seek the much lower elevation of Dr. Reynold's hospital in Esperanza. He simply moved to that coastal, semi-tropical area of Sonora and again began working there. Moreover, Dr. Reynolds had become ill and once more could use assistance.[21]

Dr. Ritchie even continued to travel, although the trips may have been considerably shorter in duration and in the number of miles covered than had sometimes previously been the case. In a letter to his wife, he described a trip to Huatabampo, some 65 miles south of Esperanza, to help a pneumonia patient:

Left at 4:P.M., arrived at 9:P.M. Stayed all night. We came back through a wild country near the ocean. Full of wild pigeons, parrotts [sic], deer, and smaller game. Dr. Stilson sat on the fender with his 22 rifle and another young man on the other fender with his shotgun while I drove. Mrs. Reynolds was in the back seat. It kept us

---

[20] [Anna Lula Ritchie] to Dear Precious Children [Iner S. and Inelda Ruth Ritchie], 16 January 1936, Ritchie Papers, SCLSU.

[21] Inelda May Christianson, daughter of Dr. Iner S. Ritchie, telephone interview by Maritza Durán, 19 September 2003, Norco, California; Clarence E. Nelson, "Iner S. Ritchie Dies," *The Journal of the Alumni Association, School of Medicine, College of Medical Evangelists*, vol. 21, No. 1 (January 1950), 16; and Iner [S. Ritchie] to My Darling Sweetheart [Inelda Ruth Ritchie], 13 March 1936, Ritchie Papers, SCLSU. The elevation of Ciudad Obregón and Esperanza was approximately 150 feet above sea level. Cajeme, "Cronología de Hechos Históricos," http://www.cdob1.com/cajeme/historia/cronologia.php.

busy stopping and picking up quail, pigeons & [etc.] that the boys shot! They winged a beautiful parrott [*sic*] and I got out and put my hat over it and folded it in it and he chewed and clawed it pretty bad but we got him home so now the youngsters here have a polly but they don't dare get near it. The country is very pretty there and there is plenty of big fish besides the hunting.[22]

Some might cringe at the thought of a double-barreled killing machine rolling up the Mexican coast, but we must remember that what might be considered environmentally detrimental and very politically incorrect today, in the twenty-first century, was often quite acceptable—even fashionable—seventy-five years ago.

Only four days later he wrote again after a short pleasure outing in a different direction. After commenting that he wished Iner William could visit because "He would like it here," he described some of what he and those with him had seen.

I drove East of the hospital a few miles and it surely was the devil's garden we got into. I never saw so many kinds of cactus before, both big and small varieties. They are blooming now and it is surely beautiful. I never saw so many doves and quail before and they are so tame evidently no one has ever hunted them. There were beautifully colored parrotts [*sic*], wrens, woodpeckers, great horned owls and all kinds of birds. There is also

---

[22] Iner [S. Ritchie] to My Darling Precious Sweetheart Inelda [Ruth Ritchie], 9 March 1936, Ritchie Papers, SCLSU. Five hours to travel 65 miles may seem excessive today, especially when on a house call, but the roads in the area left much to be desired. Most inter-city travel was by rail. It would be another two decades before the first roads there were paved.

deer, lion, catamounts, coyotes, foxes, coons, badgers, and many other animals.[23]

The missionary-evangelist physician appears to have been quite impressed with the area around Esperanza.

For several weeks after leaving Mexico City Dr. Ritchie attempted to continue to serve on the Mexican Union Mission Committee and to direct medical services at the Tacubaya Clinic and elsewhere, while actually practicing medicine independently of the church in Esperanza.[24] In time, though, he realized that he could not return to his post in the capital. He also concluded that he could not adequately handle his duties from afar. As much as he hated doing it, he understood that it was time to let someone else take over his job.

He retained only his membership on the Mexican Union Mission Committee, where his knowledge and ideas, and his contacts with Mexican government officials could—and very definitely did—continue to be useful to the church. When he died in 1949 he still was an active and valued member. At first he usually traveled by train to committee sessions. Later, especially after the Union offices were transferred to Monterrey, Nuevo León, he generally made the trip by commercial airline.[25]

---

[23] Iner [S. Ritchie] to My Darling Sweetheart [Inelda Ruth Ritchie] 13 March 1936, Ritchie Papers, SCLSU.

[24] Inelda May Christianson, interviewed by Maritza Durán, 4 August 2003.

[25] [Inelda May Christianson], *Iner Sheld-Ritchie, Founder of Liga, 1885-1949* (no place, publisher, or date), [3], Ritchie Papers, SCLSU.

After apparently selling in Mexico City as much as she could of what they did not need, on Dr. Ritchie's instructions, Inelda Ruth packed up their remaining personal medical equipment and other belongings and shipped them to California. Then she and Inelda May and Robert traveled to Loma Linda. There she learned that the boxcar bringing their possessions from Mexico had been completely unloaded and inspected by U.S. Agriculture Inspectors even though it had already been cleared by U.S. Customs. That was only an annoyance. What hurt was that the Ritchies had to pay for the unexpected additional handling involved and for a higher freight rate charged by the railroad for some "laboratory instruments" found during the inspection! Fortunately, the added charges were not great.[26] After a brief visit with her parents in Loma Linda, Inelda Ruth left the children under their care and returned to Mexico to be with her husband in Esperanza.

When the summer vacation began, Iner William and Anna, pre-medical and pre-nursing students at Southern California Junior College—today's La Sierra University—in Riverside, drove their grandparents' Model A Ford south to Esperanza, Sonora. Although Dr. Ritchie had toyed with the idea of staying and working in Esperanza, when Iner William and Anna returned they brought both parents back to California with them. By late summer 1936

---

[26] Laboratory instruments required a higher freight rate than did household goods. Antonio M. Ferrer to Inelda Sheld Ritchie, 6 February 1936, Ritchie file, WebbLLU.

the Ritchies were reunited in Loma Linda, but not before a few more adventures in Mexico.[27]

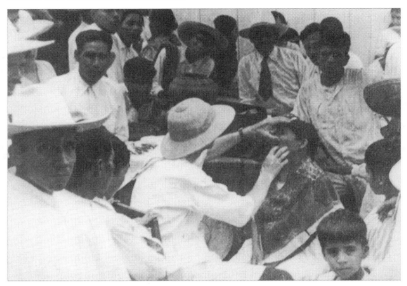

Dr. Ritchie treating a Totonac Indian woman while on a visit to central Mexico in 1934.

A month or so after Dr. Ritchie had seen all the cactus in bloom he made another short trip. This time, apparently accompanied by his son, Iner William, and by Dr. Reynolds and a railroad engineer, he traveled to a nearby, yet still relatively unexplored, area of Sonora to try to become better acquainted with the Yaqui Indians. In the process, he was informed, he became the first

---

[27] [Anna Lula Ritchie] to Precious Children [Iner S. and Ineld Ruth Ritchie] 16 January 1935, Ritchie Papers, SCLSU; Iner [S. Ritchie] to Darling Precious Mine [Inelda Ruth Ritchie], 21 March 1936, Ritchie Papers, SCLSU; [Inelda May Christianson], "Iner Sheld-Ritchie, 1885 - 1949;" and "In Memorium," Programme: Liga Mexico-Pan-American Festival October 29, 1949, Ritchie Papers, SCLSU.

person allowed to take moving pictures of any of their ceremonial dances.[28] While most of his trips had some medical purpose, he obviously enjoyed exploring, too.

After their trip, in a letter to his fiancé, Iner William provided some interesting details about the Yaqui Indians and their visit. He started out by indicating he understood that "The Yaquis are the only unconquered Indians left in the Americas and are really very savage." He then explained that only five years earlier even rail traffic going through the region had to be guarded by two carloads of soldiers—one in front and the other bringing up the rear of each train. But that was not all. Soldiers also rode on the roofs of the coaches and "airplanes were used as an advance guard to clear the track ahead and warn the train of attacks."[29]

Travel by automobile was equally dangerous. "You can see crosses all along the highway where people have been killed," he wrote, "and only a year ago they burned a man to death." He added that they did not dare travel at night because "a fellow got shot at the other night—broke his windshield—narrow escape. He said he sure stepped on the gas."[30] Apparently he had reason enough to do so!

---

[28] Aureliano Y. Campoy to [T. Gordon] Reynol[d]s and [Iner S.] Ri[t]chie, 8 April 1936, Ritchie Papers, SCLSU; [Inelda May Christianson], "Iner Sheld-Ritchie, 1885 - 1949;" and *Iner S. Ritchie and Miscellaneous Ritchie Family Videorecordings* composite, prod. by [Iner W. Ritchie and Don Cicchetti], 1 hour, 24 min., [Loma Linda University Media Services], 1989, videocasstte.

[29] Iner [W. Ritchie] to Sweetest Heart [Marian Hester], 1 June 1936, 1, Ritchie Papers, SCLSU.

[30] Ibid., 1, 4.

Iner William's explanation of why they were allowed to visit the Yaquis and of what they saw may be enlightening:

The reason for all this, that is our being able to take these pictures and to make friends with these people is that Dad cured Pluma Blanca (White Feather), chief of all the Yaqui tribes, when he was very sick. Consequently Dad has been the first man to take moving pictures of one of these ceremonies with their approval and was the first foreign doctor to be asked to treat them. . . . I took some movies of them while Dad was treating them. I shook hands with Pluma Blanca and two sub-chiefs. He surely is a hard looking customer and . . . the old boy [is said to have] killed many a man. Anyway, they were all in pretty good spirits and I got a big kick out of listening to them jabber Yaqui lingo. . . ."

We left a lot of Adventist literature and prophecy books with the Yaquis, . . . [the] first [Adventist] missionary work that has been done for them.[31]

Although Iner William apparently felt safe enough, and nothing sinister or even threatening happened to him or to anyone in their party, in describing the Yaqui Indians he wrote,

They are very superstitious and cruel people. Their religion is a strange mixture of Catholicism and paganism. The dance of which Dad took the movies was a heathen ceremony in which they had Judas Iscariot mixed

---

[31] Ibid., 1-4.

up in some way. I suppose they chose him so they could justly punish him.[32]

At the end of his account he wrote, "Without the medical work one couldn't do a thing hardly in Mexico." Then, referring more specifically to the Indians they had just visited, he added, "A Hollywood man tried to take some pictures of the Yaquis and barely got away with his life."[33]

Not long after Iner William joined him in Esperanza, Dr. Ritchie took him to the beach. They spent enough time there for the younger man to become sunburned. Then, on the way back, with his twenty-two rifle Iner William shot seven quail from the running board of the car. Both father and son enjoyed hunting, and some of their talk revolved around the possibility of fixing up a den in whatever home they might have after leaving Esperanza for Riverside. They wanted a room where they could display their animal skins, "of which we have a good assortment."[34]

Dr. Ritchie had been quite successful during the two years he had worked for the church in Mexico. He had reopened the Tacubaya Clinic and, keeping in mind its goals, had managed it more successfully than it had ever operated previously, improving its medical care and expanding its teaching program. He had developed close working relationships with a number of government officials, and he had acquainted them and many others with

---

[32] Ibid., 1.

[33] Ibid., 4.

[34] Ibid.

Adventist institutions and beliefs. In the process of accomplishing that, he also helped lay the groundwork for what eventually was to become the best known and perhaps most successful Seventh-day Adventist church institution in Mexico, the University of Montemorelos, of which more in a later chapter. His adoptive mother had once strongly urged him to be responsible for contacting and taking God's message to government officials instead of risking his health and life by making long excursions to help those in remote areas of Mexico.[35] Dr. Ritchie did both.

---

[35] Mamma and Amma [Anna Lula Ritchie] to Beloved Children [Iner S. and Inelda Ruth Ritchie], 11 August 1935, 7-8, Ritchie Papers, SCLSU.

Return to California

Dr. Ritchie and his family returned to California in 1936. There, in Riverside, he first began a private medical practice in his two-story home on Seventh Street—today known as Mission Inn Avenue. His wife acted as office nurse until he could afford to hire one. The whole family helped, each member in his or her own way. Inelda May later recalled,

> I spent summer Mondays . . . putting washed clothes from the Maytag through the wringer into the rinse tub, sloshing them up and down then through the wringer again into the second rinse, finally from that through the wringer again into the clothes basket, and out to hang on the clotheslines. The shirts and dresses and blouses had to be starched first. Tuesdays were spent sprinkling, then ironing out all those wringer creases.[1]

---

[1] Inelda Ritchie Christianson, "Ritchie Family Life in Riverside," 1, Ritchie Papers, SCLSU. Dr. Ritchie's mother-in-law, Anna Lula Ritchie, located and helped him arrange a lease-to-purchase agreement for the structure at 4146 Seventh Street while he still was in Mexico. Ibid.

It was a procedure not unlike that experienced by literally millions of other American families of the time. So also was the way they spent their leisure time, when they would listen to a home-built radio or walk the short distance to downtown Riverside for ice cream cones at Cupid's Ice Cream Fountain. One difference, however, was the aviary Dr. Ritchie maintained in the back yard for the benefit of some canaries, a black squirrel, and, until a nosy neighbor complained, a gila monster. Another difference occurred every Saturday when, after church services, and in order to avoid the ringing of the telephone or patients who had forgotten or perhaps disbelieved the "Closed Saturday" sign, they often went for a drive. They drove to the desert to see wild flowers, to Loma Linda or other nearby towns to visit with relatives, or to ranches in Chino and Prado where Dr. Ritchie had spent his youth. They usually took a simple lunch, the main course of which was a loaf of bread. It generally was whole wheat or rye bread because Dr. Ritchie believed, as he often put it, "The whiter your bread, the sooner you're dead." They would spread peanut butter and jelly on the bread, open a can of Heinz Vegetarian Beans, pour glasses of milk, and peel some fruit, and their meal was ready.[2]

On occasion they drove down to Newport Beach for a day. While Inelda fished off the pier the others played on the beach. One day Dr. Ritchie became acquainted with the owner of a sporting goods store there and bought some archery equipment—bow, arrows, and a target. He then had the target leaned

[2] Ibid., 1-3, 5.

against bales of hay stacked in their back yard so that they could practice.[3]

For many years the big event each week for Dr. Ritchie's parents had been going to the library every Saturday evening and reading the newspapers until closing time at nine p.m. While Dr. and Mrs. Ritchie no longer practiced this, whenever the children stayed at their grandparent's place in Loma Linda—which was often—they all visited the public library in Colton to read newspapers.[4]

As the Ritchie family walked downtown from their home, one of the stores they passed was a small Goodwill Store. While Dr. Ritchie got his new Riverside practice going the family patronized the store, where they sometimes could buy nearly new clothes very inexpensively. Inelda May remembers that her best Sabbath dress that first year in Riverside came from the Goodwill Store. They also bought clothes and other items from pawn shops as far away as Los Angeles. While as a result of careful management and economizing wherever possible it would not take them long to recover, as satisfying as it had been, Dr. Ritchie's stint as a church employee in Mexico had cost the family a great deal financially.[5]

Fortunately, it did not cost much to keep a family fed in those days. At the Safeway store a block away a one-pound loaf of bread

---

[3] Ibid., 4.

[4] Ibid., 6.

[5] Ibid., 2.

cost 9 cents. Larger, pound-and-a-half sized loaves cost 12 cents each. The *Family Circle* magazine was free.[6]

Like most other physicians, Dr. Ritchie generally had as much work as he could reasonably handle. He realized, though, that sometimes he needed rest. Consequently he took occasional vacations. Most were taken nearby—at first Newport Beach appears to have been a favorite destination. Later—after at Inelda's insistence he had purchased two duplexes that had been part of the old Corona del Mar Hotel complex—Corona del Mar, only a few miles southeast of Newport Beach, became the favored locale. They often spent weekends at one of the four apartments which they kept vacant for the purpose.[7] Except for an occasional brief visit, they no longer frequented Big Bear because of its high altitude and its possible effect on Dr. Ritchie's heart.

Some vacations involved greater distances and required more time. For example, in 1939 after Inelda May had graduated from the eighth grade, the Ritchie family drove to Yosemite National Park and the San Francisco Bay area for a vacation. They towed a two-wheeled utility trailer behind their car. In addition to food for several days the trailer carried mattresses, bedding, and other camping equipment such as a camp stove and utensils. Having approached Yosemite from the east, they found the high area of

---

[6] Ibid., 2-3.

[7] Ibid., 4-5. After staying in their home in the La Sierra area for about a decade following Dr. Ritchie's death, Inelda Ruth moved to Corona del Mar where she spent most of the remainder of her life close to her younger son, Robert, and his family. Ibid., 10. She passed away at age 95, on January 5, 1993.

Tuolumne Meadows uncomfortably cold at night, but Yosemite Valley was just right. They rode horses and attended a campfire program. It was at the program that they overheard a lady from back east tell someone that the cowboy performers had been "Simply superb, my dear." For years thereafter, the Ritchie family response to anything uniquely interesting, particularly enjoyable, or of outstanding quality was "Simply superb, my dear."[8]

From Yosemite the Ritchies drove to Hayward, where they visited relatives. Parking the trailer there, they then went on to the 1939 World's Fair on Treasure Island in San Francisco Bay. Inelda May later recalled, "Iner Wm. and Anna . . . got stuck with little sister, so I was taken in to see Sally Rand do her famous Fan Dance. The fans were huge and indeed feathery, so we saw a lot of the fans [but] very little of Sally."[9] When all was said and done, it had been a memorable family vacation.

While the place and time were different, in Riverside Dr. Ritchie soon developed a routine that was similar to what he had done in Calexico and even earlier. He rose early and went to the Riverside Community Hospital for surgery and daily rounds. Then he returned home for a breakfast of cornmeal mush and graham muffins with his family. For variety they might have graham mush and cornmeal muffins. On occasion—mainly on Saturday mornings before church—they had corn flakes and bananas or other fruit. Breakfast on Sunday morning was special because it often consisted of waffles or pancakes with maple-flavored syrup. After

---

[8] Ibid., 4.

[9] Ibid., 5.

breakfast Dr. Ritchie opened his office while Mrs. Ritchie drove the two younger children, Inelda May and Robert, to school. He saw patients through the noon hour until he paused to take a short nap before dinner at two in the afternoon.

Dinner was the main meal of the day and usually consisted of either white potatoes or sweet potatoes and chicken. Occasionally they had steak, stew, or beans instead of chicken. On special occasions they had tamale pie made with lots of black olives. There usually was cornbread or some other kind of bread, sliced tomatoes or peaches, and cottage cheese. They sometimes had green vegetables, but apparently because ever since he had contracted amoebic dysentery on one of his trips into the jungle of southern Mexico they seemed to upset his digestive tract, Dr. Ritchie himself rarely ate them.[10]

Dinner was the last meal of the day for Dr. and Mrs. Ritchie, but she fixed a light supper for the children. After supper they drove throughout Riverside and nearby areas as Dr. Ritchie made evening house calls. Friday evenings were different. Dr. Ritchie often made presentations on the medical and educational needs in Mexico, and when he could he took the children, who sometimes dressed in Mexican folk costumes for the occasion. When he was not speaking somewhere, he and his wife enjoyed resting at home

---

[10] Although there appears to be little doubt that certain vegetables irritated his alimentary system, that may have been more of an excuse than a reason. Dr. Ritchie simply did not care much for green vegetables. He sometimes joked about fruit, nuts, and grains being the original diet, while vegetables did not appear on the menu until after the first sin. Ibid., 3.

while the children attended Friday-evening youth meetings at the church.[11]

Dr. Ritchie later moved his practice to more suitable permanent quarters he had built on Walnut Street—today's Brockton Avenue—where he established the "Monterrey Medical Clinic" in September 1942.[12]

He had the structure on Walnut built so that he had ample room for his practice on the ground floor. The front part of the second story became their living quarters. While Dr. Ritchie called it the "Monterrey" clinic and had a wrought iron sign to that effect erected above the entryway, the printer used the word "Monterey"

The Ritchie children in Mexican charro and china poblana costumes.

on the stationery. To avoid waste the physician frugally used the incorrectly spelled letterheads for years. Then later, when they were reprinted to add son Iner William's name, the new letter-

---

[11] Ibid., 3, 8.

[12] The second location was 3742 Walnut Street. Dr. I.S. Ritchie, Card Announcement, no date, Ritchie Papers, SCLSU.

heads intentionally displayed the misspelled name.[13] The end result, if anyone noticed, was that the name of the building was different from that of the clinic.

When the Ritchies moved into the Monterrey Medical Clinic building, Mrs. Ritchie had the home and office on Seventh Street made into apartments which she rented out. She especially liked to rent to officers from nearby March Field because they generally were uncomplaining and paid their rent on time. She also let an apartment over the garage behind the medical clinic building as well as the duplexes at Corona del Mar. The income from the rentals helped her pay the bills when Dr. Ritchie was away on his many and sometimes lengthy trips to Mexico.[14]

There were problems with their new home, though. Located as it was above the clinic, patients started coming by at any time after hours, sometimes even in the middle of the night. Worse, there seemed to be no way to stop them. Dr. Ritchie often began the new day needing to go to bed and sleep. The problem grew so serious they determined to move.

They bought and moved into a beautiful home on Arroyo Drive in 1945, but after living there for about a year, Dr. Ritchie

---

[13] Inelda May Christianson, telephone interview by Delmer G. Ross, 23 November 2003; I.R. Christianson, "Ritchie Family Life in Riverside," 8; and Stationery letterheads, Monterey Medical Clinic, Ritchie Papers, SCLSU.

[14] I.R. Christianson, "Ritchie Family Life in Riverside," 8. Dr. Ritchie's income from his medical practice generally diminished to virtually nothing whenever he was away. His office nurse, Ora Leisenring, carried on with patients who arrived for weekly treatments or shots, but she could do little more than that. Physicians to whom his patients were referred while he was away kept whatever fees they thus earned. Ibid., 9.

decided that both the house and the mortgage were larger than they needed, especially as the children left home. Moreover, he did not feel well. So in mid-1946 they moved back into the apartment above the Monterey Medical Clinic until something more suitable could be found. In a letter to his son, Iner William, Dr. Ritchie wrote,

> Right now we are in the midst of moving, and it is a gigantic ordeal for us. It will probably take several weeks before we are settled back upstairs from where we started. . . .
> We are spending the day at Corona del Mar. This constant grind and worry is too much for me and I feel that I will be unable to stand it much longer as my B.P. [blood pressure] keeps climbing up and my heart bothers me at night, a thing it has seldom ever done before.[15]

Not long after moving back into quarters above his office, and after the late-hours patients began trying to take advantage again, the physician located a small, derelict Victorian home on Seventh Street that had to be moved or torn down. Bought for very little, he had it moved to a lot he and Inelda purchased on Bonita Street in the La Sierra area of what was then known as Arlington. There he had it placed on a foundation and renovated. At Inelda Ruth's

---

[15] Daddy [Iner S. Ritchie] et al. to Iner [William Ritchie] et al., 18 May 1946, 1, Ritchie Papers, SCLSU.

insistence he had two small rental apartments built above the garage behind the house. He and his wife moved there in 1947.[16]

At the Monterey Medical Clinic Dr. Ritchie continued to help the large Spanish-speaking community in Riverside and nearby towns by providing health services to even the poorest of Mexican laborers. To those he felt might find them beneficial he also offered free health-related pamphlets in Spanish such as, *Consejos para Señoras Encinta* [sic] *y Cuidado de los Niños*, which was filled with advice for pregnant women and for others involved in childcare. Such health pamphlets were supplied at no direct cost to Dr. Ritchie by a drug company, which even imprinted his name on the covers. He never forgot that he was a Christian missionary. In his waiting room, which was decorated with a large print of Jesus with his hand on the head of a child, were a number of prominently placed racks of free religious literature where his patients and others could pick up Seventh-day Adventist pamphlets in Spanish as well as English. He hoped his patients would take them home to study. He also furnished his waiting room with a display case where his patients could see various mementos of his time in Mexico.[17]

---

[16] Located at 1945 Arroyo Drive in Riverside, it is known as Casa Arroyo. The lot was located at 11651 Bonita. Today Bonita is known as Carmine Street. I.M. Christianson, telephone interview by D.G. Ross, 23 November 2003. At the time they purchased Casa Arroyo, the Ritchies sold the apartments on Seventh Street. I.R. Christianson, "Ritchie Family Life in Riverside," 9.

[17] *Consejos para Señoras Encinta* [sic] *y Cuidado de los Niños* (no place, no date), copy in Ritchie Papers, SCLSU; Inelda May Christianson, daughter of Dr. Iner S. Ritchie, interview by Delmer G. Ross, Riverside, California, 17 July 2000. A black-and-white copy of the picture which later hung on Dr. Ritchie's office wall graces the cover of *The Medical Evangelist*

As had been the case previously when he practiced in Riverside and in Calexico, Dr. Ritchie treated members of other minority groups—not only Mexicans and Mexican Americans. Asians and Asian Americans soon were also seeing him at the Monterrey Medical Clinic. In fact, the very last resident of Riverside's Chinatown, Wong Ho-Leun, who had arrived from China in 1914 and had become better known as George Wong, became one of Dr. Ritchie's patients during the 1940s.[18]

Another minority patient was fellow Adventist Omar L. Stratton, founder of the Riverside chapter of the National Association for the Advancement of Colored People (NAACP). Stratton arranged accommodations for health lectures for blacks given by Dr. Ritchie and other CME graduates. Along with effective Bible work by Stratton and others, those lectures eventually led to the formation of the Kansas Avenue church in Riverside, one that by 2005 had more than 1,300 members. Moreover, results continued because the Kansas Avenue church was instrumental in the formation of three other nearby churches, in Rubidoux, Moreno Valley, and Perris.[19]

---

of December 1919.

[18] H. Vincent Moses and Brenda Buller Focht, *Life in Little Gom-Benn: Chinese Immigrant Society in Riverside, 1885-1930* (Riverside: Riverside Museum Press, 1991), [16-17]; and I.M. Christianson, interview by D.G. Ross, 10 June 2003.

[19] Omar W. Stratton, M.D., to Inelda Christianson, 13 September 2004, Ritchie Papers, SCLSU; and Lucille-Stratton-Taylor to Inelda [Christianson], no date, Ritchie Papers, SCLSU. After Omar L. Stratton passed away in 1972, the Community Center at Bordwell Park in Riverside was named for him. "Omar L. Stratton Community Center Dedicated by Officials at Bordwell," *The*

The physician and his wife began attending the Riverside Seventh-day Adventist Church, and it was not long before he became an active member. His leadership ability soon led to his being voted a church elder.

Although Dr. Ritchie now lived and practiced medicine in California, he continued his involvement with Mexico, making literally dozens of trips to various parts of that republic as he participated in medical and educational missionary work. For example, *The Medical Evangelist* relates that the physician had returned from a particularly extensive medical missionary trip in early 1938.[20] He must have felt fully recovered from the heart attack that less than two years earlier had forced him to leave Mexico City for he now spent several weeks in a region that was approximately as high in elevation. Traveling some 2,800 miles, he visited a variety of places—some quite remote—in north central Mexico. Dr. Ritchie, along with other Seventh-day Adventist officials and local native workers journeyed by train, auto, and horseback, and apparently at least once in an old fashioned, horse-drawn, mining-company stagecoach.[21] They first visited the "Aztec" Indians in the mountainous section of the central and gulf regions of Mexico. The group of medical mission-

---

Riverside (California) Press, 19 February 1973, B1.

[20] [Iner S. Ritchie and O.R. Staines], "Itinerating in Old Mexico," *The Medical Evangelist,* Vol. 24, No. 34 (17 February 1938): 1-3; Vol. 24, No. 35 (24 February 1938): 1-2; and Vol. 24, No. 36 (3 March 1938): 2-4.

[21] Miscellaneous Ritchie family videorecordings composite, produced by [Iner W. Ritchie and Don Cicchetti], 1 hour, 24 min., [Loma Linda University Media Services], 1989, videocassette.

aries then visited the "Chichimeca" Indians in the highlands of San Luis Potosí. They carried a small but impressive array of letters of introduction from government officials in an attempt to insure safety as well as success.[22]

The last native group they visited on the trip included the Tarahumara tribe in the mountainous country of western Chihuahua. Many of the people of these tribes lived isolated from the rest of Mexican society and needed medical help more than those living in other areas. The group, under the direction of Dr. Ritchie, treated hundreds of natives with different medical problems. It gave vaccinations, extracted teeth, performed minor surgery, and conducted lectures on health and temperance.[23] In a letter he sent by Tarahumara Indian runner some 75 miles from Baquiachic to the nearest post office at Cusihuiriachic, Chihuahua, where it could be mailed to his family in Riverside, he mentioned that his group had been following the headwaters of the Conchos River for three days. They were high in the Sierra Tarahumara, not far from the famous Barranca del Cobre, at an elevation he estimated to be between 7,000 and 9,000 feet, where it was cold—especially at night. After briefly describing the scenery as "magnificent," he

---

[22] Included were letters from Gustavo L.Talamantes, governor of the state of Chihuahua, from Dr. Jesús Olmos M., chief of the Chihuahua state sanitary services office, and from Carlos A. Nieto, manager of the Chihuahua chamber of commerce. Gustavo L. Talamantes to Whom it May Concern, 15 November 1937, Ritchie Papers, SCLSU; Jesús Olmos M. to Whom it May Concern, 15 November 1937, Ritchie Papers, SCLSU; and C.A. Nieto to Whom it May Concern, 15 November 1937, Ritchie Papers, SCLSU.

[23] [Iner S. Ritchie and O.R. Staines], "Itinerating in Old Mexico," *The Medical Evangelist,* Vol. 24, No. 34 (17 February 1938): 1-3; Vol. 24, No. 35 (24 February 1938): 1-2; and Vol. 24, No. 36 (3 March 1938): 2-4.

wrote about wildlife: "Yesterday 3 deer were drinking in the Gorge from a pool in the river as we passed by. . . . Up on a grass covered mesa with big oaks & pines I got real near a flock of about 20 big black turkeys."[24] He went on, writing about the Indians they were meeting,

> We are now with the wild indians sure enough. . . .
> There are many cliff dwellers here and they build and inhabit houses exactly as we see in ruins in Arizona and New Mexico. So possibly they are descendents [*sic*] of the same people.
> They spear fish in the river and also build sand and rock dams to form pools and run the fish into these traps. Then . . . [they] dam it off and put [in] the leaves of any of 3 kinds of trees that grow here which stupefies or kills the fish. They hunt with bows & arrows. Guns and especially ammunition is too expensive and they cannot buy it. They raise corn and have sheep and cattle. They are independent and do not want foreigners in their country. I took a picture of one fellow who had killed 12 white men.[25]

While the Tarahumaras preferred to avoid strangers, for some the possibility of free medical treatment broke down barriers. Dr. Ritchie exulted in the fact that "Today I succeeded in treating a family"! Adding that "our mission in here is to give them the Gospel of the coming kingdom . . . and they surely need it and

---

[24] Iner [S. Ritchie] to Inelda Sheld-Ritchie & children, 14 November 1937, Ritchie file, WebbLLU.

[25] Ibid.

must hear it,"[26] he implied that Indian reticence might make their ultimate goal difficult to achieve.

Prolonged travel to such remote areas was tiring, as was his medical practice itself. In a letter to his elder son, Iner William, the medical evangelist acknowledged not feeling well. "We have spent the day at the beach house [in] Corona del Mar. I have been overworking and not feeling or sleeping so good lately," he wrote. "Guess I will have to have a rest or else something will happen to my cardiac system."[27] It was an unusual disclosure, but perhaps he felt he could be frank with his son who was also a medical doctor.

Having indicated that he felt poorly, he went on to describe a 125-acre property that was available in central Mexico near Cuernavaca. It already had a girls' school on it, and among other structures, had "a large mansion which could easily be converted into a hospital." Waxing enthusiastic, Dr. Ritchie thought his son might be interested in practicing there where the climate is like that of Guadalajara, which "is the finest in the world."[28] Even when tired, feeling poorly, and supposedly resting, the missionary physician could not escape thoughts of his chosen mission field. Like countless other possibilities, though, nothing came of the Cuernavaca project.

On April 21, 1946, Dr. Ritchie left California for an unusual trip to the recently established Adventist agricultural and industrial

[26] Ibid.

[27] Daddy [Iner S. Ritchie] et al. to Iner Wm. [Ritchie] et al., 16 March 1946, 1, Ritchie Papers, SCLSU.

[28] Ibid., 2.

school at Montemorelos. This time he traveled by automobile with
Inelda Ruth and their friends, Curt and Dora Effler, from Calexico.
The Efflers owned Calexico Cotton Products, Inc., which manu-
factured mattresses, over-stuffed furniture, comforters, and even
overalls. They were very missionary-minded, and wanted to look
into the possibility of establishing a mattress factory at the new
school. Such an industry could employ quite a number of students,
offering them a way to pay for their studies. After entering Mexico
and clearing customs at Laredo, they visited with church officials
in Monterrey, then continued southward to Montemorelos. They
spent a few days there, touring the farm on a tractor and visiting
the carpenter shop and the nearly completed hospital, which Dr.
Ritchie reported "is getting a finished look on it now."[29] As they
drove back to Calexico they paused several times to do some
sightseeing. They were locked into one of the Catholic churches
they visited in Monterrey. The Efflers evidently were quite
concerned, but Dr. Ritchie laughed the incident off as "just an old
Mexican . . . custom" designed to separate tourists from their
money, and he quickly paid to have someone unlock the door so
they could leave.[30] Apparently they were most impressed by
Carlsbad Caverns and Tombstone, Arizona. All in all, it was an
interesting trip, but it did not result in a mattress factory for
Montemorelos. The Efflers were unable to sell their business in
Calexico in time to do what they hoped to accomplish in Mexico.
Not all of Dr. Ritchie's trips produced the expected or desired

[29] Daddy [Iner S. Ritchie] et al. to Iner [William Ritchie] et al., 18 May
1946, 3.

[30] Ibid.

results.[31] Still, as the favorably impressed Efflers admitted in a brief note, "you made new boosters for your Sanitarium and school."[32]

Dr. Ritchie himself was favorably impressed with the progress he saw, leading him to predict, "I believe that this school will become our principal advanced training center for the Mexican Union, where workers will qualify to go out by the hundreds and thousands to all the Spanish speaking fields."[33] He could not have been more accurate.

The medical-evangelist missionary made two additional trips to Mexico in September 1946. The first was a fairly routine one to Mexico City to deal with government officials on behalf of the new Adventist sanitarium and hospital then under construction in Montemorelos. The second—to attend a youth congress in Tlalchapa, Guerrero, and to assess medical needs in that area—very nearly cost Dr. Ritchie his life.[34]

A party of three left Mexico City for Tlalchapa late in the month. They traveled approximately eighty miles south into the north central part of Guerrero, then an equal distance west, nearly

---

[31] Curt Effler, trip log, April 1946, 1-11, copy in Ritchie Papers, SCLSU; Daddy [Iner S. Ritchie] et al. to Iner Wm. [Ritchie] et al., 16 March 1946, 2; and I.M. Christianson, telephone interview by D.G. Ross, 15 June 2004.

[32] Curt and Doris [Effler] to Inner [sic[and Inelde [sic] [Ritchie, 5 May 1946, Ritchie Papers, SCLSU.

[33] Daddy [Iner S. Ritchie] et al. to Iner [William Ritchie] et al., 18 May 1946, 2.

[34] Harold House, "In Guerrero," 7-page undated manuscript, 1-3, Ritchie Papers, SCLSU.

to the adjoining state of Michoacán. In addition to Dr. Ritchie, Dr. Vernon Nickel, Dr. Ritchie's son-in-law and a captain in the United States Army, and Harold F. House, Secretary of the Mexican Union Mission, were along. After a long day of travel by bus, they reached the town of Arcelia, where they spent the night.[35]

Early the next morning they departed on horseback for Tlalchapa. Not far from their destination they were joined by a rider who told them of an ancient relic that had recently been discovered nearby. He offered to guide them to its location. Because the horseman acted so strangely, members of the medical group were suspicious of the horseman's motives and turned down his offer. They later learned that their caution was justified because their proposed guide was a member of a fanatically Catholic faction in Tlalchapa that hoped to be able to accuse the Adventists of attempting to steal the relic and thus be able to turn an angry mob loose on them. Despite such schemes, the Adventists safely reached their destination late in the afternoon. Upon unloading their baggage at the home of a merchant where they planned to stay, they visited the municipal offices where they presented their credentials and letters of recommendation to the *presidente municipal*—roughly the equivalent of mayor of an American town. Although the *presidente* appeared to react favorably, he commented that some of the people of the town had begun to threaten trouble because of their opposition to the youth

---

[35] Ibid., 2; Stephen Kumar and David Olivares, "Expect the Unexpected" (term paper presented for HIST 294/494, History Colloquium, La Sierra University, Riverside, California, 6 December 1995), 1.

congress in progress that was sponsored by the Central Mexican Mission of Seventh-day Adventists.[36]

Drs. Vernon Nickel (second from left) and Iner S. Ritchie (third from right) traveling to Tlalchapa, Guerrero.

After returning to the home where they were staying, the two physicians began treating patients who were waiting for them. Tlalchapa had no doctor, nurse, nor any other type of medical service, so people needing help began congregating at the merchant's home as soon as they learned of the arrival of *los médicos* (the doctors). As Harold House put it, "The news of their arrival seemed to spread like wildfire because many suffering from ailments of all kinds flocked in from different directions." Some of their patients warned the visitors about the local priest who the

---

[36] House, "In Guerrero," 1-2.

previous day had incited a hostile mob to march by the Adventist church chanting "Death to the Protestants!" and yelling curses and insults. Homes of Adventist church members had been stoned. That sounded ominous, but the busy doctors worked late into the night and therefore had little time to think about what might face them. Patients began arriving again shortly after daylight the next morning, so once more the two physicians were busy until it was time for them to go to the Adventist church for the final session of the youth congress.[37]

An angry crowd had been gathering at the nearby Catholic church and, shortly before noon, about 500 persons strong and armed with everything from sticks and stones to knives and firearms, the mob headed toward the Adventist church which it quickly surrounded, attacked, and looted. Although many of the youth and others in the church and its adjacent patio suffered injuries, most were not of a serious nature. Dr. Ritchie, however, was knocked unconscious by "a terrific blow from a rock which struck him behind the ear." He soon regained his senses and, with the help of a Catholic youth, was able to get away.

It was not long before it became apparent that the *presidente municipal,* the local priest, and leaders of the Catholic Action political party had all been responsible for the tumult. A warning that because Dr. Nickel was a captain in the United States Army the riot might have international repercussions quickly sobered the *presidente* and his cohorts. Then, with the assistance of two federal soldiers, by leaving at midnight and traveling over little

[37] House, "In Guerrero," 2.

used trails so as to avoid the conspirators' aroused followers, the out-of-town Adventists were able to slip away from the area of greatest danger. It had been a close call.[38]

In some ways, though, the incident was not yet over. The man who threw the stone that hit Dr. Ritchie during the riot lost virtually all his material possessions and became a beggar. The priest who had incited the riot set fire to his own church, then blamed Protestants. The truth came out during the course of the following trial. The priest later was forced to leave Tlalchapa ignominiously after being accused of sodomy by a choir boy. Certain misdeeds of the leader of the Catholic Action Party were exposed by his angry wife, with the result that he was chased out of town, after which he drowned in a nearby river. The *presidente municipal* lost his position, became ill, and died in poverty. In fact, a great number of those who participated in the riot suffered serious illnesses and accidents from which several died. Rightly or wrongly, the fanatical rioter whose thrown stone had felled Dr. Ritchie came to the conclusion that he and his fellow brawlers were being punished by God for their actions against the Adventists. A number of others reached the same conclusion, repented, and begged their former victims for help and forgiveness. Some even joined the Adventist church.[39]

Late in 1948 Dr. Ritchie took on an additional duty and title, that of consultant to the Director of Public Health for the State of

---

[38] House, "In Guerrero," 2-7.

[39] Henry J. Westphal to Mrs. [Inelda Ruth] Ritchie, 12 May 1950, copy in Ritchie Papers, SCLSU; and Kumar and Olivares, "Expect the Unexpected," 3-4.

California. The director from 1943 to 1954, Dr. Wilton L. Halverson, had received his medical degree from the College of Medical Evangelists in 1929. He and Dr. Ritchie were friends and fellow members of Liga, an organization created to promote medical and educational work in Mexico. Exactly what tasks Dr. Ritchie was expected to perform are unclear. For the record, though, they were related to various types of diseases, "especially the virus diseases of the central nervous system."[40]

It appears that the position was largely honorary, but for that very reason the good doctor considered it ideal. His actual duties would be light to non-existent—as also would be his pay—but the title of consultant would give him more credibility and influence than ever, particularly in Mexico. That much he tacitly admitted when in the letter he wrote from Mexico City accepting the position he stated, "Only today I had occasion to use your letter [of appointment] in the Dept. of Hygiene and Education of Salubridad Pública."[41] While the doors of many Mexican government officials were already open to him, he realized that his welcome was precarious, especially in a largely Roman Catholic nation with a socialist government. A little more clout could not hurt.

[40] Iner Sheld Ritchie to Wilton L. Halverson, 7 December 1948, Ritchie Papers, SCLSU.

[41] Ibid.

Liga and the Flying Doctors of Mercy

Although health problems had forced Dr. Ritchie to return to the United States from Mexico in 1936, in his heart he remained a medical missionary to Mexicans. He continued making trips to Mexico and participating in medical missionary work there. During the course of such trips large numbers of people with almost every imaginable complaint would flock to his clinics. It was not unusual for him and his native health-worker assistants to see fifty to one hundred patients in a single day.

During a particularly arduous trip of two months duration late in 1937, he decided to appeal for temporary assistance—for physicians who might be able to spend only a few weeks or even days providing medical service to those who otherwise would have none. Such doctors would be able to handle cases the health workers could not. A few weeks after his return to the United States he wrote, "I am wondering if there are not some of our doctors here [in California] near the home base who would be willing to go down and rough it for a few weeks, spending their vacation in this helpful way.[1] Although it was several years before it was formally begun, the California chapter of Liga—later known as Liga International—was already taking shape in Dr. Ritchie's mind.

In addition to his inability to cover as much territory as he felt was needed during his own trips, Dr. Ritchie was unable to travel as often or as much as he would have liked because of the distance and terrain to be covered and the often extremely poor quality of transportation facilities. Sometimes the best to be had was a horse or a mule, and occasionally he had to walk.[2] Such difficulties and the obvious needs led Dr. Ritchie to dream of flying to his Mexican destinations. So much time could be saved. So many additional people could be served. Then he asked himself the question, "Why not?"

Dr. Ritchie's first contact with flying had taken place years earlier with his friend and fellow medical missionary, Dr. Ralph Smith, in the late 1920s. He later flew to various destinations in the United States and Mexico on regularly scheduled commercial

---

[1] [Ritchie, Iner S., and Staines, O.R.] "Itinerating in Old Mexico." *The Medical Evangelist,* Vol. 24, No. 34 (17 February 1938): 1-3.

[2] Ernie Dass, "The Flying Doctors of Mercy" (term paper presented for HIST 294/494 History Colloquium, 26 May 1994), 1, D.G. Ross Collection, Department of History, Politics and Society, La Sierra University, Riverside, CA; and Clarence E. Nelson, "Iner S. Ritchie Dies," *The Journal of the Alumni Association, School of Medicine, College of Medical Evangelists*, vol. 21, No. 1 (January 1950), 16.

flights offered mainly by American Airlines. Flying, he had quickly perceived, was a real time saver.[3]

Moreover, while working in Mexico City and traveling throughout the remainder of the country, Dr. Ritchie had become aware of certain commonly used legal methods of circumventing the intent of Mexican law, including even the national constitution. Accordingly he and other church officers, in consultation with Francisco Ramírez Villarreal, an attorney from the Department of the Interior and one of the original signers of the Mexican Constitution of 1917, created the Asociación Civil Filantrópica y Educativa (Civil Philanthropic and Educational Association), perhaps better known by its acronym, ACFE.[4] Chartered in 1934, the ACFE enabled denominational entities to get around some of the anticlerical provisions of the Mexican Constitution and the following enabling laws known collectively as Ley Calles (the Calles Law) that had gone into effect in 1926—and to do so quite legally. Because such enactments prohibited church organizations from owning real property, title to virtually all denominational real estate outside of the church buildings themselves was transferred to the ACFE. The new association also made it easier for philanthropic organizations to donate funds to projects in Mexico.[5]

[3] Inelda May Christianson, interview by Delmer G. Ross, Riverside, California, 17 July 2000.

[4] [Iner William Ritchie], "History of Liga," three-page typescript, no place or date, 1, Ritchie Papers, SCLSU.

[5] Ritchie, Iner W. S., "Liga México-Pan-Americana Medico [*sic*] Educacional," three-page typescript, Riverside, California, 23 July 1974, 1, Ritchie Papers, SCLSU. According to Mexican law at that time, all church buildings, along with the ground on which they stood, were the property of the

Unfortunately, in only a few years this use of ACFE had become so well known in certain instances—for example, the Adventist school and hospital at Montemorelos—that some people who opposed the work of the Seventh-day Adventist church began to demand publicly that there be an investigation and that punishment be imposed. The penalty, if applied, would have included the confiscation of the property in question. Perhaps the letter of the law was still being observed—in fact, there was little doubt of that—but the church obviously used ACFE to circumvent at least part of the law's intent.

In 1947, at the suggestion of the Mexican Minister of Public Health, the day had been saved by creating another, apparently more health related organization, the Liga México-Americana Médico Educacional y de Trabajadores Sociales (Mexican-American League of Medical, Educational and Social Workers), to take some of the public attention and pressure from the ACFE. The new organization had such a long, tongue twister of a name that it was soon shortened by common usage to "Liga." Within months of the creation of the new body, even its "official" name evolved to a shorter form, Liga México Panamericana (Mexico Pan-American League). The popular short version, though, Liga, remained in use. With the realignment of property that took place after the organization of the Liga, by using both the ACFE and the Liga, the church was able to continue to circumvent many of the anticlerical provisions of Mexican law. The method was simplicity

---

Mexican nation. Religious organizations could use such buildings only after they had successfully formally petitioned to do so. The Seventh-day Adventist church fully complied with the law.

itself, and perfectly legal. Because the church itself did not own any real property—technically, all titles were held by either the ACFE or the Liga—there was none for the government to confiscate.[6]

The ACFE and Liga cooperated closely and successfully. In fact, in 1949 the managing board of the Mexican Union voted that the ACFE should draw up an agreement with the Mexico Pan-American League to manage Liga properties.[7] Obviously, although both the ACFE and the Liga were legally separate entities, they were managed directly by the church.

As the former head of Seventh-day Adventist medical work for the Mexican Union and General Manager of the ACFE, Dr. Ritchie had become the vice president and general manager of Liga. He knew how it had been created and why. He knew how it worked and how successful it had been. All the same, he was among the first to recommend caution and a carefully correct approach. Writing of Liga and its relationship with government officials and the Mexican government Dr. Ritchie stated:

---

[6] Iner [William] Sheld Ritchie to Augustin [sic] Olachea, 14 August 1963, Ritchie Papers, SCLSU; Liga México-Americana Medico [sic] Educacional y de Trabajadores Sociales, *Purpose and Function of the "Liga,"* (Coyoacán, D.F., [1948], 1-2, Ritchie Papers, SCLSU; and Carrol S. Small and Elsa Lonergan, "Alumni and Missions: 'Go Ye into All the World,'" *AIMS Journal,* Vol. 22, No. 1 (2001), 9. Some Liga literature gives 1924 as the year when "We began this humanitarian work." To state that Dr. Iner S. Ritchie began his work in Calexico and Mexicali in 1924 may be correct, but to imply that Liga was started then is misleading. Liga began in 1947. See, for example, [Iner W. Ritchie], "Liga México-Americana Medico [sic] Educacional y de Trabajadores Sociales (no place, no date), 1.

[7] Junta de la Unión Mexicana, "Minuta de la junta de la Unión Mexicana," México, D.F., 24 June 1949, 1275, copy in Ritchie papers, SCLSU.

We must safeguard the men, their reputation, and the high position of power they occupy in the nation, not only for their good, but for our own safety and the welfare of this church.

We must respect their laws and do everything in our power to obey them, and avoid catastrophe and even the appearance of evil. I have heard people get up and say in our U.S. churches, "Oh, we can do anything we please down there in Mexico, and the officials just wink at it."

Nothing [is] farther from the truth. We are in [t]here because they tolerate us, for we are just another problem for them.[8]

Not only was he absolutely right, but he showed great perception. If Liga was to prosper it would need to cooperate with government officials, rather than to antagonize them. Dr. Ritchie had noted that, as a result of just such a considerate attitude on the part of Liga, a significant number of American physicians had joined its membership ranks and that their identification with Liga had enabled some to be allowed to practice medicine in Mexico.[9]

As early as 1948 Liga was receiving commendations from Mexican government officials. For example, General Juan A. Castelo, chief of military operations in Northern Baja California, wrote to Dr. Ritchie in 1948:

I am thoroughly acquainted with the philanthropic work which this worthy institution has been accomplish-

---

[8] Iner S. Ritchie, 3 pages handwritten notes, np, nd., 1. Ritchie Papers, SCLSU.

[9] Ibid., 1-3.

ing in our country, a work which consists principally in the establishment and founding of rural clinics and agricultural and industrial schools which have been so beneficial in raising the moral, social and cultural standards of our country. On giving you my affirmation, I wish to take this occasion to show, now as on other occasions, that you will always find me ready to give to you both my moral and material support, as much as I am able, for the noble ends which this Liga is pursuing.[10]

It was high praise, indeed, and most welcome for Liga and Dr. Ritchie. He could rest assured that he was doing something right. But he also concluded it might be possible to do even better.

He thought that perhaps another similar organization, but based in the United States, could help even more. It could cooperate with the Mexican Liga and could possibly make that association a considerably more effective health and educational league than it already was. Perhaps some of the airplane pilots and medical personnel returning from military service at the end of World War II could get together under the auspices of such an organization and cooperate to provide medical assistance to remote areas of Mexico that could not be reached otherwise except by walking or riding on horseback.

Translating thoughts into action, Dr. Ritchie began to promote the creation of another Liga. He found that not only were physicians and airplane pilots willing to cooperate in the endeavor, but there were many physicians who were also pilots who were willing to join. He discovered that dentists, nurses, and other health

---

[10] Juan A.. Castelo Encinas to Iner S. Ritchie, 9 February 1948.

professionals were equally willing to offer their services. Therefore, after a few months of unofficial, experimental operation, in 1948 he organized an American chapter of the Liga México Panamericana Médico Educacional. Early the next year the new chapter was doing its best to acquire funds by noting the tax deductible nature of its membership dues as well as all donations up to fifteen percent of personal income.[11] Its goal was to bring together health professionals and others such as pilots, interpreters, educators, and, as one of its modern promotional brochures indicates, "anyone interested in lending a helping hand."[12]

Additionally, and more specifically, the American chapter also hoped to provide facilities for researching tropical medicine and hygiene and to provide scholarships for those studying such fields. At the same time it might offer a means for the exchange of scientific information among the countries served. Another goal was to start and support medical-educational institutions for the underprivileged. Finally, it hoped to provide funds to establish and operate agricultural and industrial schools.[13]

Thus there came to be two Ligas. The first, the Mexican Liga, was basically a holding company for the ownership of certain types of property in Mexico. The second, the American version,

[11] Membership application form, *Official Bulletin of the American Chapter, Liga México-Pan-American Médico Educacional*, No. 1 (January-February 1949), 3.

[12] Liga International, Inc., *Hands Across the Border*, nd, Santa Ana, CA.

[13] "Aims and Objectives of the Liga," *Official Bulletin of the American Chapter, Liga México-Pan-American Médico Educacional*, No.1 (January-February 1949), 3.

would provide financing and personnel for medical services and medical and educational projects.

Most of the approximately 200 original members of the American Liga were connected in some way with the College of Medical Evangelists, better known today as Loma Linda University. Many, like Dr. Ritchie, were graduates. Others were employees who worked there at various different tasks. One, for example, was W.E. Macpherson, a medical doctor who was president of the college.[14] Together they would do what they could to deliver free or extremely low cost health care to the rural poor of northwestern Mexico.

At CME's Clinical Congress and Post Graduate Assembly held in Loma Linda and Los Angeles early in 1949, exhibits sponsored by Liga were as honored as were at least four of its guests: Dr. Raymundo Garza, Dean and Professor of Anatomy of the School of Medicine at the University of Monterrey in Nuevo León, Mexico, and the president of Liga; Dr. Luis de la Rosa, Director of Public Health Education for the Federal Government of Mexico; Dr. Clarence J. McCleary of the Seventh-day Adventist hospital in Puerto Cabezas, Nicaragua; and Dr. Iner S. Ritchie, founder and General Manager of Liga. Dr. Ritchie, "well known for the humanitarian work he has been doing for the past 20 years in remote areas of the Mexican Republic," was in charge of the exhibits. Of considerable interest were plans to erect and equip a small clinic and school at Teapa, in the state of Tabasco, and to create a new "Mobile Medical Unit." Purchased as Army surplus,

---

[14] Signature sheets, no place or date, Ritchie Papers, SCLSU.

the unit, consisting of a truck and trailer, was not new, but it was newly furnished. The truck offered rather austere living quarters, while the trailer was equipped with a generator, an x-ray machine, an operating table, and related equipment and supplies.[15]

In addition to noting Liga plans for the future, at the Clinical Congress Dr. Ritchie was delighted to receive vindication for what he had been preaching for years. It came in the form of a statement from President Anastasio Somoza García of Nicaragua who was quoted as saying of Dr. McCleary's work, "His hospital is the best ambassador of good will which the U.S. has in this country."[16] Although they might not say so, even highly placed non-Adventists could see the usefulness of medical evangelism. It was the "entering wedge" of the gospel.

While the formation and operation of the two branches of Liga proved useful to the church, some denominational leaders shook their heads in dismay. They acknowledged that Liga "fulfilled Mexican legal constraints, allowing money to finance schools and medical units 'untainted' by official church connections," but they also viewed it as "a threat to denominational

[15] Clarence E. Nelson to Our Fellow Alumni, Members and Friends, [February 1949], Ritchie Papers, SCLSU. When funds were available, Liga could move forward rapidly. By late 1949 the Mobile Medical Unit was in Mexico and plans were under way to use it in a public health education drive in five different towns in the state of Oaxaca. Stephen Youngberg, "Tribute to Dr. Ritchie." México, D.F., 28 October 1949, a transcription from tape copied from wire by Inelda May Christianson, 25 November 1995, Ritchie Papers, SCLSU.

[16] Quoted in Clarence E. Nelson to Our Fellow Alumni, Members and Friends, [February 1949], addendum, Ritchie Papers, SCLSU.

Destined for service in Mexico, Liga's newly acquired mobile medical unit in 1948. Pictured left to right, Dale Rosheim, Dr. Stephen Youngberg, and Verlene Youngberg.

control."[17] Such issues eventually were resolved, although perhaps not to the complete satisfaction of everyone involved.

Just as Dr. Ritchie had dreamed more than two decades earlier, by the 1950s the American chapter of Liga was flying missions to Mexico. The first Liga president to have an airplane was Paul Freeman, a physician from Santa Ana, California. By then the Great Depression and World War II were both just memories, and quite a number of prosperous southern California physicians were buying their own airplanes. Some were Liga volunteers. They would fly into Mexico, land on back country landing strips needy villagers had prepared for the purpose, then operate a medical clinic. Once it became necessary, Velma, Paul Freeman's wife, coordinated volunteers, pilots and airplanes, and clinics.[18]

Another reorganization took place early in 1965, when the American Liga became Liga International, Inc., a California non-profit corporation with the slogan, "The Helping Hand." It also became officially non-sectarian as well as non-political. Its mission and work, however, remained essentially the same—service to suffering humanity.[19]

---

[17] Floyd Greenleaf, *The Seventh-day Adventist Church in Latin America and the Caribbean,* Vol. 2, *Bear the News to Every Land* (Berrien Springs, Michigan: Andrews University Press, 1992), 250.

[18] I.M. Christianson, interview by D.G. Ross, Riverside, California, 17 July 2000.

[19] Peter H. Morgan, Jr., "President's Message," *Liga High Flying Times,* January-February 1980, 1,4; and [Inelda May Christianson], *Iner Sheld-Ritchie, Founder of Liga, 1885-1949* [Riverside: The Stahl Center, La Sierra University, ca. 1996], [4]. The charter of Liga International proposed four ways of being

Considering that Dr. Ritchie's own personal goal always had been to serve others in the most compassionate way, it should be no surprise that the first objective of Liga International was, and still is, to provide "compassionate service" through medical assistance to individuals. Another mission is to offer health care in clinics in rural Mexico and other areas outside the United States. By the mid-1970s it supported health, agricultural, and industrial education through its medical clinics and the establishment of self-supporting schools. Liga offered health evaluations and care as well as food, clothing, and other types of assistance to victims of natural disasters such as floods, hurricanes, and earthquakes. Moreover, it provided opportunities for professional exchange and training of medical professionals. Finally, although Liga itself was non-denominational, in an effort to help spread the gospel, it sponsored or helped to sponsor various religious enterprises and projects. While its projects still were concentrated in northwestern Mexico, they were by then scattered all over the world.[20]

Just as Dr. Ritchie had hoped, the use of airplanes greatly facilitated access to remote areas. Where he had tried to go on at

---

of service to others: through medical assistance, by sponsoring educational projects, through charity, and by sponsoring religious activities. John Baerg, "Liga International, Inc.," *ASI News,* Vol. 25, Nos. 7, 8, 9, (July-September 1975), 4-5; and Richard W. Schwarz and Department of Education of Seventh-day Adventists, *Light Bearers to the Remnant: Denominational History Textbook for Seventh-day Adventist College Classes,* (Mountain View, California: Pacific Press Publishing Association, 1979), 558.

[20] Ibid., 558-59; Liga International, Inc., *Hands Across the Border;* and Dass, "The Flying Doctors of Mercy."

least one trip to rural Mexico to hold clinics every year, air transportation made it possible to conduct one or more almost every month. Consequently, in response to requests from local people eager to have access to health services, Liga International started many new clinics. Each was staffed once per month, usually for nine months every year—from October through June.[21] While each patient may have had some small transportation costs involved in reaching the clinic, there was no charge for medical or dental care. Liga's popular name, "The Flying Doctors of Mercy" certainly seems appropriate.

Those who joined Liga to provide health care to the poor often were very much like Dr. Ritchie himself. They had a great burden to serve, and they would not be deterred by minor obstacles. Moreover, they kept returning to the clinics. Many followed the example of Dr. Clarence E. Nelson, who was installed as the first president of Liga International in 1948, and who continued to participate in trips to rural Mexican clinics until 1986, when he passed away at age 92.[22]

In actual practice, a tremendous amount of planning goes into the function of each of Liga's clinics. Having determined that a particular region is in dire need of health assistance, if at all possible, and with the help of local people, a suitable building will

---

[21] Liga International, Inc, *Flying Doctors Operating on Hope,* Santa Ana, CA, nd. Because of the usual great number of storms, from July through September the weather is bad for flying in the small craft used by Liga. Moreover, because of the high tropical heat and humidity during those months, it can be difficult to put together viable medical teams.

[22] Liga International, Inc., *Hands Across the Border.*

be acquired through loan, lease, or some other means. If no existing structure will do, Liga volunteers may build one—or have it built. It should be adequately supplied with electric power and water, although in the past many have not enjoyed such amenities. The clinic building will then be supplied with medical equipment that has been donated for the purpose. Through word of mouth as well as through the media local people will be notified that The Flying Doctors of Mercy will be holding free medical clinics on the first weekend of each month, from October through June. They will also be asked to watch for notices indicating what types of specialists will be arriving in any given month so that individuals who need the attention of such professionals can plan to show up on the weekend most appropriate for them. Flights do not take place during July, August and September because of the risky nature of flying during the monsoon season.

Meanwhile, people at Liga International headquarters in California line up volunteers for each of the monthly clinic sessions. Physicians, from those who specialize in family practice to plastic surgeons, dentists, nurses, teachers, students, translators, and airplane pilots, among others, sign up, indicating when they will be available. Liga personnel arrange all of this so that each clinic is adequately staffed. All volunteers are told to meet at various appropriate airports, usually early Friday morning before the first weekend of the month. After paying between $150 and $185 for their transportation, they board their planes and fly to their destinations in Mexico. The same aircraft carry medical supplies. Upon arrival, or soon afterwards, a group of perhaps twenty people, from various different American cities, and often from Mexican cities as well, get to work with local Red Cross and other local community groups to prepare for each of the clinics that begin early in the morning. The next two days are exhausting for all concerned as hundreds of patients are examined, diagnosed, and helped as required at each location. By the time they are through they will have dealt with just about every conceivable human malady, from birth defects to leprosy. Patients they are unable to help at the clinics are often referred to specialists who can deal with the problem, and who usually will do so free of charge. On Sunday afternoon they start their journeys homeward, tired, but happy in the knowledge that they have helped others in the same way that Christ himself often did two thousand years ago.[23] What Dr Ritchie was able to do during the course of a yearly three-month-long trip, Liga volunteers often have accomplished several times over in a single weekend.

Although because of improving health care in Mexico and various other changes it may have grown little in recent years, Liga has expanded tremendously since its founding in 1948.[24] On each monthly clinic weekend as many as thirty single- and twin-engine airplanes have left from various airports in the southwestern part of the United States. Each one carried four to six individuals whose goal was to provide health services in as many as seven rural clinics throughout northwestern Mexico. Some delivered

[23] "LLU alumni provide humanitarian health service in Mexico with Liga, International," *Loma Linda University Today*, 9 October 1996, http://www.llu.edu/news/today/oct9a.html.

[24] Liga sometimes gives 1934 as the date of its founding. That was the year Dr. Ritchie made his first trip to southern Mexico to hold clinics in villages that had no medical service, but that hardly marked the founding of Liga. I.M. Christianson, interview by D.G. Ross, 15 July 2003.

medical care. Others offered instruction on health principles, nutrition, the prevention of gum disease, child care, and other health related topics, even agriculture. A few counted out pills or acted as interpreters. Many piloted their own planes, while a number flew aircraft owned by Liga. All, however, were volunteers.[25]

While the health professionals and others who serve humanity through Liga are not remunerated for their labor, they are rewarded. Perhaps the best way to explain is through the words of a nurse who had just assisted at the surgery on the cleft lip of a three-month-old baby:

> The child was transformed from a deformed, almost unsightly infant, to a beautiful baby with an almost completely normal lip. I handed the baby back to its mother and I shall never forget her tears of joy. Although we could barely communicate in language, there was no question that we understood each other, and I felt united with this woman whom I had never met before. Placing her beautiful baby in her arms and watching the mother weep is a joy I will never forget.[26]

Other Liga volunteers would agree. There may be no pay—in fact it always costs something to travel to Mexico or elsewhere to provide the services needed. In addition to travel and other

---

[25] "Aerospace Laureates, Operations: LIGA International, Inc., David S. Lawson, President," *Aviation Week & Space Technology,* Vol. 136, No. 4 (27 January 1992); and Liga International, *"Hands Across The Border."*

[26] Debbie Williams, "Counting My Blessings," *Liga High Flying Times,* December 1993 - January 1994.

expenses born by each volunteer, they all know that despite the safety record of travel by air in general, there always is a possibility of a fatal accident. Some Liga people have thus paid the ultimate cost.[27] The personal satisfaction gained for having helped someone in desperate need, though, is reward enough to keep Liga activists volunteering.

Over the years people in rural areas have not been the only ones to request help from Liga. As Dr. Ritchie had hoped from the beginning, highly placed government officials began to recognize the services of Liga and to ask for assistance. For example, early in 1954 Dr. Elihú J. Gutiérrez, Director of Public Health for the state of Baja California, asked for assistance in the planning of a large general hospital to be constructed in Mexicali, including its organization and operation after it was built. Ten years later a very different body, a group of 45 Seventh-day Adventist medical students at the University of Guadalajara requested similar assistance, and financial help, for a clinic and hospital they planned for nearby Ciudad Granja.[28]

As probably is only natural for an organization that is so medically oriented, Liga International is very involved in teaching medical skills. For a number of years its volunteers spent several

---

[27] Stephen Glenn Daly, "The Quality of Mercy—Life and Death on a Mexican Medical Mission," 1996, http://www.sandiegomag.com/forums/aviation/mercy2.shtml; and Ben Fox, "Friends Say Mexico Volunteers 'Wanted to Make a Difference,'" *The Riverside (California) Press-Enterprise*, 16 October 2000.

[28] Elijú J. Gutiérrez to I. [W.] S. Ritchie, 17 January 1954, copy in Ritchie Papers, SCLSU; and Charles E. von Pohle to Iner W. Ritchie, 2 February 1964, Ritchie Papers, SCLSU.

weekends every year at San José del Cabo, in the state of Baja California Sur, teaching Mexican physicians their specialties as they worked side by side to provide help for the poor. Liga also provided major assistance in the development of the schools of medicine, dentistry, and nutrition at the University of Montemorelos, the Seventh-day Adventist agricultural school Dr. Ritchie helped start in the state of Nuevo León, and for the formation and growth of the University of Navojoa in Sonora and Linda Vista University in Chiapas. In fact, if an early proposal had been put into effect, the latter would have been named "Ritchie Memorial University."[29]

In addition to providing health care and instruction to the rural poor in northern Mexico, only one year after the founding of its American chapter, Liga expanded to include medical and educational projects in the states of Oaxaca and Chiapas, in the southern part of the country.[30] In the 1950s it began to operate health clinics and to fund other programs throughout Central and South America. By 1975, in addition to continuing many of its earlier projects, it also offered programs to benefit the poor of Asia, Africa, and the South Pacific. Although headquartered in California, all of its services were, and still are, intended to help people living outside of the United States.[31]

---

[29] Liga International, Inc., *Hands Across the Border;* and Youngberg, "Tribute to Dr. Ritchie."

[30] Ibid.

[31] Schwarz, *Light Bearers to the Remnant,* 559; and "Aerospace Laureates, Operations: LIGA International, Inc.," *Aviation Week & Space Technology.*

Such a broadening of services could not have been accomplished without a significant growth in membership. From approximately 200 members shortly after its formation in 1948, Liga International expanded to approximately 2,000 members by the mid-1970s, a figure that has remained fairly static since then. Over last two decades of the twentieth century the number of Mexican clinics served on a regular basis has declined from seven to three—today all located in the state of Sinaloa. The decline occurred in part because of improvements in the delivery of health care in Mexico, but also because the number of affluent physicians has declined as the result of managed care in the United States. On the other hand, a new Liga Children's Heart Program begun in 1997 provided more than $1 million in services to children with heart defects in its first five years of operation. In 2000 the number of active volunteers—those serving on a regular basis—stood at more than 200. As was Dr. Ritchie himself for most of his adult life, "The Flying Doctors of Mercy" is a completely self-supporting missionary endeavor. It finances its activities with donations and grants, annual dues from its members, and through the personal involvement of its members and friends in its projects.[32]

---

[32] Schwarz, *Light Bearers to the Remnant*, 559; Liga International, Inc., "Hands Across the Border"; James Ott, Executive Director, Liga International, Inc., telephone interview by Delmer G. Ross, Riverside, California, 18 July 2000; I.M. Christianson, interview by D.G. Ross, Riverside, California, 17 July 2000; and Jackie Hanson, President, Liga International, Inc., telephone interview by Delmer G. Ross, 20 July 2000; and Richard Wilner, "The Liga Children's Heart Program," *Liga Flying Doctors of Mercy* (Winter 2003), 6. Liga receives grants from various sources. By 1994, for example, it had received two grants each from the Negri Foundation, the Million Dollar Round Table Foundation, and the Innovative Worthy Projects Foundation. "Grants

Sometimes the source of funding can be surprising. On one occasion a patient who had undergone surgery asked the surgeon what his fee would be. The physician explained that all medical services, including surgery were given without charge. The patient, however, insisted. So the doctor suggested that a donation to Liga would be helpful. Imagine the astonishment of Liga officials when the donation amounted to $30,000! It was used to create a revolving loan fund for students studying medicine and dentistry at schools outside the United States.[33]

Liga has worked on many projects to help people in other countries. Some have been relatively small, though not necessarily inexpensive, one-time ventures. These include providing a bulldozer for a resettlement project in Brazil, donating a small airplane to the Adventist church in Peru, improving the dairy herd belonging to River Plate College in Argentina with a donation of four thoroughbred bulls, and distributing literally hundreds of thousands of dollars worth of donated packets of seeds to help people improve their food crops on four continents. Others, like the three Adventist educational institutions of higher learning in Mexico that have received Liga support, the universities of Montemorelos, Navojoa, and Linda Vista, were major undertakings. Moreover, as can be seen, they are not all directly medically

---

Received," *Liga High Flying Times,* December 1993-January 1994, [6].

[33] Schwarz, *Light Bearers to the Remnant,* 559; and Robert N. Brown, *The Story of Liga* (Liga International, Inc., ca. 1968, 1-4.

related. They do, however, serve humanity and the church, which is exactly what Dr. Ritchie had in mind.[34]

While Liga International has accomplished much, it should be recognized that the concerns regarding control expressed by church officers were well founded. As long as Dr. Ritchie was alive, there was no problem. After his death, however, and especially after the reorganization in 1965 when it became officially non-sectarian, control of Liga International has slipped away from Seventh-day Adventists. By the year 2000 only one of its board members had any significant connection with Loma Linda University and the president was not an Adventist. Liga members continue to be very dedicated individuals, but their goals occasionally differ from those of Adventists. Although this change is regrettable, it should be recognized that Liga continues to benefit mankind.[35]

From the beginning, Liga has maintained a good working relationship with the Mexican government. Although at times a fee of as much as $130 per physician has been required before they have been allowed to practice medicine in Mexico, most of the time such fees have been waived and a simple proof of license and connection with an American hospital has been all that has been demanded.[36] Technically speaking, American health professionals from Liga serve under licensed Mexican physicians. Because of that important formality, and also because they do not charge for

[34] Schwarz, *Light Bearers to the Remnant*, 559.

[35] I.M. Christianson, interview by D.G. Ross, 17 July 2000.

[36] J. Ott, telephone interview by D.G. Ross, 18 July 2000.

their services, Liga doctors do not need to be licensed in Mexico. It is also a fact that more and more Mexican physicians are serving at Liga clinics. Jackie Hanson, who has run the San Blas clinic since 1984, notes that although one or two local physicians might have showed up in the 1980s, by 2000 it was not uncommon for there to be more Mexican than American doctors in attendance.[37] Moreover, because of Liga's cooperative attitude, the Mexican government usually waives the standard fees paid by entering airplanes and all import duties on medical equipment and supplies.[38]

One of Liga's most recent projects started late in 1999 when a physician at the El Carrizo, Sinaloa, clinic noticed that several of the children had suffered serious hearing losses. He obtained some inexpensive sound amplifiers from a Radio Shack store and took them with him a month later on his next trip. When he arrived a problem surfaced right away. Ten hard-of-hearing children showed up hoping for assistance, while he had planned on only the original four! He resolved that problem by taking another ten devices one month later. But he had the same problem because at least fifteen needy children showed up! Once it had been determined that many had suffered hearing losses as a result of childhood ear infections, the Starkey Foundation began providing refurbished hearing aids at the rate of one for every two used ones turned in, or for $50 each. By the end of the clinic season, in June 2000, Liga volun-

---

[37] J. Hanson, telephone interview by D.G. Ross, 20 July 2000; and I.M. Christianson, interview by D.G. Ross, 17 July 2000.

[38] J. Ott, telephone interview by D.G. Ross, 18 July 2000.

teers were fitting some fifty patients with hearing aids every month.[39]

Liga International has been singled out for a number of commendations and accolades, from sources as different as the editors of *Aviation Week,* which presented it with an Aerospace Laureate award; the Clergy Network, which honored it with the Clergy Network Award; and the Freedoms Foundation, which awarded Liga with its George Washington Medal of Honor.[40] Such organizations have been very favorably impressed with the unselfish dedication of Liga health professionals. In October 2003 Dr. Ritchie, founder of Liga, and Dr. Vernon Nickel, one of Dr. Ritchie's sons-in-law and a participant in Liga activities, were honored with a dedicated patio along the "Path of the Just" at La Sierra University in Riverside, California. The "Path of the Just" celebrates individuals such as Oscar Arias, Pearl S. Buck, and Mother Teresa who have performed exemplary service to humanity. If he could see what has been accomplished by the organization that he started back in the 1940s, in his humble, humanitarian way, Dr. Ritchie would have reason to be proud.

---

[39] Ibid.

[40] "Laurels 1991," *Aviation Week & Space Technology*, Vol. 136, No. 4 (27 January 1992); "Clergy Network Award," *Liga High Flying Times*, Summer 1995; and Liga, "The Flying Doctors of Mercy," http://www.liga-flyingdocs.org/liga_story.htm.

Liga and Educational Facilities

As is only appropriate for someone who had taught classes in health and hygiene for more than twenty-five years and who had taught anatomy for the school of medicine at the College of Medical Evangelists, Dr. Ritchie was very conscious of the value of education. It should not be at all surprising, therefore, that he contributed to the establishment of schools, including all three Seventh-day Adventist institutions of higher learning in Mexico. Moreover, both branches of Liga, organizations he helped found, have remained involved, providing equipment and funds for continued growth.

The University of Montemorelos is without any doubt the most prominent component of Dr. Ritchie's enduring legacy in education. From quite humble beginnings when it first opened for business as an agricultural school in 1942,[1] it has grown into a major educational and healthcare institution that offers degrees in a number of areas, including that of Doctor of Medicine. In fact, beginning in 1975 it has housed only the second full-fledged

---

[1] [Inelda May Christianson], *Iner Sheld-Ritchie, Founder of Liga, 1885-1949,* [Riverside: The Stahl Center, La Sierra University, ca. 1996], [3].

medical school operated by the Seventh-day Adventist church organization. While Dr. Ritchie was directly involved until the time of his death late in 1949, he has remained indirectly involved to the present through the influence of his fifteen years on the Mexican Union Mission Committee, through his contacts with Mexican government officials who remembered and appreciated him, and through the two organizations he helped found and which he managed for several years, the ACFE and the Liga, both of which were and are involved in continuing projects throughout Mexico.

The University of Montemorelos began as a concept and a seemingly impossible dream in the years prior to 1935 when Will K. Kellogg visited Mexico City in his private railroad car. He became seriously ill with double pneumonia, and his secretary-nurse called his friend, Dr. Ritchie, to attend him. As a result of conversations the two men had while the corn-flake entrepreneur,[2] regained his health, Kellogg reached the conclusion that schools combining offerings in agriculture, industrial science, and health might significantly alleviate rural health problems and poverty in Mexico.[3] Such an idea was not exactly new or original. A century

[2] W.K. Kellogg was best known for his Kellogg's Corn Flakes. For an often humorous yet perceptive view of the man and his times see Gerald Carson, "Cornflake Crusade," *American Heritage,* Vol. 8, No. 4 (June 1957), 65-85.

[3] Kellogg already was involved in the Kellogg Demonstration Farm at Michigan State College which was designed to help Michigan farmers. Copy of "Everybody in Michigan Owns Slice of this Farm," *Saginaw (Michigan) News,* 1 July 1948, in W.K. Kellogg to I.S. Ritchie, 20 January 1949, Ritchie Papers, SCLSU.

earlier Joseph Bates, who later became the senior founder of the Seventh-day Adventist Church, had been a part of a popular manual-labor school movement that hoped to accomplish much the same for youth in the United States.[4] Now, however, through his W.K. Kellogg Foundation, Kellogg donated funds to help build such a school at Montemorelos, Nuevo León. Dr. Ritchie was an enthusiastic and eloquent champion of the concept.[5]

It was at about this time that, in conjunction with Kellogg, Ramírez Villarreal, and others, Dr. Ritchie originated the idea that medical interns should spend a year of compulsory service in government institutions such as rural clinics and small hospitals immediately following graduation from medical school. In time this concept became Mexican policy and an integral part of the Mexican social security system.[6]

---

[4] George R. Knight, *Joseph Bates: The Real Founder of Seventh-day Adventism* (Hagerstown, Maryland: Review and Herald Publishing Association, 2004), 54, 210-212.

[5] [Iner William Ritchie], "History of Liga," three-page typescript, no place or date, 1, Ritchie Papers, SCLSU. Over the next two decades the W.K. Kellogg Foundation donated some $50,000 to the school. Iner W. Ritchie to Don Miller, 18 September 1956, copy in Ritchie Papers, SCLSU. Far more funds were channeled through Liga, especially Liga International. For example, between 1981 and 1989 it provided the University of Montemorelos with $60,000 for the establishment of a School of Dental Laboratory Technology, the first of its kind in Mexico. "Historic Review of Montemorelos," *Liga High Flying Times,* Vol 14 (December 1989); and Bill Heisler, "Ground Breaking at Montemorelos," *Liga High Flying Times,* Vol 14 (December 1989)

[6] [Iner W. Ritchie], "History," undated [ca. 1980s] 2-page manuscript, 2, Ritchie Papers, SCLSU.

After obtaining an orange grove known as La Carlota from the daughter of former Mexican president, General Plutarco Elías Calles, after construction began, and after a series of providential events involving wartime supplies steel, brick, cement, and electricity, the Escuela Agrícola e Industrial de México opened its doors to students late in 1942.[7] It was located along the Pan American Highway, less than a mile north of Montemorelos, Nuevo León. Mexican President Manuel Avila Camacho, was present for the official inauguration of the school on April 24, 1943. Other high-ranking politicians present included the state governor, General Salinas Castro Leal, and future president of Mexico, Miguel Alemán, whose sister was an Adventist and whose nephew studied at Montemorelos. Also in attendance were Dr. Ralph M. Smith and most of the members of Dr. Ritchie's family who, not knowing its future, had driven past the site of the school nearly a decade earlier on their way to Mexico City where the medical evangelist would take charge of the church's medical work in Mexico. In the beginning the new institution was only an unaccredited grade and high school, but it kept improving and growing. Progress in some areas, though, was slow. For example,

---

[7] C.P. Crager, "Providences Along the Way," *Inter-American Division Messenger,* Vol. 20, No. 6 (June 1943), 10; J. Marcos de León, "Historia de la Escuela," *Universidad de Montemorelos, Anuario 1945,* http://www.um.edu .mx/anuarios/1945/breve_historia.htm. The descendants of Dr. Ralph Smith recall that he provided the funds to purchase the grove where the school was to be built. Inelda May Ritchie, daughter of Dr. Iner S. Ritchie, telephone interview by Delmer G. Ross, Norco, California, 12 December 2003.

despite donations of modern equipment, for years it used a primitive ox-drawn cart to haul trash.[8]

Once the agricultural school was operating, what the missionary evangelist tried to get started was a church-operated medical clinic that could provide basic medical services as needed, and that would also offer courses in nursing, public health, and evangelism. Exactly how he expected to teach health evangelists is unclear. It appears probable that he expected the institution would offer classes such as those he and others had offered at the Tacubaya Clinic beginning in 1935. They had been short but intense classes that did not lead to any degree or recognized educational certificate. They had, however, resulted in the graduates receiving letters of recommendation and credentials as official government health workers. Those had proved most useful.

Already, in 1940, three Liga physicians, Drs. Ritchie, Raymundo Garza, and Harry Reynolds, had conducted an intensive medical missionary institute in Monterrey. Like the earlier Tacubaya institute, this was very well received. Dr. Garza then offered another in 1941.[9]

---

[8] Daddy [Iner S. Ritchie] et al. to Iner [W. Ritchie] et al., 18 May 1946, 4, Ritchie Papers, SCLSU; I.M. Ritchie, telephone interview by D.G. Ross, 12 December 2003; Inelda Ritchie Christianson, "Montemorelos Slide Commentary: Iner Sheld-Ritchie, M.D., Oct. 6, 1885 - Oct. 26, [sic] 1949," 7, eleven-page typescript in Ritchie Papers, SCLSU; and José Morales, "Un Día en la Escuela," *Universidad de Montemorelos, Anuario 1945,* http://www.um .edu.mx/anuarios/1945/un_dia.htm.

[9] Floyd Greenleaf, *The Seventh-day Adventist Church in Latin America and the Caribbean,* Vol. 2, *Bear the News to Every Land* (Berrien Springs, Michigan: Andrews University Press, 1992), 90-91.

What seemed lacking was a permanent place where more "health workers" and nurses could be trained to act as "entering wedges" for the gospel in communities throughout the nation, or, where Adventist churches already existed, they could establish new clinics that would help unite each church with its surrounding inhabitants. At first it had been thought that the best location would be the Monterrey Seventh-day Adventist Church where Dr. Garza was operating his very successful clinic. After two medical missionary institutes had been held there, though, it had become apparent that there simply was not enough room. Those most interested in the project then examined the possibility of establishing a new clinic at the new agricultural and industrial school already in operation in Montemorelos.[10]

Although formal action by the Mexican Union Committee was required before the decision to build the clinic at the Montemorelos site could be considered official, by mid-1944 that appeared to be the preferred location. The location gained even more acceptance when it was announced that Dr. Ritchie and his good friend and former partner, Dr. Ralph Smith, planned to move to Montemorelos to operate the clinic. Then a small hitch developed in the plans. Dr. Smith, who was chief surgeon at the church's Glendale Sanitarium and Hospital in California, decided that he could not do major surgery at a clinic. That problem was quickly resolved by upgrading the plans to provide for the construction of a hospital. Some of the Union Committee members, considering the cost and the impoverished state of Union

---

[10] Harold F. House, "The Entering Wedge in Mexico," *Inter-American Division Messenger,* Vol. 20, No. 12 (December 1943), 10.

finances, no doubt questioned the wisdom of the change. When at Dr. Smith's urging the Glendale Sanitarium and Hospital donated $15,000 for the construction of a hospital—not a clinic—their cautious approach lost support.[11]

The unexpected death of Dr. Smith in 1944 might have caused more reevaluation, but an added source of funding appeared at about the same time. Late in December 1944, after Dr. Ritchie had showed him the two proposed sites and the hospital construction in progress at Montemorelos, Emory W. Morris, president of the W.K. Kellogg Foundation, announced that his organization would be donating a significant sum to help finance the hospital project.[12]

When Dr. Ritchie arrived in Monterrey, Nuevo León, on March 2, 1945, he was already late for the annual Mexican Union Mission Committee meetings being held in that northeastern city. He arrived in time, though, to help deal with the matter that was his main concern—plans for a new hospital. The committee discussed and approved plans for construction at the school in Montemorelos and for the Mexican Union to help finance the venture.[13]

Because of Dr. Ritchie's two decades of experience and his extensive connections with people in both the public and private sectors, his would be the task obtaining necessary permissions at

[11] I.R. Christianson, "Montemorelos Slide Commentary," 7.

[12] Emory W. Morris to I.S. Ritchie, 26 December 1944, Ritchie Papers, SCLSU; and I.R. Christianson, "Montemorelos Slide Commentary," 8. The W.K. Kellogg Foundation offered as much as $45,000, half of the cost of construction, depending on matching funding from other sources.

[13] Ibid., 7.

the state and national levels. Moreover, for the same reason, and because the Union was far from wealthy, committee members looked to him to help complete the financing of the project, either through financial grants or through donations in kind.[14] Dr. Ritchie and Liga went to work. In fact, because one of the reasons for creating Liga was to help raise funds for hospital construction, it has been referred to as Liga's "first project." The missionary physician's efforts brought in a major share of the needed money, and he provided generously from his own funds as well.[15]

Once the issues of where and what to build had finally been decided, the next step was to try to obtain not only approval, but also active assistance, from the governor of Nuevo León, Arturo B. de la Garza. Because he was very much in favor of improving medical facilities for the people of his state, and the proposed facility would be in a position to distribute vaccinations and to provide needed medications to the underprivileged, it was expected that the governor would endorse the project. But would he also become a participant and provide assistance when needed? A team of physicians, including Dr. Ritchie, arranged to meet with the governor. After they had explained what they hoped to

---

[14] Elizabeth Vodeb and Andrew Howe, "Dr. Ritchie's Relationship with Mexican Governors" (term paper presented for HIST 294/494, History Colloquium, La Sierra University, Riverside, California, 29 November 1995), 2, D.G. Ross Collection, HPSLSU.

[15] F. Greenleaf, *The Seventh-day Adventist Church in Latin America,* Vol. 2, 251; and Matthew Park and Allison Rice, "The Financial Aspect of Building Montemorelos Hospital" (term paper presented for HIST 294/494, History Colloquium, La Sierra University, Riverside, California, 29 November 1995), 2, D.G. Ross Collection, HPSLSU

accomplish, he enthusiastically approved and not unexpectedly pledged to do all he could to help.[16]

Help, as it turned out, was required right away. The owner of the property needed for construction of the school hospital refused to sell it to Protestants, regardless of the reason or the offered price. Because her priest had told her not to sell, she was not going to. Period. When the governor was informed of the situation, the stalemate soon was over. The state properly expropriated the needed property and, for a price of 14,000 pesos—about U.S.$ 3,000—transferred title to the ACFE. The price was so low that the transaction was generally viewed as a gift from the state to help speed the construction of the desired medical facility.[17]

More than a year earlier, as general manager of the ACFE, Dr. Ritchie had written to President Manuel Avila Camacho informing him of the plan to use funds donated by private parties in Mexico and the United States to construct a hospital on school property in Montemorelos. The president had responded cordially, stating that once the project was under way, and acting within parameters established by law, his government would make available "the facilities necessary for the realization of your works and . . . will examine the possibilities of cooperating . . . economically."[18]

---

[16] Vodeb and Howe, "Dr. Ritchie's Relationship," 2.

[17] Hospital y Sanatorio Montemorelos, *Cofía y Azahares, 1957: X Aniversario del Hospital y Sanatorio Montemorelos* (Montemorelos, Nuevo León: Hospital y Sanatorio Montemorelos, 1959), 8; and Vodeb and Howe, "Dr. Ritchie's Relationship," 3.

[18] M. Avila Camacho to I.S. Ritchie, 16 March 1944, translated copy in Ritchie Papers, SCLSU.

Well might the president reply favorably. His administration fostered programs to reduce illiteracy, to expand industry, to introduce new techniques in agriculture, and to provide medical care for all Mexicans, with emphasis on the needs of rural areas. President Avila Camacho's goals in these areas were virtually the same as those of Dr. Ritchie and the Adventist church in Mexico.[19]

Therefore, once construction was under way, and because the institution at Montemorelos needed help with several different matters, it was time to contact the president again. Although there were a few difficulties arranging for an interview, in time a commission of five persons, including Dr. Iner S. Ritchie, Harold F. House, Dr. Raymundo Garza, and Attorney Francisco Ramírez Villarreal, all of the ACFE, met with him at his retreat, La Soledad, in the state of Veracruz. There he promised to make arrangements for the immigration of Dr. Ritchie's son, Dr. Iner William Ritchie, who was scheduled to become director of the hospital; John Ewing, who was to be school administrator; and Herald Habenicht, who was to be the farm manager at Montemorelos. The president also pledged quick delivery of an already promised printing press and related equipment needed to establish a printing industry at the school.[20]

---

[19] Norman Karlow and Antoinette Paris, "Dr. Ritchie's Relationship with President [Manuel Avila] Camacho" (term paper presented for HIST 294/494, History Colloquium, La Sierra University, Riverside, California, 24 April 1994), 2, D.G. Ross Collection, HPSLSU.

[20] Harold F. House, *Interview with President Gral. Manual Avila Camacho,* 24 May 1945, copy in Ritchie Papers, SCLSU.

While President Avila Camacho kept his word, and the men and equipment arrived, Dr. Iner William Ritchie did not become the first administrator of the hospital at Montemorelos. The hospital was not yet finished when he and his family arrived following World War II. During parts of 1945 and 1946, while he waited for his position to become active, he worked with Dr. Raymundo Garza at a clinic quartered in the basement of the Monterrey Seventh-day Adventist Church. While putting in long hours there he learned that his own father was paying his salary because of budget constraints of the Mexican Union. That would not do. It meant that Dr. Ritchie's practice in Riverside was supporting two families, and that at a time when his father's health was not good. So Iner William and his family returned to California, and Dr. Hersel Butka became the school's first medical director.[21]

The new 20-bed hospital opened in January 1947. President Miguel Alemán was present at the inaugural ceremony. The associated nursing school began in 1948, and in 1949 the hospital's occupancy rate approached 95 percent.[22] Within ten years related services had found other space and hospital capacity had

---

[21] I.R. Christianson, *Montemorelos Slide Commentary*, 10.

[22] F. Greenleaf, *The Seventh-day Adventist Church in Latin America*, Vol. 2, 252-53; Heidi Serena and Paul Negrete, "Dr. Iner S. Ritchie's Relationship with Mexican Presidents" (term paper presented for HIST 294/494, History Colloquium, La Sierra University, Riverside, California, 6 December 1995), [3], D.G. Ross Collection, HPSLSU; Barbara O. Westphal, "Good News from Mexico," *Inter-American Division Messenger*, Vol 26, No. 11-S (November 1949): 7; and Alex R. Monteith, "Our Medical Work in Mexico," *Inter-American Division Messenger*, Vol. 26, No. 12 (December 1949), 7.

increased to 64 beds, and that soon was not large enough to handle the demand. Thus a new, modern hospital with a capacity of 150 beds was built and inaugurated in 1981.[23]

The inauguration of the Montemorelos Hospital and Sanitarium in 1947.

Air ambulance service using the hospital's own landing strip was added not long after the hospital first opened for business, enabling patients in remote areas to make use of hospital facilities. Air service also made it feasible for hospital personnel to hold

---

[23] Hospital y Sanatorio Montemorelos, *Cofia y Azahares, 1957,* 8. The old hospital structure then was occupied by other university departments, including the School of Education. Inelda May Christianson, daughter of Iner S. Ritchie, interview by Delmer G. Ross, Riverside, California, 25 July 2004.

clinics and offer health presentations in isolated areas far removed from the hospital itself.[24]

Located on more than 200 acres of land and thus still having room to grow, the University of Montemorelos now provides instruction in medicine, education, engineering, business administration, theology, and other fields. Its School of Nursing recently celebrated 55 years of preparing students to serve those who are ill and hurting.[25]

Despite laws prohibiting the teaching of religion in elementary schools and prohibiting any priest or pastor from grade-school teaching,[26] in 1948 the Mexican Union Committee issued a call to Elder William Baxter to be Professor of Bible at the school in Montemorelos. There obviously was a plan afoot for the institution to provide more than just instruction in farming methods and the trades. Immediately before this particular action, the Committee had voted to facilitate a colporteur institute at Montemorelos, so that students who wished to attend might be able to earn scholarships.[27] While claiming not to teach religion in schools held by the

---

[24] David Zinke, "Hospital with Air Service," *Tropic Topics,* Vol. 5, No. 1 (January 1954), 3.

[25] Libna Stevens, "Mexico: Adventist University Celebrates 61 Years of Educating Students," http://www.interamericana.org/users/index.php?type =news&id-18&language=en.

[26] Ivan M. Angell, "Mexican Agricultural and Industrial School," *Inter-American Division Messenger,* Vol. 20, No.9 (September 1943), 4-5.

[27] Junta de la Unión Mexicana, "Minutas de la Unión," 5 May 1948, copy in Ritchie Papers, SCLSU.

ACFE,[28] it appears that some religious instruction was offered at the secondary level. In fact, it was recognized as early as 1942 that, barring problems, the school at Montemorelos would eventually become the first training school for denominational workers in Mexico. Prior to the welcome opening of that school, according to official Mexican Union sources, "The only [C]hristian education that ou[r] children and young people could acquire was by means of the Sabbath School and by means of the Missionary Volunteer Societies." The same source reported that "Most of our workers . . . have been trained in a special short course" offered at Tacubaya. "But now," it added, "our whole outlook for the future has changed because of the bright prospects at the new school."[29]   Today the University of Montemorelos remains the principal worker training school in that country, although such instruction is also offered at the University of Navojoa and Linda Vista University.

Feeling that something typically Mexican could help promote the school, Dr. Ritchie had a *marimba de lujo* (luxury marimba) built in Tuxtla Gutiérrez in 1944. He then donated it to the

---

[28] Regarding Adventist schools in Mexico a semi-official source states unequivocally, "In harmony with the law, these schools are not operated by the church but by an independent organization, the Asociación Civil Filantrópica y Educativa . . . , and religion is not taught in the classroom." Don F. Neufeld, ed., *Seventh-day Adventist Encyclopedia*, Rev. ed., (Washington, D.C.: Review & Herald Publishing Association, 1966), s.v. "Mexico, Departmental Work, Educational Work."

[29] H.F. House, *Report of the Superintendent of the Mexican Union Mission*, (Monterrey, N. L., 28 February 1944), 3. Se also Glenn Calkins, "A New Institution in Mexico," *Inter-American Division Messenger*, Vol. 19, No. 11 (1 December 1942), 3-4.

growing institution.[30] It was an inspired gift. Used by skilled marimba-playing students to provide music for everything from birthday parties for campus faculty members to sessions of the General Conference of the Seventh-day Adventist Church, it generated immeasurable quantities of recognition and good will over the years.

Dr. Ritchie was a visionary, but it seems unlikely that he seriously imagined anything like what UM has become. Thanks to funds and equipment donated by Liga and many other sources, the 1970s proved to be a time of great expansion for the school. Not only did it become an accredited university in 1973, but from 173 students at the college level at that time, enrollment quickly ballooned to 529 by 1977.[31] More recently, in 2003 enrollment very nearly reached 1,600 students.

In honor of his vision the university awarded Dr. Ritchie a posthumous Medal of Honor during its fiftieth anniversary celebration in 1992. A bronze bust of Dr. Ritchie was unveiled in the new hospital on the occasion of its fiftieth anniversary in 1996.

---

[30] Vicente Rodríguez to Y. [Iner] S. Ritchie, no date [ca. 1944]; and I.M. Christianson, telephone interview by D.G. Ross, 30 November 2003.

[31] Iglesia Adventista del 7mo. Día Apocalipsis 14, "Historia: Acontecimientos importantes en la historia de la Iglesia Adventista del Séptimo Día," 3, http://www.apocalipsis14.org/historia.html; and Walton J. Brown, "The Six Miracles of Montemorelos," *Advent Review and Sabbath Herald,* 30 June 1977, 1, 19-21. Total on-campus enrollment at all levels in 1977 was 1,212 students. Ibid.

At the same time the university announced the establishment of the Iner Sheld-Ritchie, M.D. Scholarship.[32]

During the fiftieth anniversary celebration of the Montemorelos Hospital, Inelda Ritchie Chistianson and Anna Ritchie Nickel at the unveiling of the bust of their father in the lobby of the new hospital.

Although very medically oriented, Liga International also shares in efforts to provide people with a good and useful general

[32] Universidad de Montemorelos, "Announcing the Iner Sheld-Ritchie, M.D. Scholarship," 14-16 November 1996, Ritchie Papers, SCLSU. The bust is flanked by those of Drs. Raymundo Garza and Hersel Butka, placed slightly lower than Dr. Ritchie's. I.M. Christianson, interview by D.G. Ross, 25 July 2004.

education. It has participated in the establishment of a number of self-supporting agricultural and industrial schools designed to help students learn useful skills. One of the earliest, and the second largest of these, with accommodations for several hundred students, is today's Universidad de Navojoa, in the northwestern Mexican state of Sonora. Located on property donated to Liga by Frank Byerly, an American businessman holding Mexican citizenship, it opened late in 1948. Once it had been greatly enlarged and its various industries had become profitable enough to make the school self-sustaining, Liga turned it over to the North Mexican Union so that it could concentrate on other projects. Positioned on more than 700 acres of some of the best farm land in the state, the school specializes in teaching agricultural and mechanical skills while offering courses in other disciplines as well.[33]

It all began in 1917 when Frank Byerly and his wife moved from Montana to Navojoa where he engaged in hardware and hotel businesses. He prospered, and wishing to return some of that prosperity to the people who had made it possible, he conceived a plan to open a school where youth from Navojoa and the surrounding area could develop agricultural and industrial skills

---

[33] "Liga Projects Progress on Four Fronts," *Official Bulletin of the American Chapter, Liga México-Pan-American Médico Educacional*, No. 1 (January - February 1949), 2; Harry C. Nelson, "The Navojoa Industrial School," *Official Bulletin of the American Chapter, Liga México-Pan-American Médico Educacional*, No. 2 (October 1949), 5-6; and Inelda May Christianson, daughter of Dr. Iner S. Ritchie, interview by Delmer G. Ross, Riverside, California, 17 July 2000.

and learn crafts and trades. It was the same concept that Dr. Ritchie was discussing with W.K. Kellogg at about the same time.

Byerly bought 125 acres of fertile land in the Mayo River valley. It was located along the Navojoa-Huatabampo road at a place known as El Sicoma, about eight miles southwest of Navojoa. He drilled wells, put up wind mills, developed an irrigation system, and erected several substantial brick buildings on the site. Then he hired personnel to run his school. For whatever reason, however, it did not prosper.

Eventually Byerly had to close it. School land then was used to pasture cattle, and the buildings were used as stables. Byerly, of course, was very disappointed. He did not give up his dream, though.

Several years later Frank Byerly and a friend, Alberto Maas, from nearby Alamos were discussing Mexico's various needs. Byerly told his friend about his failed technical school and his continuing belief that such an institution could be of real benefit to the entire region. Maas, a former correspondent for the *Los Angeles Times* and the Associated Press in Mexico, agreed, and wondered why the school could not be reopened. If lack of expertise in the operation of agricultural and industrial schools was the problem, he might be able to help. Only a year earlier he had become acquainted with an organization of physicians from southern California that was very interested in exactly that kind of school in Mexico. Moreover, he thought the group already operated at least one, just outside Montemorelos, in the state of Nuevo León. If Maas could arrange a meeting, would Byerly be interested in discussing the matter with one or more members of that group?

Would he be interested? Oh, yes! Indeed he would!

Maas promptly contacted Dr. Harry C. Nelson, of Santa Ana, California. Dr. Nelson then got in touch with fellow Liga members, Doctors Iner S. Ritchie and T. Gordon Reynolds. Definitely interested in trade schools for Mexico, and wondering what Byerly might have in mind, the three men boarded a train for Mexico. Upon their arrival in Navojoa, Dr. Reynolds and Byerly recognized each other immediately. Byerly had been one of Dr. Reynolds's patients several years earlier when he had been operating his hospital and nursing school in Esperanza, not fifty miles north of Navojoa.

The representatives of Liga rode out to the site of the school with Byerly. What they saw was both encouraging and discouraging. The land was as fertile as ever. The school buildings, however, while for the most part still basically sound, would require extensive repairs. The physicians could see the possibilities, though. Byerly saw in these men of experience exactly what he needed to make his dream of an agricultural and industrial school flourish. He offered to donate the property to Liga if it would reopen and operate the school.[34]

After touring the property, Dr. Ritchie and other members of the Mexican Union Committee met in the Hotel Byerly in Navojoa on March 17, 1948, and formally voted to accept Frank Byerly's

---

[34] Ed Ainsworth, "Mexican Waifs Educated in U.S.-Financed School," *Los Angeles Times,* 18 June 1950, Part 2, 1, 3.

offer. They also voted several measures designed to provide financing for the school project.[35]

Hoping to reopen the school for the upcoming school year, Liga people immediately got busy cleaning and making repairs. It was almost a month later that Liga's attorney, Francisco Ramírez Villarreal, showed up to finalize the transfer of ownership to the Mexican branch of Liga and to deal with related legal matters.[36]

Frank Byerly was delighted to see the Escuela Agrícola e Industrial del Pacífico (Pacific Agricultural and Industrial School) open for business in September, only six months after he had donated the property. The first of its 23 students on opening day was "a little bootblack waif" named Jesús "Chuy" Ramírez. Sponsored at $10 per month by Alberto Maas, young Ramírez was also the first graduate of the school, doing so with high honors and grade scores that averaged 99 percent. During its early years, many of its students were so sponsored.

The official inauguration of the school took place almost a month after the beginning of classes. After all the speeches—including one by a beaming Frank Byerly—those present were treated to sandwiches and dessert prepared by the home economics class. Unfortunately Byerly did not live to see

---

[35] Junta de la Unión Mexicana, "Minutas de la Unión," Voto 1754 - 1758, 17 March 1948, Navojoa, Sonora, copy in Ritchie Papers, SCLSU.

[36] "Una Escuela Agrícola e Industrial," *Diario del Mayo* (Navojoa, Sonora), 10 April 1948, 1, 2; Harry C. Nelson, "The Navajoa [*sic*] Industrial School," *Official Bulletin of the American Chapter, Liga México-Pan-American Médico Educacional,* No 2 (October 1949), 5-6.

any students graduate. He died in an airplane crash on his ranch in March 1949.[37]

He did have the satisfaction of seeing the school become a key distribution center for food, clothing, and other types of assistance provided by Liga during the disastrous Mayo River basin floods of early 1949. With Liga's help, Byerly's donation had already become a positive influence.[38]

The school at Navojoa grew rapidly at first. By 1950 attendance had more than doubled to 63 students.[39] In addition to donating thousands of dollars, individual members of Liga worked on specific projects to try to help the school. For example, right after the Mexican Union Committee voted to accept Frank Byerly's generous offer, Dr. Ritchie contacted his friend, General Abelardo Rodríguez. At the time the General was governor of Sonora and thus was in a position to provide state assistance as well as using his influence in Mexico City to obtain help from the national government. What Dr. Ritchie requested was for help to arrange the duty-free importation of needed materials and equipment. General Rodríguez immediately contacted a friend in the national capital, and although it took some time, such a permit was granted. Dr. Harry C. Nelson worked to acquire a government

[37] E. Ainsworth, "Mexican Waifs Educated"; and "Magnífica Fiesta Hubo en una Inauguración," *Diario del Mayo (Navojoa, Sonora),* 19 October 1948, 1, 4.

[38] "Liga Acts in Emergency Flood Relief," *Official Bulletin of the American Chapter, Liga México-Pan-American Médico Educacional,* No. 1 (January - February 1949), 1.

[39] E. Ainsworth, "Mexican Waifs Educated."

surplus bakery—and much other needed equipment over the years. Following the example of his father who had provided one to the school at Montemorelos, Dr. Iner W. Ritchie donated a marimba.[40] Others did much the same.

While most such assistance helped to stimulate the growth of the school, growth itself created problems such as inadequate dormitory space, inadequate sewage disposal systems, the need for more student employment opportunities, and the need for buildings for administration, an auditorium, and on-campus faculty. Such problems were solved over time and with the financial help of special church offerings, the Mexican Union and its component areas, the American branch of Liga, and individuals and entities such as Health Education Food Service Enterprises, Inc. (HEFSE), a non-profit corporation connected with the School of Tropical and Preventive Medicine of CME. Along with the American Liga, by fostering institutional industries HEFSE helped the school at Navojoa become largely self supporting.[41]

Strange things may happen on any airplane flight, but they seemed to happen more often than usual on Liga flights to Mexico.

[40] Abelardo L. Rodríguez to Iner Sheld Ritchie, 27 March 1948, Ritchie Papers, SCLSU; Abelardo L. Rodríguez to Nazario S. Ortiz Garza, 27 March 1948, Ritchie Papers, SCLSU; Harry [C. Nelson] to Iner [S. Ritchie], 15 April 1948, Ritchie Papers, SCLSU; and L.A. Wheeler to Iner W. Ritchie, 11 June 1958, Ritchie Papers, SCLSU.

[41] "STPM Assists Navojoa School," *Tropic Topics,* Vol. 8, No. 3 (July 1957), 2; Joseph Pierce, *The HEFSE Plan,* Health Education Food Service Enterprises, Inc., San Bernardino, California, no date, 1-4; Liga México-Pan-Americana Médico Educacional, *Semiannual Report,* Los Angeles, June 1958, 1; and Iner W.S. Ritchie, *Navojoa School Project,* Liga México-Pan-Americana Médico Educacional, no place or date), 2-4.

One such event occurred in connection with the school at Navojoa. In order to start a dairy at the school Liga members flew in registered calves to be the nucleus of the dairy herd. The calves were tranquilized to keep them quiet during the flight, but one awoke and began staggering drunkenly and unhappily about the airplane! All turned out well, though, and the dairy eventually became a major attraction at the school.[42]

Serious financial difficulties caused the school to be closed in 1965. When it reopened in 1967, it did so as the Colegio del Pacífico. At the time of reopening it had 90 students and 16 faculty members. It has grown steadily since then.

The major money crop on the school's farm turned out to be wheat. Dr. Ritchie, who had been amazed to see heads of wheat measuring as much as eleven inches long and containing as many as seventy grains each growing in the nearby Yaqui River valley back in 1929 might have predicted that. During its first year of existence the farm produced 50 tons of wheat, by 1951 after a well had been drilled it became possible to plant two crops per year, and by 1973 the net profit from wheat alone was $100,000 U.S. Mexican President Luis Echeverría visited the school on Christmas day that year, leaving a gift of U.S.$8,000 plus promises of other types of assistance. At last the school was able to support itself, and in January 1974, for the first time since 1948, there was

---

[42] Liga México-Pan-Americana Médico Educacional, Report, Los Angeles, [California], October 1963, 3-4, Ritchie file, WebbLLU.

no request for funds for the school or any related projects in the Liga newsletter.[43]

The school continued to grow. In 1995 the State of Sonora authorized it to offer higher degrees as the College of the Pacific campus of the University of Montemorelos. While that may have caused some confusion, it did not last long. In 2001 the state of Sonora authorized it to grant its own degrees as the University of Navojoa.[44] The new northwestern school remains the smallest of Adventist universities in Mexico, with an enrollment of 330 students in 2003.

Because of his death, Dr. Ritchie's direct personal involvement with the school at Navojoa stopped in 1949. He continued to be involved after his death, though, through the Liga, which is still very much alive.

Because at first glance it appears to have been started in the late1950s it might seem that Dr. Ritchie could at most have played only an indirect role in the founding of yet another institution of higher learning, Linda Vista University. That, however, was not the case. His role was both direct and prominent.

The reason that is so is that Linda Vista was not begun at its present location on the former Finca Santa Cruz near Pueblo Nuevo, Solistahuacán, Chiapas, but at Teapa, Tabasco. Beginning

---

[43] Juan Gil, "Escuela de Navojoa, Son.," *Salud y Saber,* Vol. 1, No. 4 (August 1949), 3; Juan Gil, "Navojoa Boarding School, a Living Miracle," *Inter-American Division Messenger,* Vol. 29, No. 4
(April 1952), 7-8; and John Baerg to [Liga International membership], 22 January 1974, Ritchie Papers, SCLSU.

[44] Universidad de Navojoa, "Historia de Nuestra Institución," http://www.unav.edu.mx/sec/acerca_de/historia.htm.

in 1948, the school functioned at Teapa for ten years before it was moved.[45]

Because of the tropical climate of much of the region, southern Mexico was the first area to be considered seriously by CME as a location for a field station or laboratory for the study of tropical medicine. Even though travel was difficult because WWII was yet being fought, once the proper priority had been obtained from the Mexican government, Dr. Ritchie, his son, Dr. Iner W. Ritchie, several members of the Mexican Union Mission Committee, and other interested parties toured extensively in the states of Tabasco and Chiapas to try to locate a good place to establish a school and possibly a hospital in southern Mexico. The final decision came after Dr. Ritchie and about a dozen others for several days were flown over various properties in a plane provided without charge by the Mexican airline, Compañía Mexicana de Aviación. They very closely examined a number of properties, including a ranch and other possibilities near Tuxtla Gutiérrez, the state capital of Chiapas, and at least one near Teapa, Tabasco. They also visited the state of Yucatán. Although the two-week trip doubtless was tiring, Dr. Ritchie was pleased with what they had accomplished, and in a letter written from Tapachula, Chiapas, to his "Darling Sweetheart Inelda," he wrote that he expected a final decision before the journey was over. He apparently favored a location near Tuxtla Gutiérrez, but the decision was to establish the school at Teapa. Dr. Ritchie flew home on regularly scheduled flights of Pan American Airways and Amer-

---

[45] Universidad Linda Vista, "Nuestra Historia," November 2002, http://www.ulv.edu.mx/remembranza.html.

ican Airlines, although, because of wartime conditions, the final segment of his journey had to be approved by the United States embassy in Mexico City.[46]

When members of the Seventh-day Adventist church in Chiapas learned of the possibility of the establishment of a school in Teapa, Tabasco, they were delighted. Although in a different state, Teapa was not far from where the majority of Adventist youth in Chiapas lived, and they and their parents eagerly looked forward to the day when the school would open. They hoped to be able to obtain "a good Christian education" there.[47]

Not everyone who supported a different location felt that the decision to establish the school in Teapa was final, and some continued to lobby in favor of their preferred sites. Even congressmen got in on the act. For example, Deputy Eliseo Argon R. wrote in favor of establishing "a great medical clinic for the study and cure of the endemic diseases of this region and also for the

[46]   Iner W.S. Ritchie, "Liga México-Pan-Americana Medico [*sic*] Educacional," three-page typescript, Riverside, California, 23 July 1974, 2, Ritchie Papers, SCLSU; and [Iner S. Ritchie] to Darling Sweetheart Inelda [Ruth Ritchie], Thursday, [September 1948], Ritchie file, WebbLLU. Apparently someone has added a month and year, September 1948, to date the letter, but that appears to be in error. Because it is known that Dr. Ritchie was involved in a trip to find a location for a school in southern Mexico in March 1945, because World War II was still in progress, and because the school at Teapa opened in 1948, it seems probable that the correct year is 1945. Iner Sheld Ritchie and H.F. House, "Interviews with Mexican Government Officials Relative to New Medical and Educational Institutions," a six-page typed report, no place, 1945, 3-5, Ritchie Papers, SCLSU.

[47]   Max Fuss, *Informe de la Misión de Chiapas, 1947* (Tuxtla Gutiérrez, Chiapas: Misión Adventista del Séptimo Día, December 1947): 4.

advancement of our professional youth" in his home state of Morelos.[48]

For the time being, though, the decision to locate in Teapa stood firm. In addition to a school there, plans were to establish a clinic that would expand to a hospital and would become a center for the study of tropical diseases. Of course, money had to be raised before construction could begin. In 1947 Dr. Ritchie, accompanied by Harold House and George S. Smisor traveled to Tabasco. Smisor, a photographer, took pictures to be used to help the Liga México-Pan-Americana Médico Educacional y de Trabajadores Sociales raise money for the construction program. These efforts appear to have been successful because the school began operations in 1948, with its official dedication taking place on the national *Cinco de mayo* holiday.[49]

The planned clinic, however, remained incomplete. In 1949 the California branch of Liga issued appeals that, among other things, announced the possibility of using monkeys found in the jungle surrounding Teapa in cancer research and promised that members would have access to the facility for their own related study or research once it was built. Late that year it was reported that some $4,000 yet needed to be raised.[50]

---

[48] Eliseo Argon R. to I.S. Ritchie, 28 August 1946, Ritchie Papers, SCLSU.

[49] The holiday celebrates the Mexican victory over an invading French army at Puebla on May 5, 1862.

[50] I.R. Christianson, "Montemorelos Slide Commentary," 10; Clarence E. Nelson to Our Fellow Alumni, Members and Friends, [1949], (on Liga stationery), copy in Ritchie Papers, SCLSU; Stephen A Youngberg to Iner S. Richey [*sic*], 5 May 1948, Ritchie Papers, SCLSU; and Stephen Youngberg,

The necessary funds continued to be donated, though, and the clinic and hospital building was finished in 1950. Known as "Hospital Doctor Ritchie," it did not open for business immediately because it lacked everything from laboratory equipment to patient beds—and Dr. Youngberg and his family were living in the surgical unit. Once equipment had been obtained and the physician and his family had moved into their newly constructed home, the hospital opened officially on July 27, 1952. Unfortunately, because of illness Dr. Youngberg soon was forced to leave the Ritchie Memorial Clinic. After that, because of the lack of permanent, full-time physicians and other staff members, the clinic and hospital functioned only sporadically.[51]

Unfortunately, the location at Teapa was not the best. Lowland tropical diseases were altogether too common, and students, teachers, and physicians and nurses often were laid low by them. Despite a government fumigation program designed to eradicate mosquitos, as one visitor put it, "The continual hum of the insects made it impossible to stay, either for foreigners or

---

"Liga Convoy Reaches Teapa," *Official Bulletin of the American Chapter, Liga México-Pan-American Médico Educacional,* No. 2 (October 1949), 4.

[51] I.R. Christianson, "Montemorelos Slide Commentary," 10; "Teapa, Mexico," *Bulletin* [of the American Chapter,] *Liga México-Pan-American Médico Educacional,* No. 8 (March 1952), 1; Barbara O. Westphal, "The Ritchie Memorial Clinic," *Inter-American Division Messenger,* Vol. 29, No. 6 (June 1952), 7; "News Notes from Mexico," *Inter-American Division Messenger,* Vol. 29, No. 9 (September 1952), 7; Arthur H. Roth, "The Mexican Union Session," *Inter-American Division Messenger,* Vol. 29, Nos. 10, 11 (October-November 1952), 10-11; and D.F. Neufeld, ed., Seventh-day Adventist Encyclopedia, s.v. "Mexico, Departmental Work, Medical Work."

employees." He added that even "the natives were ill."[52] More-over, the forty acres of land on which its buildings were located proved to be too small to allow for needed student industries, and there was no reasonable way to expand without involving govern-ment agencies and possibly using eminent domain and running the very real risk of negative reaction from the townspeople.

The leaders of Liga and the Mexican Union inspected the school and hospital at Teapa in 1954 and decided to try to find a more healthful location. So the search for a good site got under way again.[53]

The Teapa campus was sold in the mid-1950s and the school moved to a new location at a much higher elevation in Chiapas—ironically at a site only 100 miles east of Tuxtla Gutiérrez, much like Dr. Ritchie had favored a decade earlier.[54] Despite the change in location, the Liga continued to be very much involved in what was then known as Colegio Linda Vista. For example, when the need for a dairy herd became obvious, a group of Liga physicians from southern Texas sponsored it. In addition

---

[52] [Iner W. Ritchie], "History of Liga," no place, no date, 2, Ritchie Papers, SCLSU.

[53] Ibid.; H[orace] Kelley to Friend [Iner W. Ritchie], no date [mid-1958], 1, Ritchie Papers, SCLSU; and Gregory T. Cushman and Matthew Perry, "From Teapa to Linda Vista: Dr. Iner S. Ritchie's Vision for Southern Mexico" (term paper presented for HIST 294/494, History Colloquium, La Sierra University, Riverside, California, 27 April 1994), D.G. Ross Collection, HPSLSU.

[54] Iner W.S. Ritchie to The Max and Victoria Dreyfus Foundation, Inc., 17 March 1989, Ritchie Papers, SCLSU; and I.R. Christianson, "Montemorelos Slide Commentary," 10.

to his efforts to help through Liga, Dr Ritchie's elder son, Dr. Iner W. Ritchie, apparently donated the cost of not just one, but two marimbas for the new school.[55]

Today known as Linda Vista University, the humble institution begun more than a half century ago with about sixty elementary and secondary students has grown and prospered. In 2003 it offered advanced training in several areas—from accounting and business administration to education and theology—to nearly 400 students, mainly from southern Mexico.[56]

In any account of Dr. Ritchie's role in Liga, higher education, and Mexico some mention should be made of classes in tropical medicine at Boca del Río, a small coastal town in the state of Veracruz. The project was publicized as "the first one in denominational history that takes undergraduates from any Seventh-day Adventist college into the mission field to acquaint them with future problems they may encounter in mission life."[57] It thus anticipated modern student-missionary programs. Initially arranged by Dr. Ritchie, Liga, the National University of Mexico, and the School of Tropical and Preventive Medicine of CME as the result of an offer made by the Mexican government in 1947, it was headed by Dr. Bruce W. Halstead until 1953. It was housed in

[55] I.W.S. Ritchie, "Liga," 23 July 1974, 2; H. Kelley to Friend, no date, 2; and Mike Kelley to Inelda [May Christianson], 22 October 2004, Ritchie Papers, SCLSU.

[56] Paul and Lorna Allred to Friends [Warren and Inelda M. Christianson], 5 December 1962, Ritchie Papers, SCLSU; and U. Linda Vista, "Nuestra Historia."

[57] Milton Murray, "Boca del Río, Mexico," *Inter-American Division Messenger,* Vol. 26, No. 10 (October 1949), 8.

a new, large, two-story building located only one hundred yards from a sandy beach on the Gulf of Mexico. Staffing was provided by professors from CME and the University of Mexico and by scientists from the Institute of Tropical Diseases of Mexico City, most of whom were members of Liga. Courses taught at the Boca del Río "field station," led to a number of CME students studying tropical medicine in an almost equatorial setting beginning in 1949. Although the project was of relatively short duration, the favorable publicity it generated helped improve the reputation of CME and Adventist schools generally. Because the school at Montemorelos was one of the places visited by the students attending classes at the field station, its reputation was enhanced as well.[58]

One historian, in evaluating the role of Liga in developing institutions of higher education for the Seventh-day Adventist church in Mexico, speculated that "without Liga they might not have existed at all."[59] Certainly they would not exist in their present configuration.

---

[58] F.Greenleaf, *The Seventh-day Adventist Church in Latin America,* Vol. 2, 253; [Iner W. Ritchie], "History of Liga," 2; Milton Murray, "The School of Tropical and Preventive Medicine," *Inter-American Division Messenger,* Vol. 26, No. 11 (November 1949), 2-3; Harold N. Mozar, "School Offers Field Course in Tropical Medicine," *The Journal of the Alumni Association. School of Medicine, College of Medical Evangelists,* Vol. 20, No. 7 (July 1949), 14; "Summer Course in Tropical Medicine," *The Journal of the Alumni Association, School of Medicine, College of Medical Evangelists,* Vol. 21, No. 6 (June 1950), 12; and "Field Course in Mexico," *Tropic Topics,* Vol. 1, No. 3 (October 1950), 3-4.

[59] F. Greenleaf, *The Seventh-day Adventist Church in Latin America,* Vol. 2, 252.

Although Liga's most visible educational projects usually have involved providing funds for the founding and operation of schools, they can also be quite personal. On one occasion, for example, when a young woman born without legs asked for assistance, Liga provided her with a properly equipped wheelchair and paid her tuition so that she could learn secretarial and computer skills and become an independent and productive member of society.[60]

No account of Liga's educational projects would be complete without some mention of its efforts to promote and provide elementary education for those living in areas where there were no schools of any kind. During the late 1940s, the1950s, and the early 1960s, rural villagers often asked the American branch of Liga to help them start schools in their communities. Sometimes it was able to provide the requested assistance. Its Mountain School program, for example, provided schools in the states of Sonora and Chihuahua. It thus established and operated literally dozens of schools over the years. In 1949 it operated approximately thirty. The Mexican government sometimes helped by subsidizing such schools. On occasion, though, after Liga had hired a teacher and got the new school going well, the government would step in and take over. While such an action might be perceived by some as a disaster, it freed up funds to use to start yet another school in a

[60] Liga International, Inc., *Hands Across the Border*; and Liga International, Inc., *"Educational Influence,"* nd, http://www.liga-flyingdocs.org /education.htm.

different location. The end result was that thousands of Mexican children benefitted by learning how to read and write.[61]

Interestingly, the Mountain School plan was one of the most cost beneficial programs Liga developed. In a report prepared in 1958 it was noted that 800 persons had been "alphabetized"—that is, provided with three years of schooling—at a cost of only one dollar per student per month. It was amazingly inexpensive. The returns involved far more than 800 people knowing how to read, write, and handle basic arithmetic. One hundred of those 800 students were baptized into the Seventh-day Adventist church.[62] While he helped get the program started, Dr. Ritchie never learned of the extent of its success. Had he been able to, he would have been delighted.

---

[61] I.S. Ritchie to Luis de la Rosa, July 1949, copy in Ritchie Papers, SCLSU; Liga México Panamericana Médico Educacional, *Bulletin,* Los Angeles, California, 10 October 1959, 1; and I.M. Christianson, interview by D. G. Ross, 17 July 2000.

[62] Liga México-Pan-Americana Médico Educacional, American Chapter, "Liga Board Meeting Minutes," Arlington, California, 17 August 1958, 1-2.

The Busy Forties

The middle to late 1940s were busy years for Dr. Ritchie. He faced the daily demands of a large medical practice as well as the many speaking appointments and medical and educational missionary projects that engaged his attention. Moreover, he still was a member of the Mexican Union Mission Committee. Fortunately, there was considerable overlapping among the various obligations. Had it not been so, he would have been unable to keep up.

He was in considerable demand as a public speaker for youth meetings, church functions, and civic gatherings. His speeches usually dealt with health topics or some aspect of Seventh-day Adventist medical and educational work in Mexico, and the obvious need for more help in those areas. Such presentations could have been something less than exciting—not to say just plain boring—but Dr. Ritchie almost always illustrated his talks with accounts of his personal experiences and with most every-thing else he could find that was suitable, from maps to animal skins. Such illustrations and aids helped create interesting presentations that often led to other speaking engagements.

For years as he traveled throughout Mexico Dr. Ritchie looked for items that would help add interest to his presentations. In time he had quite a collection, from jaguar and snake skins to blankets and native costumes, the last of which he sometimes asked his children to model. One particularly effective aid was a partially stuffed monkey skin that could be used as a puppet. Children, especially, liked that one. His 16-millimeter movies were quite effective, too. Consequently, at one time it probably is safe to say that Seventh-day Adventist youth in southern California knew more about Yaqui Indian ceremonial dancing than did the vast majority of Mexicans! He used graphics, slide transparencies, and the occasional live animal in his health lectures.[1]

Therefore, while he may not have been an outstanding orator, he was an effective public speaker. As a medical evangelist Dr. Ritchie considered it his duty to be available to speak in church or elsewhere as the occasion demanded. Every such event gave him the opportunity to teach, which was something he enjoyed. When he had sufficient advance notice he prepared carefully, sometimes writing out his full presentation in advance. More often, though, he prepared the body of his lecture or sermon carefully and in detail, but merely outlined material such as medical information and illustrations with which he was personally well acquainted.[2] Like altogether too many Seventh-day Adventist preachers of the

---

[1] Inelda May Christianson, daughter of Dr. Iner S. Ritchie, telephone interview by Delmer G. Ross, Norco, California, 25 June 2004.

[2] See, for example, [Iner S. Ritchie], "The Greatest Thing in the World," three pages of notes for a talk for young people, no date, file folder: Medical Missionary Experiences in Mexico, Ritchie Papers, SCLSU.

day, his sermons and other presentations before Adventist audiences often consisted of many quotations from the writings of Ellen G. White and a few Bible texts strung together to bolster a desired conclusion, a conclusion which in his case generally dealt with how best to assist the people of Mexico with their physical and spiritual needs. Dr. Ritchie managed to be effective in spite of that formula because he enlivened it with visual aids and by adding illustrations based on his own extensive experience with Mexicans as well as stories gathered from other Seventh-day Adventist workers in Mexico.

For example, in one of his talks to which he apparently gave the title, "God's Vast Design," he gave a lengthy illustration from his own experience. At the time of the events he described he was practicing medicine along the Mexican border as a self-supporting medical missionary. He and several associates had gone eastward on a medical tour. They crossed the Colorado River into the Mexican state of Sonora where they paused at a village called San Luis. During the day they cared for a large number of people needing medical attention, then offered an illustrated health lecture in the local public school after dark. The well attended lecture was in progress when, as Dr. Ritchie put it,

> I was interrupted by a cry for help which was caused by one of the members of my audience having an epileptic seizure of convulsions. I asked the audience to keep their seats and be quiet and I would return in a few minutes. I had the patient carried into the house across the street where I attended her, and was back in a few minutes to

continue our lecture after which we had a clinic and treated the sick there.[3]

Having dealt with the setting and most of the event, the missionary evangelist introduced a possibly ominous complication when he mentioned that "Two well dressed men were present and watched the entire procedure." He told his audience that the men,

> came to me and introduced themselves, and asked, "Who is sponsoring this wonderful work?"
> "We are," I answered.
> "Yes, but who pays you for it? Who supports it?"
> "We do," I answered again.
> "But how can you do it? We want to know where we can find you. We must visit you."

By this time his listeners doubtless were expecting some complication—some problem to surface. Perhaps the physician and those with him had been thrown into jail. But no, nothing like that took place. Instead, he went on,

> In a few days these distinguished officials from Mexico City visited us at our headquarters [in Calexico] and upon leaving said, "Here are our cards and addresses. If you ever come to Mexico City look us up and we will do anything we can to help you." This proved . . . [to be a] providential thread in the Divine pattern which was

---

[3] Iner S. Ritchie, untitled 14-page handwritten manuscript with internal title, "God's Vast Design," at top of p. 12, no date, 11, Ritchie Papers, SCLSU.

being woven, and little did I realize at the time how important this was to be in my later work.[4]

Dr. Ritchie continued his talk with accounts of two obstetrical cases. The local librarian, a lady whose husband was a general who had been killed during a military campaign among the Yaqui Indians, told him about the birth of her daughter, who was one of his own patients. She had been in Yaqui country when she had gone into labor. Unfortunately, she was unable to deliver normally. Continuing the story, Dr. Ritchie explained,

> She was attended only by the Yaqui women, as there were no doctors there. In extreme cases the Yaquis place the patient on a large blanket, then hold the corners and along the edges, chanting and relaxing the blanket, then pulling together, tightening and raising the blanket with force—thus violently throwing the patient high into the air and then catching her again. By the end of the third day she was exhausted and thought it was the end when unexpectedly an American doctor from the mining country of Chihuahua came into town. . . . [He] put a stop to that procedure and delivered her of the baby girl. This woman later became the chief of policewomen in Mexico City, and she also was to form a thread of the pattern slowly being woven in God's [design].[5]

The second case he mentioned was one of his own patients, the wife of the governor's chief of staff, who had insisted that Dr.

---

[4] Ibid.

[5] Ibid., 12.

Ritchie remain in Calexico until she had her baby, even though he had made plans to travel to Mexico City. Although he was loath to delay his trip just for her, he did.

Later, when he looked back on the outcome of it all, he saw the change in schedule as providential—as the working of God's plan.[6] He had hoped to have an interview with the president of Mexico. He needed assistance with several matters, all of which had been long delayed. When he finally reached Mexico City he first visited the government officials he had met after his health lecture in San Luis, Sonora. They arranged for him to go and see the president. Then, as he explained in his presentation,

> While we were sitting in the waiting room at the Presidential National Palace, I noticed a woman . . . dressed in beautiful furs . . . looking straight at me and smiling. I looked away. The lights were dim and [I] thought she had mistaken me for someone else. I looked back and here she was . . . coming [toward me]. I felt sure both of us were going to be embarrassed. When she was within a few feet I left my chair, but to my surprise she greeted me in friendly Mexican fashion with a big "abrazo," or hug. She had moved to Mexico City and had been appointed Chief of the Mexico City Policewomen. "Qué milagro! [What a miracle!]" she said. "I have just come from Guadalajara where my mother is very ill. And I have been praying all the way on the train 'Oh if my doctor were only here,' and now here you are! But what brings you here?"
>
> "I have come to see the president," I told her.

---

[6] Ibid.

"To see the president? . . . None of these people here in the waiting room will see the president." Then she added softly, "None but you. You will see him."

She left and went into the adjoining room with the Presidential Secretary and Chief of Staff. In a few moments two lieutenants appeared at the door and called my name.[7]

Dr. Ritchie then had his interview with the president of Mexico, who helped the medical evangelist with what he needed. Two apparently chance meetings and an irritating delay had made it possible. To Dr. Ritchie it was all part of God's design to enable Mexicans to receive medical and spiritual care.

One Sabbath in 1946 he preached on "The Medical Missionary," a topic very dear to his heart. As usual, the sermon was replete with quotations from the Bible and the writings of Ellen G. White, but he illustrated it with touching stories of his own experiences. A major illustration dealt with his trip to the Totonac Indian town of Pantepec shortly after he and his family had moved to Mexico City. He told of how he had taken the trip because he felt he needed to know about health conditions in remote areas of the country, as already mentioned. Others with whom he had traveled into Indian country wrote about their adventure, but in this sermon Dr. Ritchie offered many more interesting details.

Before leaving the capital he asked Mexican Union officials about the equipment and medications he ought to take on the journey. They told him he need not bother to take anything because those Indians were very hardy. They were all healthy

---

[7] Ibid., 13-14.

because they lived outdoors and got plenty of fresh air. Knowing a little about remote areas in Mexico, he did not follow their advice. Instead he took along enough supplies and equipment to constitute a full load for a pack mule. He told about their travel, ending in a 10-hour ride on horseback that was extended an hour or so while they picked up after his bucking pack mule had "scattered all my supplies down canyon for a mile." They had been warned not to make the trip because the Indians were unfriendly and had killed three recent travelers, so when they finally reached their destination they stayed in a "large fort" where they slept on cots.

They were awakened the next morning by a lot of noise in a room adjoining theirs. Dr. Ritchie peeked through a hole in the door to determine what was happening. He saw someone making a wooden box about two feet wide and six feet long—a coffin. Recalling the earlier warning to stay out of the region, the men dressed quickly and went out to learn more. The coffin was for a woman who had died during the night after four days of labor. Dr. Ritchie asked, "Why didn't you call a doctor?" The response was, "What's that? A doctor? No doctors ever come near here. We are born, live, suffer, and die . . . [without] doctors, nurses, dentists, [or] teachers!" Appalled, the medical missionary stated, "I wish I had known it. I am a doctor, and probably could have saved her life. I have had many such cases—five in one night." He went on with the story:

> He stared at me for the first time, [then] laid his tools down and went out. The word was sent up the river into the mountains and jungle. And the people began coming:

mothers carrying two children—one in each arm; young men carrying their old fathers on their backs; some on freshly made litters of poles. By night [the place] looked like a great army encampment, [with people] standing around fires [and] sick ones lying on [the] ground. My patients filled the place . . . [and] crowded around me till I could not raise up for the press of the crowds, all day and into the night.

[On the] 3rd day [I] told them [I] had to leave. "Oh no, you can't leave us! Why, you have just come. . . ." Leaders came to me and said, "Haven't we treated you well? We have given you food and shelter, the best we have. What more can we do, so you will stay?"

The Indians weren't at all willing to allow the medical missionary to leave until he promised, "I will come back after I have trained some of your own young people to do this same kind of work," and then only reluctantly. People kept coming and begging, "Doctor, please cure me before you go." He concluded his illustration by letting his audience know that he had experienced the same type of thing when he visited other Indians in remote regions of Mexico.[8]

His listeners could and probably did soon forget the rest of his sermons, but who could resist or quickly forget the appeal implied in his very personal illustrations? Dr. Ritchie's obvious sincerity and enthusiasm was contagious. As a consequence, during the 1930s and 1940s he could be counted among the more persuasive

---

[8] [Iner S. Ritchie], "The Medical Missionary Work," an 18-page unpaginated handwritten manuscript, 5 January 1946, [7-8], Ritchie Papers, SCLSU. Some punctuation and words added because this was taken from sometimes cryptic sermon notes.

speakers in favor of medical evangelism in the entire church. He effectively interested many others in donating their services and of their means to that cause in Mexico and elsewhere, as the work of Liga attests even today.

Although Dr. Ritchie may not consciously have been witnessing for his faith when he wrote letters to members of his immediate family—after all, they were all Seventh-day Adventist Christians—he did so anyway. This custom, which he apparently began when he was writing love letters to Inelda Ruth, continued throughout his life. Portions of his letters often were quite "preachy." Take, for example, a five-page letter he wrote to his son, Iner William, in 1946, in which he wrote:

> It will take a lot of sacrifice if we do our part in this final program for earth's last message to be finished in this generation. We need to get a new vision, I fear, before we can fulfill God's plan for our full part in this work, and what a wonderful work it is and what an incomprehensible reward we will receive. I hope you keep all these eternal values in mind in your preparation for your part in this great country of Mexico. . . .
>
> The signs in our country & the world in general surely indicate that we are on the very verge of the end of time. The forces of evil are all set for the final crisis. "The final moments will be rapid ones," we are told. I am glad to hear you are doing missionary work where you are. We must be busy at that wherever we are and then, come

when it may, the end will find us on duty and ready to meet our Lord and Redeemer.[9]

Even when he simply provided news, it often revolved around Mexico and medical and educational missionary work there, and the advancement of God's work. He was, after all, a medical-evangelist graduate of the College of Medical Evangelists, and he never forgot that fact.

As exhausted as he sometimes became, he worked tirelessly for the church and for its institutions in his chosen mission field of Mexico. In the just quoted letter, for example, he reported that he had already accumulated some $7,000 worth of equipment for the hospital yet under construction at the school in Montemorelos. He also indicated that CME alumni were planning to give $10,000 toward the same goal. Moreover, he indicated that he had talked several times recently with W.K. Kellogg and that the breakfast-cereal magnate would "take up the matter" of providing additional needed equipment.[10] Then, in a final report on a trip to Montemorelos from which he had just returned, he jubilantly wrote,

On our way back we stopped at the Customs broker . . . in Laredo . . . and saw the big shipment of boxed equipment on the [railroad] platform. We went over to the Mexican Federal Customs office & saw the chief who told us that there was an order there for all goods coming

[9] Daddy [Iner S. Ritchie] et al. to Iner [William Ritchie] et al., 18 May 1946, 4-5, Ritchie Papers, SCLSU.

[10] Ibid., 4.

in for the Montemorelos Hospital . . . to be passed
through duty free.[11]

Dr. Ritchie not only worked hard, he worked effectively toward
achieving what he believed was needed. Obtaining approval for
the duty-free importation of anything for a religious institution in
Mexico in those days was quite simply miraculous. The violence
of the Mexican Revolution and the Cristero War—the fight of the
Catholic church against the government and the full implementa-
tion of the Constitution of 1917—remained fresh in the memory
of many of those in positions of power. Working alongside other
Adventist church officers, however, Dr. Ritchie had approached
government officials several times and, explaining the benefits to
Mexicans, he had tried to obtain such a concession. They had
made their request the subject of much prayer. Finally, the
government had granted their request. The miraculous had taken
place. Moreover, this particular concession set a precedent that
could be—and was—followed in the construction of other church
institutions that would be of similar benefit to Mexico. The
missionary physician had every reason to feel jubilation.

It did not take much for jubilation to become anxiety, though.
Early in 1947 some church officers managed to obtain from
Francisco Ramírez Villarreal, the attorney, copies of a number of
Mexican government officials' letters to Dr. Ritchie. Just how they
managed it is unclear, but considering that the medical evangelist
was connected with the church, Ramírez Villarreal probably did
not believe there would be a problem. There soon was, though.

---

[11] Ibid., 5.

Without thinking that there was to be no legal connection between the church and the ACFE or Liga, these church officers copied the letters and began using them to help them publicly solicit money for the church. Dr. Ritchie was outraged. These unthinking individuals threatened to undo more than twenty years of hard work and good will. If, as they should have, they had been willing to ask him, the attorney, or any of dozens of church officials who were acquainted with the facts, the situation could have been explained to them. The almost unbelievable thoughtlessness of those officials could have pushed the Mexican government to rigidly enforce all of the anticlerical provisions of Mexican law, just as the *cristero* rebels had during the Cristero War in the 1920s. The missionary physician somehow got the use of the letters stopped, but the next few weeks and months were anxious ones for him and for church leaders.[12]

In a way, though, thoughtful church leaders and even Dr. Ritchie may have been at least partly to blame for what had happened. They could have been warned if they had paid close attention to the Mexican Union annual report of 1944. Oh, it quite correctly pointed out on the very first page that "it might be well to explain that all religious bodies found it expedient to move very cautiously in all their activities during recent years."[13] It went on to note that "Even yet we must take every step cautiously if we aim to escape the danger of being publicly denounced as violators

[12] Anna Nickel to Honey & Warren [Inelda May and Warren Christianson], May 1947, Ritchie Papers, SCLSU.

[13] H.F. House, *Report of the Superintendent of the Mexican Union Mission,* Monterrey, N. L., 28 February 1944, 1.

of the law." On the same page, however, it stated, "Our clinics and dispensaries have accomplished untold good and they have served as a basis for campaigning the whole country for assistance and support, during the Ingathering program." That statement should have been warning enough, but the report continued, "It is most encouraging to find so many government officials and influential business men [sic] sympathetic and complimentary of this work."[14] The next step was to put letters from those government officials to use in collecting funds, which is exactly what happened. Responsible church leaders had two years, or longer, to prevent what was bound to happen, but they did not. Fortunately, use of the letters appears to have caused no serious problem.

Another project that took a considerable amount of Dr. Ritchie's time was the preparation of a health textbook. The project began in the late 1930s and continued into the 1940s before it was abandoned. The book was to be based on twelve health lectures Dr. Ritchie had given at various different times, including especially those given at the Tacubaya Clinic in Mexico City. It was to be published by Associated Lecturers, Inc., which operated Madison College, an Adventist institution located in Nashville, Tennessee.

Its appears that Dr. Ritchie submitted a rough draft of at least a major portion of the proposed text to the publishers early in 1939. That elicited a constructive three-page response from the president, who evidently had undertaken the task of editing the planned text. He wrote,

[14] Ibid., 3.

> I have a feeling that you would make better progress in your work there [in Riverside] if you would . . . arrange your book to cover the principles of *health in general before* jumping into the strong presentation of Christianity and the Adventist doctrines direct from the Bible as you have done. . . . I fear that you are taking too great a risk in putting such direct religious teaching into the book and that it will bring a ban against it[s] use.[15]

Such a ban, obviously enough, could have a detrimental result on book sales, an effect publishers generally attempt to avoid. Considering, however, that the book was to have been based on his lectures at the Tacubaya Clinic, and that the goal of those lectures was to prepare Adventist workers to make health presentations of their own, the problem could and should have been foreseen. The lectures served their original purpose very well. Transforming them into a textbook on health was asking rather much unless they were considerably modified.

After receiving the letter Dr. Ritchie apparently worked some more on his manuscript, making revisions and preparing illustrations. Some of the illustrations he drew himself; others were clipped from various published sources, making the manuscript appear rather like a scrapbook.[16] Despite the effort he put into it, the expected textbook was not published, whether because the

---

[15] Julius Gilbert White to I.S. Ritchie, 9 July 1939, Ritchie Papers, SCLSU.

[16] Iner S. Ritchie, untitled, unfinished book manuscript, no date, Ritchie Papers, SCLSU.

author could not find enough time to revise it, because he simply lost interest, or because the publisher gave up on it, is unclear.

Playing himself, Dr. Ritchie in a riverbank scene from
Bajo el cielo tropical.

Many of the incidental tasks he undertook—those not directly related to his medical practice in Riverside—required Dr. Ritchie to travel. For example, in 1948 he made no fewer than seven air trips to Mexico.[17]

One of those trips was particularly arduous because it involved the filming of *Bajo el Cielo Tropical (Under the Tropical Sky)* by the Department of Health and Welfare of the Mexican national government. The film depicted Dr. Ritchie's efforts to

---

[17] "Obituary," 4, Ritchie file, WebbLLU.

bring health and healing to remote areas of the republic and his attempt to multiply and to provide a continuation of those efforts by teaching others. Dr. Ritchie hoped that the film might stimulate those who were able to provide of their means to promote such work.[18]

Liga was an organization that was often foremost in his thoughts and that demanded a major share of Dr. Ritchie's time. As the general manager of Liga, he was directly involved in providing medical attention to those in need as well as most of the organization's special projects, from starting an agricultural school on the west coast of Mexico to outfitting a mobile clinic to be used in the southeastern part of the country. One of his trips to Mexico in 1948 involved traveling with several members of Liga, and others, to help set up the Boca del Río field station for the study of tropical medicine for CME. Flying in an airplane provided free of charge by the Mexican government, Dr. Ritchie marveled that they could so rapidly reach a destination that had taken him and a companion ten arduous days of travel by canoe on the Coatzacoalcos River only a few years earlier.[19]

Dr. Ritchie worked diligently to expand the scope and influence of Liga. For example, in June 1949 he and Mrs. Ritchie

---

[18] Mexico, Department of Health and Welfare. *Bajo el Cielo Tropical.* Documental No. 6. 8 min. Dirección General de Educación Higiénica de la Secretaría de Salubridad y Asistencia, México, [1948]. Copy of film on videocassette in Ritchie Papers, SCLSU.

[19] Daddy [Iner S. Ritchie] to Inelda [Ruth Ritchie] & Children, 6 September [1948]; and Cordelia P. Reynolds, "The League at Work for Mexico," *The Journal of the Alumni Association, School of Medicine, College of Medical Evangelists,* Vol. 20, No. 2 (February 1949), 14.

participated in the Mexican portion of a goodwill tour of Mexico and Central America designed to acquaint government officials with the organization and its aims. Their Mexican hosts expressed their desire that Liga should sponsor educational facilities "like that of La Sierra"—today's La Sierra University in Riverside, California—in their country. The touring Liga members were delighted to be able to point out that their organization was already working on similar educational projects in Montemorelos, Navojoa, and Teapa.[20]

Of course, a lot of his travel was local, involving driving to and from work and making house calls. For such local as well as longer drives Dr. Ritchie came to prefer to drive a Cadillac. It was not a case of pretentiousness; it was because it was a better built and more comfortable automobile than most. Therefore, except for a time during World War II, throughout the 1940s he drove Cadillacs. During the war he drove a Chevrolet with wartime louvers over the headlights. While the louvers enabled him to drive at night during blackouts, he detested the car. Simply put, it was not built to Cadillac standards.[21]

[20] Clarence E. Nelson, "Good Will Tour in Inter-America," *The Journal of the Alumni Association, School of Medicine, College of Medical Evangelists,* Vol. 22, No. 10 (October 1949), 11-13.

[21] Inelda Ritchie Christianson, "Transportation," undated 5-page handwritten manuscript, 5, Ritchie Papers, SCLSU.

A Life Well Spent

Monday, October 24, 1949, started out like most other October days in rural Arlington: sunny and cool. As the sun beat down, though, the temperature rose rapidly until it was quite warm. By early afternoon it was unusually hot—especially for so late in the month.

Dr. Ritchie, as was his custom, had wakened, shaved, eaten a hearty breakfast of hot cereal and fruit, then driven to his office in Riverside. He arrived a little before nine o'clock, in plenty of time to deal with his first appointment of the day which was scheduled for nine.

As he prepared for his first patient, he wondered if he should take a vacation. He had felt tired lately. Very tired. It was the kind of exhaustion that might be appropriate for an old man who had overworked for many consecutive days. He felt like he needed to sleep nights and days for a week. He did not suppose he would need it, but he was glad he had already made out his will.[1]. His fatigue had been noticeable at a Liga meeting held earlier, in July.

---

[1] It was a brief holographic will granting everything to his wife. Iner Sheld-Ritchie, "Last Will," 1 March 1944, copy in Ritchie Papers, SCLSU.

After listening to a recording of the conference, Dr. Ritchie's younger daughter, Inelda May Christianson, later commented, "In contrast to the strong, cheerful voice Dad recorded on other tapes a few months before this, his voice was faint and he spoke slowly, as though he were tired and not well."[2] In fact, he had felt fatigued for months, and he was only 64—no longer young, but not so old either. In February the Mexican government had honored him with an award of merit in appreciation for his quarter century of service to the Mexican people, and in June the Distrito Federal—the Federal District that comprises the Mexican capital—had awarded him a gold medal.[3] Besides, he had just enjoyed a fairly restful weekend. Despite the recognition and the relaxing weekend, on this October morning, even before he had seen a single patient, he was already looking forward to going home for the day. He wondered how many patients he might need to see. Then, as work got under way, he almost forgot his weariness as he examined, diagnosed, advised, and sometimes prescribed treatment or medication for those who arrived to see him.

Between patients he thought about an upcoming Liga meeting. He was scheduled to make a short speech that would steer his

[2] Inelda May Christianson, "Note," added to Stephen Youngberg, "Tribute to Dr. Ritchie," Mexico, D.F., October 28, 1949, a transcription from tape copied from wire by Inelda May Christianson, 25 November 1995, Ritchie Papers, SCLSU.

[3] Iner W.S. Ritchie, "Liga México-Pan-Americana Medico [*sic*] Educacional," three-page typescript, Riverside, California, 23 July 1974, 2, Ritchie Papers, SCLSU; and Clarence E. Nelson, "Iner S. Ritchie Dies," *The Journal of the Alumni Association, School of Medicine, College of Medical Evangelists*, Vol. 21, No. 1 (January 1950),16.

listeners from the founders of the organization to opportunities for the future. He had made that type of speech before, so this one should not involve much additional new preparation. For that he was thankful.[4]

He left the office at about three in the afternoon. As he turned his car into the driveway of his home on Bonita Street, he discovered an automobile blocking his way. His next-door neighbor, Henry Norton, the manager of the Southeastern California Book and Bible House, was toweling off his just-washed vehicle in the shade of a tree. Norton quickly moved his car, and Dr. Ritchie proceeded up the driveway to a point just short of the garage door. When the physician got out, the two men conversed briefly. Norton explained that it was so hot in the sun that he had hoped to dry his car in the shade so that it would not end up water-spotted. The weary physician smiled wanly and indicated that he understood and that his neighbor was welcome to use the shade, then he went into the house where he lay down to take a nap. After a few minutes of sleep he hoped he might feel less fatigued and thus be ready to eat his final meal of the day and to make any necessary house calls.

Norton finished wiping off his car, changed clothes, then drove to his office. He had barely got to work when, at four, the phone rang. The call was from his wife who informed him that Dr. Ritchie, with whom he had conversed less than an hour earlier, had passed away.

---

[4] Liga México-Pan-Americana Médico Educacional, "Programme: Liga Mexico-Pan-American Festival," 29 October 1949, Ritchie file, WebbLLU.

Aside from the doctor himself, Mrs. Ritchie was the first to realize something was seriously wrong. She had walked by and looked into the room where her husband lay on a bed. She saw that he was in some kind of trouble and immediately called Henry Norton's son, Bill, who had been a medic in the armed forces. Both suspected a heart attack. While Inelda Ruth looked in the bathroom medicine cabinet, the former medic searched Dr. Ritchie's medical bag. They hoped to find his supply of heart medication. By the time they realized they would not find it, the physician had died. Even had they located and been able to administer the medicine right away, the heart attack was so advanced that they probably would not have been able to forestall the outcome.[5]

The voice of the medical evangelist who loved Mexico and Mexicans so was at last silenced. What a handful of enemies had been trying to accomplish for many years was at last a reality. Dr. Ritchie's legacy, though, lives on.

That such was likely to be the case became apparent as early as his funeral, if not even before. It was held in the Riverside Seventh-day Adventist church on the Sabbath following his death. The church was full, with people who were unable to find seats standing in the aisles. Elder Glenn A. Calkins, who had recently completed his first stint as president of the Inter-American Division of the Seventh-day Adventist Church—which was in

---

[5] Henry Norton to Inelda [May Christianson], 31 October 1949, Ritchie Papers, SCLSU; and Certificate of Death, 29 October 1949, Ritchie Papers, SCLSU.

charge of the church in Mexico—led out.[6] Among those in attendance was Dr. Clarence E. Nelson, a friend and, like Dr. Ritchie, a true medical evangelist, and the Mexican consul.[7] As her mother described it in a letter to Inelda May Christianson who was in Washington, D.C., and who could not attend because of pregnancy, "The whole front of [the] church was banked with beautiful flowers." She went on to say, "We have 92 cards which came with flowers and some cards had several names." She described the coffin as "of plain polished mahogany, it looked so fitting for a man like our Daddy. He loved beautiful woods."[8]

The funeral procession from the Riverside church to the Ritchie family burial plot in Corona contained some 200 vehicles. Stretching at least two miles, it was described by one of the motorcycle policemen who helped with traffic control as being the longest he had ever seen.[9]

Inelda Ritchie received dozens of cards and letters of condolence from church functionaries, Mexican government officials, friends, and former patients. One of the most touching was from a former patient, a Mrs. Thyra N. Ishoy, of Sunnymead, part of today's Moreno Valley, California. She wrote that Dr. Ritchie had

---

[6] Calkins served as president of the Inter-American Division from 1941 to 1947 and from 1951 to 1954. "Calkins, Glenn Alwin," *Seventh-day Adventist Encyclopedia,* Rev. ed. (1976).

[7] Henry Norton to Inelda [May Christianson], 31 October 1949.

[8] Mother [Inelda Ruth Ritchie] to Dearest Children [Warren and Inelda May Christianson], 4 November 1949, Ritchie Papers, SCLSU.

[9] Inelda May Christianson, daughter of Dr. Iner S. Ritchie, telephone interview by Delmer G. Ross, 23 November 2003.

been her physician for twelve years and that she missed him every time she had to go in for her shots. She described him as a kind and sincere person who "was always the same and readdy [sic] to help anyone in need." She indicated that as a result of a dream she had been inspired to write a poem which she hoped would "comfort you a little."[10] She called it "Another Shining Star in Heaven."

> God needed another star in Heaven
> To shine for Him so bright.
> So He took back what He once had given,
> And who had a better right?
> God needed your loved one in Heaven,
> Of that you may be sure.
> Some day you shall meet and greet him,
> Be with him for ever more.
> So do not weep for your loved one.
> He is now in Christ's tender care,
> Loved by everyone in Heaven
> As he was loved by everyone here.
> I ask our Father to bless you
> And comfort your aching heart
> And whisper someday in the future
> That you'll be with him and never part.[11]

---

[10] Thyra N. Ishoy to Mrs. [Inelda Ruth] Ritchie, 13 January 1950, Ritchie Papers, SCLSU.

[11] Thyra N. Ishoy, "Another Shining Star in Heaven," included in Thyra N. Ishoy to Mrs. [Inelda Ruth] Ritchie, 13 January 1950, Ritchie Papers, SCLSU.

While this former patient obviously had views about death that differed from those of most Seventh-day Adventists who believe that death is a sleep that will last until the resurrection of the faithful at Jesus' second advent, what is important here is the author's thoughtfulness. Moreover, her poem doubtless was reassuring, exactly as intended. Who would not receive comfort from thoughts so kindly and sincerely expressed?

Within ten days of Dr. Ritchie's death, his son, Dr. Iner William Ritchie, who practiced medicine in Blythe, California, had begun arrangements to spend three days each week in his father's office. He would take over full time as soon as he could sell his own practice in Blythe.[12] He also became a major force in Liga, carrying out many of his father's plans for that organization.

How does one summarize a life well spent?

Dr. Ritchie was a visionary—a dreamer. He dreamed of establishing schools and medical clinics in every state of Mexico. He dreamed of teaching health workers in those clinics so that they could go into rural areas and help people who literally were dying for lack of medical attention. They might not be physicians, but they could help. They could offer comfort and hope. It was a fine goal. Like most people discover as they attempt to accomplish something in this life, though, he faced many obstacles and hardships on the way. Moreover, at the time of his death only one of the many permanent clinics he had envisioned existed, although a second seemed about to materialize.

Had he failed? Not at all.

---

[12] Mother [Inelda Ruth Ritchie] to Dearest Children [Warren and Inelda May Christianson], 4 November 1949.

Anyone who helps to establish three universities is outstand-
ingly successful! Of course, they were only agricultural schools at
the time they were started, but they became universities. Additionally, the medical missionary's dream of providing medical
assistance to people throughout Mexico is at this moment being
fulfilled by dozens of physicians—not graduates of six weeks of
courses, as useful as that was—but well trained medical doctors
who can and do follow Dr. Ritchie's example. Every year the
Medical School at the University of Montemorelos graduates as
many medical doctors as most of those early teaching clinics did
"health workers." The work of "El Doctor," as many of those who
appreciated him often referred to him, continues despite his
absence. Instead of fading, his dream evolved, growing into
something beyond his own imagination, something so advanced
that he might have considered dreaming about it a waste of time.

For twenty-five years, from 1924 when he became involved
in work along the Mexican border, his goals had been to help
provide health and educational facilities for Mexicans who needed
them, and to expose as many as possible to the gospel of eternal
salvation through Jesus. During his lifetime he reached thousands
of people. Since his death the institutions and work he helped put
in place have influenced hundreds of thousands.

Although it may seem strange to some, Dr. Ritchie, the
visionary, was also a firm believer in dreams as guides for
behavior. He sincerely believed that the Bible was the word of
God and that it offered an overview and interpretation of events
from the distant and recent past, practical direction for the present,
and an accurate prediction of the future. He interpreted quite
literally Joel 2:28 as repeated in Acts 2:17, "And it shall come to

pass in the last days, saith God, I will pour out of my Spirit upon all flesh: and your sons and your daughters shall prophesy, and your young men shall see visions, and your old men shall dream dreams."[13]

So, why not take dreams seriously? Moreover, a dream had led to his being taken in by the Ritchies, who had encouraged him to improve himself. Because of them he had become a Seventh-day Adventist. Because of them he had gone through medical school and had become a physician. The results of Anna Lula Ritchie's dream had quite literally changed his life. Had she not heeded her dream he might never have been anything but a ranch hand, working for a pittance until death or retirement on even less provided by the county or state. As she once put it in a letter when she commented on a dream Dr. Ritchie had experienced and related to her:

> It was just such a dream as that that made you our own. It changed the whole course of your life and ours. Without the dream and subsequent dreams I never would have taken you and we would never have been more than passing acquaintances. Nothing in our lives that is so dear to us all now would have happened. Neither your splendid devoted wife nor any of [your] darling children would have been in your life.[14]

---

[13] King James Version.

[14] Mamma and Amma [Anna Lula Ritchie] to Iner and Inelda [Ritchie], 28 August 1935, 7, Ritchie Papers, SCLSU.

With such an example of the importance of dreams—and, of course, their proper interpretation—it would have taken a very strong-minded, stubborn individual indeed to totally disregard the value of dreams as factors in the direction of lives.

Exactly what Anna Lula Ritchie dreamed about young Iner to influence her and her husband in his favor is not known. It may have been a dream she recounted to him in a birthday letter she wrote to him in 1935:

> Perhaps nothing could be more fitting for this day than to remind you of my dream of you, of the snowy white garment which was dipped in perfume and was ever after to radiate perfumed incense. The incense represents your influence. My wish for you from my very heart . . . is that the dream may be fully fulfilled in your life.[15]

The dream and its interpretation dovetailed perfectly with Dr. Ritchie's own desire to serve both God and suffering humanity. Moreover, Dr. Ritchie's influence has radiated far beyond what he, personally, was able to accomplish during his lifetime.

For some time after he had become involved in the border area around Calexico and Mexicali Dr. Ritchie had been pondering the possible significance for him of the command of Jesus to Simon and Andrew who were fishing in the Sea of Galilee, "Come ye after me, and I will make you to become fishers of men."[16] It sounded like Jesus wanted his disciples to attract even more

---

[15] Mamma [Anna Lula Ritchie] to Our Beloved Son [Iner S. Ritchie], 2 October 1935, Ritchie file, WebbLLU.

[16] Mark 1:16-17, KJV.

followers, and, of course, many other texts confirmed that interpretation. For years he had felt impressed to help disseminate the salvation story in Mexico, but Mexican law forbade proselytizing by foreigners and it imposed numerous other restrictions and outright prohibitions on those who might wish to spread the gospel. How should he react? Could he be mistaken? He came to no immediate conclusion.

One night, though, he had a dream. It was one of those memorable dreams that can make a person wonder if what he or she had seen might have some meaning. He dreamed that he was standing near the center of a pond shaped like Mexico. The water was quite murky, which he felt symbolized trouble of some kind. Then the water began to evaporate, and as it did so the pond became fairly shallow and the water even muddier. It also became very turbulent. While he observed what was happening, the phrase, "fisher of men," kept going through his mind.

This, he felt, must have some meaning, perhaps a significant meaning for him and his family. As Dr. Ritchie later explained,

> I began reaching down in the water and catching fish with my hands. I worked fast, throwing handfuls of small fish upon the bank. As long as I would work I could . . . catch fish—and the faster the more I caught. When I would stop to rest the commotion continued; the pond was full of fish. Someone said "if you go careful you will catch big fish." So I reached down deeper among all the

little fish and I felt big fat fish. These took more time, but I caught them and landed them on the bank also.[17]

A voice told him, "Follow me and I will make you a fisher of men." Dr. Ritchie, still dreaming, responded with, "I won't worry any more, Lord, I'll follow you."[18]

His immediate interpretation of the dream was straightforward: he was to go to Mexico and, trusting God to open the way despite laws and prohibitions, he was to be a fisher of men by taking them the good news of salvation and eternal life. Moreover, instead of concentrating on the poor, lower-class people—the small fish in the pond—he was to use his contacts with government officials and other highly placed individuals to help convert big-fish upper-class people. Then God could, as he put it, "multiply my efforts."[19]

When told about it, Anna Lula Ritchie had her own ideas about his dream, and was quite emphatic in her interpretation:

> This dream is clearly given of the Lord. To dream of fish always has meant people. . . . There is no question in my mind that this dream was given to you both to correct your methods and to direct you in the better way, and to encourage you and me as well.
>
> For a long time your plan has been to lecture and contribute your strength and mind to a class of people of

---

[17] Iner S. Ritchie, "Fish Dream," handwritten manuscript, no date, 2, Ritchie Papers, SCLSU.

[18] Ibid.

[19] Ibid., 3.

a grade that were really unable intellectually to grasp what you presented. . . .

God is not condemning you for working with the poor and ignorant, the little fish, the smelt, but that is NOT what HE WANTS you to do. What he WANTS you to do is to catch BIG FISH. And it is not going to be a wholesale job like visiting Indians and treating a hundred a day. It is going to be a ONE BY ONE job.[20]

After offering a specific example from his own recent experience—he had discussed the Bible for some two hours with a government official—and again pounding away on the same theme, his opinionated adoptive mother and mother-in-law continued with her apparent clincher: "There is no question what ever [sic] about it. This dream is as clear as any thing [sic] can be and if you disobey it you will be disobeying God and will not have his protection and blessing."[21] She continued in the same vein for another two single-spaced typewritten pages, offering more examples, including that of the Biblical Joseph.

Being a medical doctor and quite aware of the numerous physical reasons for dreams, including an overfilled stomach, Dr. Ritchie might have taken what Anna Lula wrote with the proverbial grain of salt. It was his own dream, though, and his and his mother-in-law's interpretations did not differ in any significant way. Moreover, he dreamed the same dream a number of times.

---

[20] Mamma and Amma [Anna L. Ritchie] to Dear Beloved Children [Iner and Inelda Ritchie], 11 August 1935, 7-8, all capitals for emphasis in original, Ritchie Papers, SCLSU.

[21] Ibid., 8.

That no doubt had the effect of giving it added importance in his own mind.

He later also interpreted his dream to mean that when he needed something—say a place to hold meetings or authorization to conduct classes on health and hygiene—he should go to the highest-placed person available for assistance. Thus, instead of dealing only with local officials, he called on state governors, cabinet ministers, or the president himself. And why not? Decisions made by local people could always be countermanded by someone higher up. If the decision came from the president himself, though, while some local people might be unhappy about it, they generally would cooperate, even if only grudgingly.

Of course, some might adamantly refuse to cooperate no matter who ordered them to do so. On one occasion he needed the help of the Minister of Public Health, but, despite the fact that the president had ordered him to provide all necessary assistance, he treated Dr. Ritchie and those with him coldly and claimed he could do nothing to support what they hoped to do. The petitioners made the issue a matter of prayer, and two months later when the defiant minister was replaced with another who was very sympathetic and helpful, Dr. Ritchie's comment was, "God honors those who honor him."[22]

The medical evangelist was a man of great faith. Some might have called it presumption, but his trust in God was rewarded so often that to call it anything but faith seems inappropriate and misleading.

---

[22] I.S. Ritchie, "Fish Dream," 3.

It seems unlikely that anyone knows the meaning of his dream. At the same time, it appears that Dr. Ritchie responded to what he considered to be its significance for him. He made numerous efforts to get to know those in a position to help advance God's work, and he was quite successful. Influential people he had come to know often opened doors that might otherwise have remained tightly closed for many years.

That Dr. Ritchie took the dream and his interpretation of it seriously cannot be doubted. His actions speak as clearly as words. After his death Inelda Ruth found in his wallet a slip of paper on which was written a single sentence, "You will have to open doors which you thought were closed." It was a thought—and a burden—he carried wherever he went.

Not everyone agreed with his approach. Someone once said to him, "You are a pretty good politician to get into places where you do." In a backhanded way, he was thus accused of spending too much time hobnobbing with the rich and powerful. Dr. Ritchie dealt with all kinds of people, from presidents and cabinet ministers and governors to the utterly destitute—in fact, with far more of the latter than of the former. But, in the final analysis, their positions in society did not matter to him. His response spelled out what truly did matter:

> Yes I am, if that is what you call it. I am an ambassador, if you please, for my King, sent down there to that country [Mexico] to tell the people to get ready to meet him in peace, for He is coming soon. . . . We are living in the last days. The end of all things is at hand. There are stormy times before us but let us not utter one word of unbelief or discouragement. He who understands the

necessities of the situation arranges that advantages should be brought to our workers in various places to enable them to more effectively arouse the attention of the people.

That was a refrain he was to repeat many times over the years. He wanted it to be clear that he was not representing himself, but a far higher authority. His message came from the source of all power. He also wanted it known that he was quite unlike most ordinary politicians:

There is a vast difference between the worldly politician and the heavenly. I used to feed the pigs on the ranch and try to pour the milk into their trough. Every pig was putting himself forward and trying to be first and squealing the loudest for his hog's share. That reminds me of the way some politicians are. . . . Egotism and forwardness are obnoxious not only to God but to most people. It is the hardest task for me to force myself into some of the openings that the Lord has made for me.[23]

He went on to recount how he had been very bashful as a youth. When he attended school he would not even eat with other students. At school picnics, instead of playing with the other children, he would sit alone and hold his head. He had a terrible inferiority complex.

That changed when he met Jesus. After learning of and accepting the truth he, as he put it, "determined to fit myself for some part in it." But he was too bashful and lacked any real talent.

---

[23] I.S. Ritchie, Handwritten notes, 5-6.

Medical doctors on a trip to the Boca del Río field station in 1948, (l-r): Miguel B. Lomali, of Mexican Public Health; Harold N. Mozar, Bruce W. Halstead, and George T. Harding, of CME; Alonzo E. Hardison, of the Institute if Inter-American Affairs; Iner S. Ritchie, of Liga (holding his impressive and generally helpful album of letters of recommendation); Theodore R. Flaiz, of the General Conference of SDAs; and Clarence Nelson, of Liga.

He went to a phrenologist who supposedly could "read" his head and tell him what he was best fitted to do. Before being checked, he told the phrenologist that he hoped to become a minister or a doctor. After an examination of the bumps on his head he told Iner to forget about those professions because he was best suited to become a mechanical draftsman. God had other plans for him, though, and had opened the way for him to become a doctor and a lay minister. He was determined to stay in the path God wished for him to follow.[24]

To some, the name of Dr. Ritchie's medical school—College of Medical Evangelists—sounded strange and uniquely unpretentious. It almost sounded like the name of some kind of unaccredited, diploma-mill Bible college. But he was proud of the name and considered it to be divinely inspired. Moreover, he saw it as fitting in every way. "We are Evangelists," he wrote, "Medical Evangelists. Our message to the world is not a medical message mainly. It is a saving message, mainly spiritual but includes as a part the physical."[25] Although the name of his alma mater was changed to Loma Linda University several years after his death, from the beginning of his medical studies to the end of his life he always viewed himself as a medical evangelist, and he acted accordingly. He served God and humankind.

In that service Dr. Ritchie was backed wholeheartedly by his wife. While, like most couples, he and Inelda Ruth had their disagreements, and even though he considered himself to be the

---

[24] Ibid., 6.

[25] I.S. Ritchie, "Fish Dream," 4.

boss of their household, he earned her support by encouraging her in her own management skills—she handled their finances, including real estate investments—and by never deliberately mistreating her or their children. She once stated, "He never talked to me like I've heard other people talk. Never." She went on to say that despite his early cowboy and ranch associates "I never heard him use an oath in my life." She added, "when he died, I didn't think I could live anymore. I was crazy in love with him from the time I was a little child. And he was a good husband, and very, very affectionate."[26]

Dr. Ritchie's work continues not only in institutions such as the University of Montemorelos, the University of Navojoa, and Liga International that he and others working with him started, but it carries on in the work of those who were inspired by him. His own grandson, Warren Ritchie Christianson—better known as Ritchie Christianson—offers a good example.

Although because he was born in 1948 he does not remember meeting his grandfather, Ritchie Christianson wrote,

My early life was influenced by stories of how my grandfather, Dr. Iner Ritchie[,] went into the jungles of Mexico working for the poor Indians in that country. I remember as a child seeing a 16mm movie of his work

---

[26] Inelda Ruth Sheld-Ritchie, widow of Dr. Iner S. Ritchie, transcript of interview by her granddaughter, Cheryl Ann Nickel Leathers, 2 March 1986, [La Jolla, California], 23-25 [9-11], Ritchie Papers, SCLSU

there. Although I never went to a foreign country as a missionary, the concept was planted in my mind.[27]

What was planted grew to fruition following Hurricane Mitch which caused an estimated 10,000 deaths and a tremendous amount of damage in Central America in 1998. The Adventist Development and Relief Agency (ADRA) asked for medical volunteers to provide assistance, and Ritchie Christianson, who is a registered nurse and a general building contractor, decided to join the relief effort. He recruited two other registered nurses and got a hospital to provide immunizations, then flew to Nicaragua. Assigned by ADRA to conduct health clinics in Las Maderas and the surrounding communities, he also helped teach health principles and benefits and methods of water purification. Observing a need for computers in the Seventh-day Adventist church school in Las Maderas, he acquired two of them for the school and taught all seven teachers how to use them. Today, years after the devastation caused by Hurricane Mitch back in 1998, he continues to help that and other nearby schools.[28] Ritchie Christianson honestly admits, "I can trace my desire to help in Nicaragua to the influence of my grandfather . . . who did so much to help in Mexico."[29]

---

[27] Warren Ritchie Christianson to Warren [and] Inelda Christianson, 28 September 2003, Ritchie Papers, SCLSU.

[28] Susan Everett, "Nicaragua Trips Mean More than Healing," *The Sonora (California) Union Democrat,* 8 June 2001, 16A; and Warren Ritchie Christianson to Warren [and] Inelda Christianson, 28 September 2003, Ritchie Papers, SCLSU.

[29] Ibid.

Another example of the continuation of Dr. Ritchie's work is the Pan American Health Service run by Dr. Stephen Youngberg and others in Central America. Inspired by Dr. Ritchie's life of service, Dr. Youngberg served for a time as a medical missionary at Liga's operation in Teapa, Tabasco, Mexico. As a matter of fact, in a kind of impromptu and narrowly symbolic passing of the torch, he crossed the border from the United States into Mexico during the very hour that Dr. Ritchie passed away. Because of health problems Dr. Youngberg had to leave Teapa, but he continued to serve elsewhere. Now conducting a full-time medical missionary endeavor in Peña Blanca, Honduras, the Pan American Health Service which he sponsored operates a Children's Nutritional Hospital. More than a half century after his death, Dr. Ritchie's gift of service to humanity lives on in something that he never personally touched.[30]

It may be true that Dr. Ritchie died prematurely, but during his life he created a legacy that lives on in the countless lives he saved. Moreover, it endures in the lives of their children, and their grandchildren—even though they may never even have heard of him—and it will continue until the end of time itself. It lives on in the educational institutions he encouraged and helped to found and the young minds shaped by them. It persists in the lives of those he inspired to adopt lives of service to God and to fellow humans. Such a legacy is unmistakable evidence of a life well spent.

---

[30] "A Solid Faith: The Youngbergs Live a Life of Healing and Teaching," *Scope,* Vol. 36, No. 1(Summer 2000); Stephen Youngberg, "Tribute to Dr. Ritchie," October 28, 1949, Ritchie Papers, SCLSU; and "Alumni Notes," *Scope,* Autumn 2000, http://www.llu.edu/news/scope/aut00/NSalumni.htm.

Bibliography

In an effort to prevent this bibliography from becoming excessively long, rather than listing each item used from a collection, unless the item itself is several pages long or of particular significance, it will be found only in the appropriate footnote or footnotes. The collection, however, will be identified in the note, usually in abbreviated form. For example, anything used from the Ritchie Papers in the Stahl Center for World Service at La Sierra University—by far and away the most significant source of documents used in the preparation of this volume—will show "Ritchie Papers, SCLSU." Likewise, any series of interviews will be listed with dates for the initial and final interviews; the appropriate footnote must be consulted for the date of a specific interview.

The first time a source is used in any chapter the footnote will provide a full reference. Unless it might prove confusing, subsequent use in that chapter will generally offer only abbreviated names and titles.

Published Sources: Books and Pamphlets

The Alumni Association, LLU School of Medicine. *Loma Linda School of Medicine 1909-1989 Celebrating 80 Years of Classes*. Undated pamphlet (ca. 1989).

Brown, Henry F. "The Medical Situation in Mexico." *The Medical Evangelist,* Vol. 10, No. 19 (1 November 1923): 1-2.

Brown, John, Jr., and James Boyd, eds. *History of San Bernardino and Riverside Counties,* Vol 1. The Western Historical Association, 1922.

Brown, Robert N. *The Story of Liga.* Liga International, Inc., no place or date (ca. 1968). Copy of pamphlet in Ritchie Papers, SCLSU.

Christian, Peggy. *Historic San Timoteo Canyon: A Pictorial Tour, Myths and Legends.* Morongo Valley, California, 2002.

[Christianson, Inelda May]. *Iner Sheld-Ritchie, Founder of Liga, 1885-1949.* [Riverside: The Stahl Center, La Sierra University, ca. 1996].

The College of Medical Evangelists: Founders Day. Loma Linda, California, 26 May 1955. Copy of pamphlet in Ritchie Papers, SCLSU.

Consejos para Señoras Encinta [sic] y Cuidado de los Niños. No place or date. Copy in Ritchie Papers, SCLSU.

Greenleaf, Floyd. *The Seventh-day Adventist Church in Latin America and the Caribbean,* Vol. 2, *Bear the News to Every Land.* Berrien Springs, Michigan: Andrews University Press, 1992.

Hospital y Sanatorio Montemorelos. *Cofia y Azahares, 1957: X Aniversario del Hospital y Sanatorio Montemorelos.* Montemorelos, Nuevo León: Hospital y Sanatorio Montemorelos, 1959.

House, H.F. *Report of the Superintendent of the Mexican Union Mission.* Monterrey, N. L., 28 February 1944.

Iglesia "El Mesías." *Semana de Higiene.* Iglesia "El Mesías": Mexico, D.F., 6-10 May 1935. Copy in Ritchie Papers, SCLSU.

Knight, George R. *A Brief History of Seventh-day Adventists*. Hagerstown, Maryland: Review and Herald Publishing Association, 1999.

_____. *Joseph Bates: The Real Founder of Seventh-day Adventism*. Hagerstown, Maryland: Review and Herald Publishing Association, 2004.

Kyle, Douglas E. *Historic Spots in California*, 4th ed. Stanford, California: Stanford University Press, 1990.

Liga International, Inc. *Flying Doctors Operating on Hope*. Undated pamphlet. Santa Ana, California.

_____. *Hands Across the Border*. Undated pamphlet. Santa Ana, California.

Loma Linda University Medical Center. *Ritchie Mansion*. Loma Linda, California, 12 December 2002. Copy of invitation to grand opening in Ritchie Papers, SCLSU.

Mexico. Departamento de Salubridad Pública. *Lista de los Médicos Cirujanos, Homeópatas, Veterinarios, Cirujanos Dentistas, Farmacéuticos, Parteras y Enfermeras que han registrado su título profesional en este Departamento durante el año de 1929, Suplemento al Directorio General*. México, D.F.: Imprenta del Departamento de Salubridad Pública, 1930.

Meyer, Michael C. and William L. Sherman. *The Course of Mexican History*, 5th ed. New York: Oxford University Press, 1995.

Moses, H. Vincent, and Brenda Buller Focht. *Life in Little Gom-Benn: Chinese Immigrant Society in Riverside, 1885-1930*. Riverside: Riverside Museum Press, 1991.

Neufeld, Don F., ed. *Seventh-day Adventist Encyclopedia,* Revised ed. Washington, D.C.: Review & Herald Publishing Association, 1966.

Pierce, Joseph. *The HEFSE Plan.* Health Education Food Service Enterprises, Inc., San Bernardino, California, no date.

Pomona Valley Genealogical Society, Mary Swank, ed. *Pomona Cemeteries,* Vol. 1. Pomona, California, 1973.

Rathus, Spencer A. *Psychology in the New Millennium,* 6th ed. Fort Worth, Texas: Harcourt Brace College Publishers, 1996.

Reynolds, Keld J. *Outreach: Loma Linda University, 1905-1968.* [Loma Linda, California: Loma Linda University], 1968.

_____. *Sunshine, Citrus and Science: Loma Linda from Indian Village to Charter City, An Informal History.* Loma Linda, California: City of Loma Linda, 1985.

Rhodes, Edwin. *The Break of Day in Chino.* Chino, California: Edwin Rhodes, 1951.

Rice, Richard B., William A. Bullough, and Richard J. Orsi. *The Elusive Eden: A New History of California.* New York: McGraw-Hill Companies Inc., 1996.

Ritchie, Iner W.S. *Navojoa School Project.* Liga México-Pan-Americana Médico Educacional, no place or date. Copy in Ritchie Papers, SCLSU.

Schaefer, Richard A. *Legacy: The Heritage of a Unique International Medical Outreach.* Mountain View, California: Pacific Press Association, 1977.

Schwarz, Richard W., and Seventh-day Adventists, Department of Education. *Light Bearers to the Remnant: Denominational History Textbook for*

Seventh-day Adventist College Classes. Mountain View, California: Pacific Press Publishing Association, 1979.

Small, Carrol S., ed. *Diamond Memories.* Loma Linda, California: Alumni Association, School of Medicine of Loma Linda University, 1984.

Smith, Dunbar W. *The Travels, Triumphs & Vicissitudes of Dunbar W. Smith, M.D.* Loma Linda, California: Dunbar W. Smith, 1994.

Utt, Richard H. *From Vision to Reality, 1905-1980: Loma Linda University.* Loma Linda, California: Loma Linda University, 1980.

White, Ellen G. *Counsels on Health and Instruction to Medical Missionary Workers.* Mountain View, California: Pacific Press Publishing Association, 1923.

_____. *The Ministry of Healing.* Washington, D.C.: Review & Herald, 1905.

_____. *Testimonies for the Church,* Vol. 6. Oakland, California: Pacific Press, 1901.

_____. *Testimonies for the Church,* Vol. 8. Kansas City, Missouri: Pacific Press Publishing Co., 1904.

White, Julio Gilbert. *Aprenda Cómo Estar Bien.* Translated by A.J. Calderón. [Clinica Tacubaya]: Tacubaya, D.F., no date. Copy in Ritchie Papers, SCLSU.

Wood, Clarence E. *In the Land of the Aztecs.* Takoma Park, Washington, D.C.: Review and Herald Publishing Association, 1939.

Published Sources: Articles

"1991 Aerospace Laurel Awards Presented," *Aviation Week and Space Technology* (27 April 1992): 15.

Adventist Health System/West. "From Clinic to Medical Center: White Memorial Celebrates 80 Years of Making a Difference in Los Angeles." *Pacific Union Recorder,* Vol. 93, No. 16 (16 August 1993): 6-7.

"Aims and Objectives of the Liga." *Official Bulletin of the American Chapter, Liga México-Pan-American Médico Educacional,* No.1 (January-February 1949): 3.

Ainsworth, Ed. "Mexican Waifs Educated in U.S.-Financed School." *Los Angeles Times,* 18 June 1950: Part 2: 1, 3.

"Aerospace Laureates, Operations: LIGA International, Inc., David S. Lawson, President." *Aviation Week & Space Technology,* Vol. 136, No. 4 (27 January 1992): 14-15.

Andross, E.E. "A Visit to Mexico." *Inter-American Division Messenger,* Vol. 12, No. 6 (June 1935): 9-10.

Angell, Ivan M. "Mexican Agricultural and Industrial School." *Inter-American Division Messenger,* Vol. 20, No.9 (September 1943): 4-5.

Baerg, John. "Liga International, Inc." *ASI News,* Vol. 25, Nos. 7, 8, 9, (July-September 1975): 4-5.

Brown, Walton J. "The Six Miracles of Montemorelos." *Advent Review and Sabbath Herald,* 30 June 1977: 1, 19-21.

Burke, I.M. "Dr. Ralph M. Smith." *The Medical Evangelist.* Vol. 31, No. 12 (December 15, 1944).

"California Items." *Pacific Union Recorder.* Vol. 5, No. 13 (26 October 1905): 7.

Calkins, Glenn. "A New Institution in Mexico." *Inter-American Division Messenger,* Vol. 19, No. 11 (1 December 1942): 3-4.

Carson, Gerald. "Cornflake Crusade." *American Heritage,* Vol. 8, No. 4 (June 1957): 65-85.

"Chino and the Sugar Factory." *Riverside (California) Daily Press Annual,* Souvenir ed., Vol. 7, No. 1711 (9 January 1892): 7.

Christianson, Inelda Ritchie. "Anna Lula Joseph: Romance and Responsibility in Early Adventism." *Adventist Heritage,* Vol. 17, No. 2 (1997): 23-29.

Cicchetti, Christina. "El Doctór [sic]." *Journal of the Riverside Historical Society,* Vol. 2 (February 1998): 1-9.

"Clergy Network Award." *Liga High Flying Times.* Summer 1995: 1.

"College News." *The Medical Evangelist,* Vol. 7, No. 2 (September 1920): 19.

"College News," *The Medical Evangelist,* Vol. 8, No. 1 (July 1921): 26.

Corbett, Peter. "Mission of Mercy." *The Scottsdale Daily Progress/Saturday Magazine* (Scottsdale, Arizona), 8 December 1984: 5-6.

Crager, C.P. "Providences Along the Way." *Inter-American Division Messenger,* Vol. 20, No. 6 (June 1943): 10.

Dobbs, Jennifer M. "A Safe Harbor." *The San Bernardino County Sun,* 24 December 2001: D1, D5.

[Donaldson, Arthur N.,ed.] "News Notes." *The Medical Evangelist,* Vol. 7, No. 1 (June 1920): 24.

"Elders Hare and Adams. . . ." *Pacific Union Recorder.* Vol. 5, No. 11 (5 October 1905): 11.

Everett, Susan. "Nicaragua Trips Mean More than Healing." *The Sonora (California) Union Democrat,* 8 June 2001: 16A.

"Everybody in Michigan Owns Slice of this Farm," *Saginaw (Michigan) News,* 1 July 1948, typescript copy with W.K. Kellogg to I.S. Ritchie, 20 January 1949, Ritchie Papers, SCLSU.

"Field Course in Mexico." *Tropic Topics,* Vol. 1, No. 3 (October 1950): 3-4.

Fox, Ben. "Friends Say Mexico Volunteers 'Wanted to Make a Difference.'" *The Riverside (California) Press-Enterprise,* 16 October 2000.

Gil, Juan. "Navojoa Boarding School, a Living Miracle." *Inter-American Division Messenger,* Vol. 29, No. 4 (April 1952): 7-8.

[Gil, Juan]. "Escuela de Navojoa, Son." *Salud y Saber,* Vol. 1, No. 4 (August 1949): 3.

"Grants Received." *Liga High Flying Times,* December 1993-January 1994: [6].

Heisler, Bill. "Ground Breaking at Montemorelos." *Liga High Flying Times,* Vol 14 (December 1989).

"Historic Review of Montemorelos." *Liga High Flying Times,* Vol 14 (December 1989).

Hotchkiss, Ron. "Kelloggs of Battle Creek." *American History,* Vol. 29, No.6 (February 1995): 62-66.

House, Harold F. "The Entering Wedge in Mexico." *Inter-American Division Messenger,* Vol. 20, No. 12 (December 1943): 10.

Innis, C.F. "The Loma Linda Dispensary." *The Medical Evangelist,* Vol. 11, No. 52 (25 June 1925): 2-3.

Jackson, Helen. "Hospital in Mexican Jungles a Memorial to Riverside Physician." *Riverside (California) Enterprise,* 22 September 1950: 17.

Kellogg, J.H. "An Appeal for Mexico." *Advent Review and Sabbath Herald,* Vol. 74, No. 26 (29 June 1897): 408.

"Laurels 1991." *Aviation Week & Space Technology,* Vol. 136, No. 4 (27 January 1992): 11.

"Liga Acts in Emergency Flood Relief." *Official Bulletin of the American Chapter, Liga México-Pan-American Médico Educacional,* No. 1 (January - February 1949): 1.

Liga México Panamericana Médico Educacional. "Because it has been several months . . . ." *Bulletin,* Los Angeles, California, 10 October 1959: 1.

"Liga Projects Progress on Four Fronts." *Official Bulletin of the American Chapter, Liga México-Pan-American Médico Educacional,* No. 1 (January - February 1949): 2.

"Loma Linda University: 'a miracle that should open the eyes of our understanding.'" *Loma Linda University Scope,* Vol. 27, No.1 (January-March 1991): 6-13.

"Magnífica Fiesta Hubo en una Inauguración." *Diario del Mayo (Navojoa, Sonora),* 19 October 1948: 1, 4.

Membership application form, Liga. *Official Bulletin of the American Chapter, Liga México-Pan-American Médico Educacional,* No.1 (January-February 1949): 3.

"Mercy Flights in the Mountains of Mexico." *These Times,* Vol. 76, No. 10 (15 September 1967): 3.

"Mexico Topic Dr. I.S. Ritchie Able Address." *Rialto (California) Record,* Vol. 21, No. 22 (4 October 1929): 5.

"A Mission Field at Our Door." *The Medical Evangelist,* Vol. 10, No. 32 (31 January 1924): 1-2.

Monning, L. "The Guadalajara Sanitarium." *Advent Review and Sabbath Herald,* Vol. 76, No. 17 (25 April 1899): 269.

Montieth, Alex R. "Our Medical Work in Mexico." *Inter-American Division Messenger,* Vol. 26, No. 12 (December 1949): 7.

Moon, C.E. "Dispensary at Tacubaya, D.F., Mexico." *The Medical Evangelist,* Vol. 18, No. 14 (1 October 1931): 1.

_____. "Healing the Paralytic." *Inter-American Division Messenger,* Vol. 12, No. 9 (September 1935): 7.

Morgan, Peter H., Jr. "President's Message." *Liga High Flying Times,* January-February 1980: 1, 4.

Mozar, Harold N. "School Offers Field Course in Tropical Medicine." *The Journal of the Alumni Association. School of Medicine, College of Medical Evangelists,* Vol. 20, No. 7 (July 1949): 14.

Murray, Milton. "Boca del Río, Mexico." *Inter-American Division Messenger,* Vol. 26, No. 10 (October 1949): 8.

_____. "The School of Tropical and Preventive Medicine." *Inter-American Division Messenger,* Vol. 26, No. 11 (November 1949): 2-3.

Nelson, Clarence E. "Good Will Tour in Inter-America." *The Journal of the Alumni Association, School of Medicine, College of Medical Evangelists,* Vol. 22, No. 10 (October 1949): 11-13.

_____. "Iner S. Ritchie Dies." *The Journal of the Alumni Association, School of Medicine, College of Medical Evangelists,* Vol. 21, No. 1 (January 1950): 16.

Nelson, Harry C. "The Navajoa [*sic*] Industrial School." *Official Bulletin of the American Chapter, Liga México-Pan-American Médico Educacional,* No. 2 (October 1949): 5-6.

"News Notes." *The Medical Evangelist,* Vol.6, No. 4 (March 1920): 27.

"News Notes from Mexico." *Inter-American Division Messenger,* Vol. 29, No. 9 (September 1952): 7.

"Obituaries," Ritchie—Anna Lula Joseph. *Pacific Union Recorder,* Vol. 48, No. 8 (27 September 1948).

"Omar L. Stratton Community Center Dedicated by Officials at Bordwell." *The Riverside (California) Press,* 19 February 1973: B1.

"Our Graduates in Medicine—Where are they?" *The Medical Evangelist,* Vol. 7, No.1 (June 1920): 6-7.

Pavicic, Sandy. "Medicine Mixes with Compassion in Poorest Mexico." *The (Riverside, California) Press-Enterprise,* 15 April 1984: B1, B4-5.

_____. "Surgeon Offers to Perform Operation to Try to Save "Doomed" Mexican Girl." *The (Riverside, California) Press-Enterprise,* 18 April 1984: B1, B7.

"Progress in Mexico." *The Medical Evangelist,* Vol. 19, No. 1 (7 July 1932).

Reaser, G.W. "Southern California Items." *Pacific Union Recorder,* Vol. 4, No. 51 (13 July 1905): 3.

Recer, Paul. "Flu that Killed 20 Million Traced." *The (Riverside, California) Press-Enterprise,* March 21, 1997: A17.

Reynolds, Cordelia P. "The League at Work for Mexico." *The Journal of the Alumni Association, School of Medicine, College of Medical Evangelists,* Vol. 20, No. 2 (February 1949): 14.

Ritchie advertisement. *Pacific Union Recorder,* Vol. 4, No. 21 (15 December 1904): 8.

Ritchie, Iner S. See also Sheld-Ritchie, Iner.

Ritchie, I.S. "Another Appeal From Mexico." *The Medical Evangelist,* Vol. 15, No. 38 (21 March 1929).

_____. "Medical Missionary Work in the Homeland." *The Medical Evangelist,* Vol. 10, No. 26 (December 20, 1923): 1-4.

_____. "Sins Against Our Kidneys." *The Medical Evangelist,* Vol. 8, No. 4 (January-February 1922): 12-14.

Ritchie, I.S., and C.F. Innis. "Loma Linda Dispensary." *The Medical Evangelist,* Vol. 11, No. 35 (February 26, 1925): 4.

[Ritchie, Iner S.]. "Working in Old Mexico." *The Medical Evangelist,* Vol. 13, No. 47 (19 May 1927), 1-3.

[Ritchie, Iner S., and O.R. Staines]. "Itinerating in Old Mexico." *The Medical Evangelist,* Vol. 24, No. 34 (17 February 1938): 1-3; Vol. 24, No. 35 (24 February 1938): 1-2; and Vol. 24, No. 36 (3 March 1938): 2-4.

Roth, Arthur H. "The Mexican Union Session." *Inter-American Division Messenger,* Vol. 29, Nos. 10, 11 (October-November 1952): 10-11.

Sheld-Ritchie, Iner. See also, Ritchie, Iner S.

Sheld-Ritchie, Iner. "The Alumni." *The Medical Evangelist,* Vol. 7, No. 5 (March 1921): 9-10.

_____. "'But by My Spirit.' Zech.4:6." *The Youth's Instructor,* Vol. 62, No. 42 (20 October 1914): 5-8.

_____. "Parting Tribute From Dr. Iner Ritchie, Lifelong Friend and Chum of Dr. Ralph Smith." *The Medical Evangelist,* Vol. 31, No.12 (15 December 1944): 2.

_____. "The Stranger At Our Gates." *The Medical Evangelist,* Vol. 10, No. 34 (14 February 1924): 1-2.

_____. "Work for All Classes." *The Medical Evangelist,* Vol. 11, No. 32 (February 5, 1925): 1-2.

Shepard, Betty. "Riversiders Take Part in Mexican Philanthropy." *Daily (Riverside California) Press,* 29 August 1944: 3.

Small, Carrol S., and Elsa Lonergan. "Alumni and Missions: 'Go Ye into All the World.'" *AIMS Journal,* Vol.22, No. 1 (2001).

Smith, Chauncey L. "The Value of Membership." *Lome Linda University School of Medicine Alumni Journal,* Vol. 66, No. 1 (January-February 1995): 28.

"A Solid Faith: The Youngbergs Live a Life of Healing and Teaching." *Loma Linda University Scope,* Vol. 36, No. 1 (Summer 2000).

Staines, O.R., ed. "Dr. Hersel E. Butka, Class of '17." *The Medical Evangelist,* Vol.19, No. 43 (27 April 1933).

_____, ed. "Dr. Orley Van Eman, Class of '24." *The Medical Evangelist,* Vol. 11, No. 43 (23 April 1925).

_____, ed. "Dr. Ritchie Working in Mexico." *The Medical Evangelist,* Vol. 18, No. 45 (5 May 1932).

_____, ed. "From Here and There." *The Medical Evangelist,* Vol. 12, No. 31 (28 January 1926).

_____, ed. "Items." *The Medical Evangelist,* Vol. 19, No. 19 (10 November 1932), 4.

_____, ed. "Loma Linda Dispensary." *The Medical Evangelist,* Vol. 12, No. 11 (10 September 1925): 1.

_____, ed. "News Flashes." *The Medical Evangelist,* Vol. 20, No. 45 (10 May 1934): 4.

_____, ed. "News in Brief." *The Medical Evangelist,* Vol. 12, No. 36 (4 March 1926).

_____, ed. "News Notes." *The Medical Evangelist,* Vol. 12, No. 48 (27 May 1926): 1.

_____, ed. "Pencilgrams." *The Medical Evangelist,* Vol. 19, No. 18 (3 November 1932).

[Staines, O.R., ed.] "News Flashes." *The Medical Evangelist,* Vol. 20, No. 45 (10 May 1934): 4.

[_____, ed.] Untitled news items. *The Medical Evangelist,* Vol. 11, No. 23 (4 December 1924).

[_____, ed.] Untitled news items. *The Medical Evangelist,* Vol. 11, No. 43 (23 April 1925).

"STPM Assists Navojoa School." *Tropic Topics,* Vol. 8, No. 3 (July 1957): 2.

"Summer Course in Tropical Medicine." *The Journal of the Alumni Association, School of Medicine, College of Medical Evangelists,* Vol. 21, No. 6 (June 1950): 12.

Sutton, Arthur E. "Weekend in Sonora." *These Times,* March 1965: 26-27.

"Teapa, Mexico." *Bulletin* [of the American Chapter,] *Liga México-Pan-American Médico Educacional,* No. 8 (March 1952); 1.

Thomas, Larry. "A Look Back to the Future." *Loma Linda University School of Medicine Alumni Journal,* Vol. 65, No. 1 (January-February 1994): 26, 32.

"Una Escuela Agrícola e Industrial." *Diario del Mayo (Navojoa, Sonora),* 10 April 1948: 1, 2.

"Wanted," [advertisement]. *The Medical Evangelist,* Vol. 18, No. 45 (5 May 1932).

Westphal, Barbara O. "Good News from Mexico." *Inter-American Division Messenger,* Vol 26, No. 11-S (November 1949): 7.

_____. "The Ritchie Memorial Clinic." *Inter-American Division Messenger,* Vol. 29, No. 6 (June 1952): 7

White, J.G. "The Redlands Campaign." *The Medical Evangelist,* Vol. 8, No.4 (January-February 1922): 8-9, 12-14.

"Whole Family Dead." *Arlington (California) Times,* 2 November 1917.

Wilcox, F.M. "The Opening of Our Work in Mexico." *Advent Review and Sabbath Herald,* Vol. 71, No. 8 (20 February 1894): 116-17.

Williams, Debbie. "Counting My Blessings." *Liga High Flying Times,* December 1993 - January 1994: 1.

Wilner, Richard. "The Liga Children's Heart Program." *Liga Flying Doctors of Mercy,* Winter 2003: 6.

Wood, C.E. "Itinerating with Our Doctor in Mexico." *Inter-American Division Messenger,* Vol. 11, No. 12 (December 1934): 9-10.

_____. "Medical Missionary Work in Mexico." *Inter-American Division Messenger,* Vol. 14, No. 17 (15 September 1937): 6.

_____. "Mexican Union Mission: Report of the Union Committee Session." *Inter-American Division Messenger,* Vol. 16, No. 9 (1 May 1939): 4.

"The Work in Many Lands: Operations in Mexico." *Advent Review and Sabbath Herald,* Vol. 71, No. 28 (10 July 1894): 437.

Youngberg, Stephen. "Liga Convoy Reaches Teapa." *Official Bulletin of the American Chapter, Liga México-Pan-American Médico Educacional,* No. 2 (October 1949): 4.

Zinke, David. "Hospital with Air Service." *Tropic Topics,* Vol. 5, No. 1 (January 1954): 3.

Published Sources: The Internet

"Alumni Notes." *Scope,* Autumn 2000. Http://www.llu.edu/news/scope/aut00/NSalumni.htm.

"Butterfield Stage Route." Http://www.ku.edu/heritage/trails/bsroute.html.

Cajeme. "Cajeme: Una Historia de Orgullo, Antecedentes." Http://www. cdob1.com/cajeme/historia/cronologia.php.

_____. Cajeme. "Cronología de Hechos Históricos." Http://www. cdob1. com/cajeme/historia/cronologia.php.

Chino Chamber of Commerce. "California Resource Guide, City or Community of Chino." Http://www.pe.net/~rksnow/cacountychino.htm.

Daly, Stephen Glenn. "The Quality of Mercy—Life and Death on a Mexican Medical Mission," 1996. Http://www.sandiegomag.com /forums/aviation /mercy2.shtml.

De León, J. Marcos. "Historia de la Escuela," *Universidad de Montemorelos, Anuario 1945.* Http://www.um.edu.mx/anuarios/1945/breve_historia.htm.

"E.J. 'Lucky' Baldwin." Http://www.socalhistory.org/Biographies/baldwin. htm.

Iglesia Adventista del 7mo. Día Apocalipsis 14. "Historia: Acontecimientos importantes en la historia de la Iglesia Adventista del Séptimo Día," 3. Http://www.apocalipsis14.org/historia.html.

Liga International, Inc. *"Educational Influence."* Http://www.ligaflyingdocs. org/education.htm.

"LLU alumni provide humanitarian health service in Mexico with Liga, International." *Loma Linda University Today*, 9 October 1996. Http://www.llu.edu/news/today/oct9a.html.

Loma Linda University. "History." Http://151.112.2.51/heritage/Collections. htm#LLU.

Morales, José. "Un Día en la Escuela," *Universidad de Montemorelos, Anuario 1945*. Http://www.um.edu.mx/anuarios/1945/un_dia.htm.

Pasadena Tournament of Roses. "Rose Parade History." Http://www. tournamentofroses .com/photogallery/timeline/TL-1890s.htm.

Stevens, Libna. "Mexico: Adventist University Celebrates 61 Years of Educating Students," 27 November 2003. Http://www. interamericana.org/users/index.php?type=news&id-18&language=en.

Universidad de Navojoa. "Historia de Nuestra Institución." Http://www.unav.edu.mx/sec /acerca_de/historia.htm.

Universidad Linda Vista. "Nuestra Historia," November 2002. Http://www. ulv.edu.mx/remembranza.html.

Published Sources: Videorecordings

Iner S. Ritchie and Miscellaneous Ritchie Family Videorecordings composite. Produced by [Iner W. Ritchie and Don Cicchetti]. 1 hour, 24 minutes. [Loma Linda University Media Services], 1989. Copy of film on videocassette in Ritchie Papers, SCLSU.

Mexico, Department of Health and Welfare. *Bajo el Cielo Tropical*. Documental No. 6. 8 min. Dirección General de Educación Higiénica de la Secretaría de Salubridad y Asistencia, México, [1948]. Copy of film on videocassette in Ritchie Papers, SCLSU.

Universidad de Montemorelos. *Universidad de Montemorelos, 50 Aniversario Hospital la Carlota*. Produced by Inelda Ritchie, directed by Liliana Henao. 26 min. Centro de Producción Unión Mexicana del Norte, 1996. Videocassette.

Unpublished Sources: Interviews

Christianson, Inelda May, daughter of Dr. Iner S. Ritchie, interview by Chris Johnston and Christine Yoon, 6 April 1994, Riverside, California. Transcript. Ross Collection, HPSLSU.

Christianson, Inelda May, daughter of Dr. Iner S. Ritchie. Interviews by Delmer G. Ross, 17 July 2000 to 15 August 2004, Riverside, California.

Christianson, Inelda May, daughter of Dr. Iner S. Ritchie. Telephone interviews by Delmer G. Ross, 18 June 2000 to 12 December 2004, Norco, California.

Christianson, Inelda May Ritchie, daughter of Dr. Iner S. Ritchie. Interviews by Maritza Durán, 2 November 1999 to 4 August 2003, Riverside, California.

Christianson, Inelda May Ritchie, daughter of Dr. Iner S. Ritchie, telephone interviews by Maritza Durán, 7 June 2000 to 19 September 2003, Norco, California.

Hanson, Jackie, President, Liga International, Inc. Telephone interview by Delmer G. Ross, 20 July 2000, Santa Ana, California.

Ott, James, Executive Director, Liga International, Inc. Telephone interview by Delmer G. Ross, 18 July 2000, Santa Ana, California.

Sheld-Ritchie, Inelda Ruth, widow of Dr. Iner S. Ritchie, interview by her granddaughter, Cheryl Ann Nickel Leathers, 20 November 1985 and 2 March 1986, [La Jolla, California]. Transcript. Ritchie Papers, SCLSU.

Unpublished Sources: Miscellaneous Documents and Papers

Banfield, Gloria, and Ken Kurts. "Dr. Ritchie Paper: His Education and Medical Missionary Work in Mexico" (term paper presented for HIST 294/494, History Colloquium, La Sierra University, Riverside, California, 6 December 1995). D.G. Ross Collection, HPSLSU.

[Christianson, Inelda May]. "Iner Sheld-Ritchie, October 6, 1885 - October 24, 1949." Undated chronology. Ritchie Papers, SCLSU.

Christianson, Inelda Ritchie. "Montemorelos Slide Commentary: Iner Sheld-Ritchie, M.D., Oct. 6, 1885 - Oct. 26, [sic] 1949." Eleven-page typescript. Ritchie Papers, SCLSU.

_____. "Ritchie Family Life in Riverside." Ten-page typescript. Norco, California, 27 April 2004. Ritchie Papers, SCLSU.

_____. "The Ritchie/Joseph Who's Who." Undated four-page typescript. Ritchie Papers, SCLSU.

Cushman, Gregory T., and Matthew Perry. "From Teapa to Linda Vista: Dr. Iner S. Ritchie's Vision for Southern Mexico" (term paper presented for HIST 294/494, History Colloquium, La Sierra University, Riverside, California, 27 April 1994). D.G. Ross Collection, HPSLSU.

Dass, Ernie. "The Flying Doctors of Mercy" (term paper presented for HIST 294/494, History Colloquium, La Sierra University, Riverside, California, 26 May 1994). D.G. Ross Collection, HPSLSU.

Diploma. Southern California School of Physical Therapy. San Gabriel, California, 1 December 1930. Ritchie Papers, SCLSU.

Durán, Maritza. "Iner Sheld-Ritchie, a Paradigm of Service" (honors thesis, La Sierra University, 2000). D.G. Ross Collection, HPSLSU.

Effler, Curt. Trip log, April 1946, 1-11. Copy in Ritchie Papers, SCLSU.

Fuss, Max. *Informe de la Misión de Chiapas, 1947*. Tuxtla Gutiérrez, Chiapas: Misión Adventista del Séptimo Día, December 1947.

Garbutt-Quistiano, Joel R., and Leslie Reeves. "Sweethearts Always" (term paper presented for HIST 294/494, History Colloquium, La Sierra University, Riverside, California, 25 April 1994). D.G. Ross Collection, HPSLSU.

Gonzalez, Marc, and Todd Cooper. "The Romance of Iner and Inelda Sheld-Ritchie" (term paper presented for HIST 494 History Colloquium, 6 December 1995). D.G. Ross Collection, HPSLSU.

Johnston, Chris, and Christine Yoon. "The Religious and Educational Influence of the Ritchie Family on Iner Sheld" (term paper presented for HIST 294/494, History Colloquium, La Sierra University, Riverside, California, 10 May 1994). D.G. Ross Collection, HPSLSU.

Junta de la Unión Mexicana. "Minuta de la junta de la Unión Mexicana." México, D.F., 24 June 1949. Copy, Ritchie Papers, SCLSU.

_____. "Minutas de la Junta de la Unión Mexicana." Navojoa, Sonora, 17 March 1948. Copy, Ritchie Papers, SCLSU.

Karlow, Norman, and Antoinette Paris. "Dr. Ritchie's Relationship with President [Manuel Avila] Camacho" (term paper presented for HIST 294/494, History Colloquium, La Sierra University, Riverside, California, 24 April 1994). D.G. Ross Collection, HPSLSU.

Kumar, Stephen, and David Olivares. "Expect the Unexpected" (term paper presented for HIST 294/494, History Colloquium, La Sierra University, Riverside, California, 6 December 1995). D.G. Ross Collection, HPSLSU.

Liga México-Americana Medico [sic] Educacional y de Trabajadores Sociales. *Purpose and Function of the "Liga,"* Coyoacán, D.F., [1948]. Copy in Ritchie Papers, SCLSU

Liga México-Pan-Americana Médico Educacional. *Semiannual Report,* Los Angeles, June 1958. Copy in Ritchie Papers, SCLSU.

Liga México-Pan-Americana Médico Educacional, American Chapter. "Liga Board Meeting Minutes," Arlington, California, 17 August 1958. Copy in Ritchie Papers, SCLSU.

Mexican Union Mission Committee. "Minutes." México, D.F., 5 July 1933 - 16 August 1934: 147-181. Copy, Ritchie Papers, SCLSU.

Mexico. Servicio de Migración. "Registro de Extranjeros." México, D.F., 3 May 1934.

Meyer, Earl, and Hazel Meyer. "La Obra Adventista en la Frontera." No date. Ritchie Papers, SCLSU.

Nassimian, Deborah, and Roxana Maddalena. "Dr. Ritchie and His Patients" (term paper presented for HIST 294/494, History Colloquium, La Sierra University, Riverside, California, 5 December 1995). D.G. Ross Collection, HPSLSU.

Order of Adoption, Inelda Ruth Ritchie, a minor. February 26, 1912. Superior Court, Riverside, California.

Park, Matthew, and Allison Rice. "The Financial Aspect of Building Montemorelos Hospital" (term paper presented for HIST 294/494, History Colloquium, La Sierra University, Riverside, California, 29 November 1995). D.G. Ross Collection, HPSLSU.

Pettey, J[ames] G. "Diary, Aug.25, 1927 — ." Archives and Special Collections, WebbLLU.

[Ritchie, Iner S.]. "The Medical Missionary Work." 18-page, unpaginated handwritten manuscript dated Sabbath, 5 January 1946. Ritchie Papers, SCLSU.

[_____]. Untitled 14-page hand written manuscript with internal title, "God's Vast Design," at top of p. 12, no date. Ritchie Papers, SCLSU.

Ritchie, Iner Sheld, and H.F. House. "Interviews with Mexican Government Officials Relative to New Medical and Educational Institutions." Six-page typed report, no place, 1945. Ritchie Papers, SCLSU.

[Ritchie, Iner W.]. "Liga México-Americana Medico [sic] Educacional y de Trabajadores Sociales. No place, no date. Ritchie Papers, SCLSU.

[_____.]. "History of Liga." No place, no date. Ritchie Papers, SCLSU.

Ritchie, Iner W. S. "Liga México-Pan-Americana Medico [*sic*] Educacional." Three-page typescript, Riverside, California, 23 July 1974. Ritchie Papers, SCLSU.

Serena, Heidi, and Paul Negrete. "Dr. Iner S. Ritchie's Relationship with Mexican Presidents"(term paper presented for HIST 294/494, History Colloquium, La Sierra University, Riverside, California, 6 December 1995). D.G. Ross Collection, HPSLSU.

Sheld, Dan. "Story of Dan Shelds—1914 Start of Married Life to 1964 Golden Wedding Anniversary." Undated scrapbook text transcription. Ritchie Papers, SCLSU.

Vodeb, Elizabeth, and Andrew Howe. "Dr. Ritchie's Relationship with Mexican Governors" (term paper presented for HIST 294/494, History Colloquium, La Sierra University, Riverside, California, 29 November 1995). D.G. Ross Collection, HPSLSU.

Youngberg, Stephen. "Tribute to Dr. Ritchie." México, D.F., October 28, 1949. Transcription from tape copied from wire by Inelda May Christianson, 25 November 1995. Ritchie Papers, SCLSU.

Collections

Ritchie Collection. Women's Resource Center, La Sierra University, Riverside, California; abbreviated: WRCLSU.

Ritchie, Iner S., File. Archives and Special Collections, Del E. Webb Library, Loma Linda University, Loma Linda California; abbreviated: WebbLLU.

Ritchie Papers. Stahl Center for World Service, La Sierra University, Riverside, California; abbreviated: SCLSU.

Ross, D.G., Collection. Department of History, Politics and Society, La Sierra University, Riverside, California, abbreviated: HPSLSU.

Index